ıllııllıı
CISCO™

Course Booklet

Routing and Switching Essentials

Version 6

cisco press.com

Cisco | Networking Academy
Mind Wide Open

Routing and Switching Essentials v6 Course Booklet

Copyright © 2017 Cisco Systems, Inc.

Published by:
Cisco Press
800 East 96th Street
Indianapolis, IN 46240 USA

Printed in the United States of America

2   17

Library of Congress Control Number: 2016954043

ISBN-13: 978-1-58713-427-2

ISBN-10: 1-58713-427-6

Warning and Disclaimer

This book is designed to provide information about the Cisco Networking Academy Routing and Switching Essentials course. Every effort has been made to make this book as complete and as accurate as possible, but no warranty or fitness is implied.

The information is provided on an "as is" basis. The authors, Cisco Press, and Cisco Systems, Inc. shall have neither liability nor responsibility to any person or entity with respect to any loss or damages arising from the information contained in this book or from the use of the discs or programs that may accompany it.

The opinions expressed in this book belong to the author and are not necessarily those of Cisco Systems, Inc.

Editor-in-Chief
Mark Taub

Alliances Manager, Cisco Press
Ron Fligge

Product Line Manager
Brett Bartow

Executive Editor
Mary Beth Ray

Managing Editor
Sandra Schroeder

Project Editor
Tonya Simpson

Editorial Assistant
Vanessa Evans

Cover Designer
Chuti Prasertsith

Composition
codeMantra

This book is part of the Cisco Networking Academy® series from Cisco Press. The products in this series support and complement the Cisco Networking Academy curriculum. If you are using this book outside the Networking Academy, then you are not preparing with a Cisco trained and authorized Networking Academy provider.

For more information on the Cisco Networking Academy or to locate a Networking Academy, Please visit www.cisco.com/edu.

CISCO.

Trademark Acknowledgments

All terms mentioned in this book that are known to be trademarks or service marks have been appropriately capitalized. Cisco Press or Cisco Systems, Inc., cannot attest to the accuracy of this information. Use of a term in this book should not be regarded as affecting the validity of any trademark or service mark.

Feedback Information

At Cisco Press, our goal is to create in-depth technical books of the highest quality and value. Each book is crafted with care and precision, undergoing rigorous development that involves the unique expertise of members from the professional technical community.

Readers' feedback is a natural continuation of this process. If you have any comments regarding how we could improve the quality of this book, or otherwise alter it to better suit your needs, you can contact us through email at feedback@ciscopress.com. Please make sure to include the book title and ISBN in your message.

We greatly appreciate your assistance.

Americas Headquarters	Asia Pacific Headquarters	Europe Headquarters
Cisco Systems, Inc.	Cisco Systems (USA) Pte. Ltd.	Cisco Systems International BV
San Jose, CA	Singapore	Amsterdam, The Netherlands

Cisco has more than 200 offices worldwide. Addresses, phone numbers, and fax numbers are listed on the Cisco Website at **www.cisco.com/go/offices.**

CCDE, CCENT, Cisco Eos, Cisco HealthPresence, the Cisco logo, Cisco Lumin, Cisco Nexus, Cisco StadiumVision, Cisco TelePresence, Cisco WebEx, DCE, and Welcome to the Human Network are trademarks; Changing the Way We Work, Live, Play, and Learn and Cisco Store are service marks; and Access Registrar, Aironet, AsyncOS, Bringing the Meeting To You, Catalyst, CCDA, CCDP, CCIE, CCIP, CCNA, CCNP, CCSP, CCVP, Cisco, the Cisco Certified Internetwork Expert logo, Cisco IOS, Cisco Press, Cisco Systems, Cisco Systems Capital, the Cisco Systems logo, Cisco Unity, Collaboration Without Limitation, EtherFast, EtherSwitch, Event Center, Fast Step, Follow Me Browsing, FormShare, GigaDrive, HomeLink, Internet Quotient, IOS, iPhone, iQuick Study, IronPort, the IronPort logo, LightStream, Linksys, MediaTone, MeetingPlace, MeetingPlace Chime Sound, MGX, Networkers, Networking Academy, Network Registrar, PCNow, PIX, PowerPanels, ProConnect, ScriptShare, SenderBase, SMARTnet, Spectrum Expert, StackWise, The Fastest Way to Increase Your Internet Quotient, TransPath, WebEx, and the WebEx logo are registered trademarks of Cisco Systems, Inc. and/or its affiliates in the United States and certain other countries.

All other trademarks mentioned in this document or website are the property of their respective owners. The use of the word partner does not imply a partnership relationship between Cisco and any other company. (0812R)

Contents at a Glance

Contents

Command Syntax Conventions

The conventions used to present command syntax in this book are the same conventions used in the IOS Command Reference. The Command Reference describes these conventions as follows:

- **Boldface** indicates commands and keywords that are entered literally as shown. In actual configuration examples and output (not general command syntax), boldface indicates commands that are manually input by the user (such as a **show** command).

- *Italic* indicates arguments for which you supply actual values.

- Vertical bars (|) separate alternative, mutually exclusive elements.

- Square brackets ([ ]) indicate an optional element.

- Braces ({ }) indicate a required choice.

- Braces within brackets ([{ }]) indicate a required choice within an optional element.

About This Course Booklet

Your Cisco Networking Academy Course Booklet is designed as a study resource you can easily read, highlight, and review on the go, wherever the Internet is not available or practical:

- The text is extracted directly, word-for-word, from the online course so you can highlight important points and take notes in the "Your Chapter Notes" section.

- Headings with the exact page correlations provide a quick reference to the online course for your classroom discussions and exam preparation.

- An icon system directs you to the online curriculum to take full advantage of the images imbedded within the Networking Academy online course interface and reminds you to perform the labs, Class activities, Interactive activities, Packet Tracer activities, watch videos, and take the chapter quizzes and exams.

Refer to **Online Course** for Illustration | Refer to **Lab Activity** for this chapter | Go to the online course to take the quiz and exam. | Refer to **Interactive Graphic** in online course | Refer to **Packet Tracer Activity** for this chapter | Refer to **Video** in online course

The *Course Booklet* is a basic, economical paper-based resource to help you succeed with the Cisco Networking Academy online course.

Course Introduction

0.0 Welcome to Routing and Switching Essentials

0.0.1 Message to the Student

Refer to
Online Course
for Illustration

0.0.1.1 Welcome

Welcome to the CCNA Routing and Switching Essentials course. The goal of this course is to introduce you to fundamental networking concepts and technologies. These online course materials will assist you in developing the skills necessary to plan and implement small networks supporting a range of applications. The specific skills covered in each chapter are described at the start of each chapter.

You can use your smart phone, tablet, laptop, or desktop to access the course, participate in discussions with your instructor, view your grades, read or review text, and practice using interactive media. However, some media are complex and must be viewed on a PC, as well as Packet Tracer activities, quizzes, and exams.

Refer to
Online Course
for Illustration

0.0.1.2 A Global Community

When you participate in the Networking Academy, you are joining a global community linked by common goals and technologies. Schools, colleges, universities, and other entities in over 160 countries participate in the program. A visualization of the global Networking Academy community is available at http://www.netacad.com.

Look for the Cisco Networking Academy official site on Facebook© and LinkedIn©. The Facebook site is where you can meet and engage with other Networking Academy students from around the world. The Cisco Networking Academy LinkedIn site connects you with job postings, and you can see how others are effectively communicating their skills.

Refer to
Online Course
for Illustration

0.0.1.3 More Than Just Information

The NetAcad learning environment is an important part of the overall course experience for students and instructors in the Networking Academy. These online course materials include course text and related interactive media, Packet Tracer simulation activities, real equipment labs, remote access labs, and many different types of quizzes. All of these materials provide important feedback to help you assess your progress throughout the course.

The material in this course encompasses a broad range of technologies that facilitate how people work, live, play, and learn by communicating with voice, video, and other data. Networking and the Internet affect people differently in different parts of the world. Although we have worked with instructors from around the world to create these materials, it is important that you work with your instructor and fellow students to make the material in this course applicable to your local environment.

Refer to
Online Course
for Illustration

0.0.1.4   How We Teach

E-doing is a design philosophy that applies the principle that people learn best by doing. The curriculum includes embedded, highly interactive e-doing activities to help stimulate learning, increase knowledge retention, and make the whole learning experience richer – and that makes understanding the content much easier.

Refer to
Online Course
for Illustration

0.0.1.5   Practice Leads to Mastery

In a typical lesson, after learning about a topic for the first time, you will check your understanding with some interactive media items. If there are new commands to learn, you will practice them with the Syntax Checker before using the commands to configure or troubleshoot a network in Packet Tracer, the Networking Academy network simulation tool. Next, you will do practice activities on real equipment in your classroom or accessed remotely over the internet.

Packet Tracer can also provide additional practice any time by creating your own activities or you may want to competitively test your skills with classmates in multi-user games. Packet Tracer skills assessments and skills integration labs give you rich feedback on the skills you are able to demonstrate and are great practice for chapter, checkpoint, and final exams.

Refer to
Online Course
for Illustration

0.0.1.6   Mind Wide Open

An important goal in education is to enrich you, the student, by expanding what you know and can do. It is important to realize, however, that the instructional materials and the instructor can only facilitate the process. You must make the commitment yourself to learn new skills. The following pages share a few suggestions to help you learn and prepare for transitioning your new skills to the workplace.

Refer to
Online Course
for Illustration

0.0.1.7   Engineering Journals

Professionals in the networking field often keep Engineering Journals in which they write down the things they observe and learn such as how to use protocols and commands. Keeping an Engineering Journal creates a reference you can use at work in your ICT job. Writing is one way to reinforce your learning – along with reading, seeing, and practicing.

A sample entry for implementing a technology could include the necessary software commands, the purpose of the commands, command variables, and a topology diagram indicating the context for using the commands to configure the technology.

Refer to
Online Course
for Illustration

0.0.1.8   Explore the World of Networking

Packet Tracer is a networking tool for learning that supports a wide range of physical and logical simulations. It also provides visualization tools to help you understand the internal workings of a network.

The pre-built Packet Tracer activities consist of network simulations, games, activities, and challenges that provide a broad range of learning experiences. These tools will help you develop an understanding of how data flows in a network.

Refer to
Online Course
for Illustration

0.0.1.9   Create Your Own Worlds

You can also use Packet Tracer to create your own experiments and networking scenarios. We hope that, over time, you consider using Packet Tracer - not only for experiencing the pre-built activities, but also to become an author, explorer, and experimenter.

The online course materials have embedded Packet Tracer activities that will launch on computers running Windows® operating systems, if Packet Tracer is installed. This integration will also work on other operating systems using Windows emulation.

Refer to **Packet Tracer Activity** for this chapter

0.0.1.10 How Packet Tracer Helps Master Concepts

Educational Games

Packet Tracer Multi-User games enable you or a team to compete with other students to see who can accurately complete a series of networking tasks the fastest. It is an excellent way to practice the skills you are learning in Packet Tracer activities and hands-on labs.

Cisco Aspire is a single-player, standalone strategic simulation game. Players test their networking skills by completing contracts in a virtual city. The Networking Academy Edition is specifically designed to help you prepare for the CCENT certification exam. It also incorporates business and communication skills ICT employers seek in job candidates.

Performance-Based Assessments

The Networking Academy performance-based assessments have you do Packet Tracer activities like you have been doing all along, only now integrated with an online assessment engine that will automatically score your results and provide you with immediate feedback. This feedback helps you to more accurately identify the knowledge and skills you have mastered and where you need more practice. There are also questions on chapter quizzes and exams that use Packet Tracer activities to give you additional feedback on your progress.

Refer to **Online Course** for Illustration

0.0.1.11 Course Overview

As the course title states, the focus of this course is on learning the architecture, components, and operations of routers and switches in a small network. In this course, you will learn how to configure a router and a switch for basic functionality. You will do the following:

- Configure and verify static routing and default routing.
- Configure and troubleshoot basic operations of a small switched network.
- Configure and troubleshoot basic operations of routers in a small routed network.
- Configure and troubleshoot VLANs and inter-VLAN routing.
- Configure, monitor, and troubleshoot ACLs for IPv4.
- Configure and verify DHCPv4 and DHCPv6.
- Configure and verify NAT for IPv4.
- Configure and monitor networks using device discovery, management, and maintenance tools.

Go to the online course to take the quiz and exam.

Chapter 0 Quiz

This quiz is designed to provide an additional opportunity to practice the skills and knowledge presented in the chapter and to prepare for the chapter exam. You will be allowed multiple attempts and the grade does not appear in the gradebook.

Chapter 0 Exam

The chapter exam assesses your knowledge of the chapter content.

Your Chapter Notes

Routing Concepts

1.0 Introduction

Refer to
Online Course
for Illustration

1.0.1.1 Routing Concepts

Networks allow people to communicate, collaborate, and interact in many ways. Networks are used to access web pages, talk using IP telephones, participate in video conferences, compete in interactive gaming, shop using the Internet, complete online coursework, and more.

Ethernet switches function at the data link layer, Layer 2, and are used to forward Ethernet frames between devices within the same network.

However, when the source IP and destination IP addresses are on different networks, the Ethernet frame must be sent to a router.

A router connects one network to another network. The router is responsible for the delivery of packets across different networks. The destination of the IP packet might be a web server in another country or an email server on the local area network.

The router uses its routing table to determine the best path to use to forward a packet. It is the responsibility of the routers to deliver those packets in a timely manner. The effectiveness of internetwork communications depends, to a large degree, on the ability of routers to forward packets in the most efficient way possible.

When a host sends a packet to a device on a different IP network, the packet is forwarded to the default gateway because a host device cannot communicate directly with devices outside of the local network. The default gateway is the destination that routes traffic from the local network to devices on remote networks. It is often used to connect a local network to the Internet.

This chapter will answer the question, "What does a router do with a packet received from one network and destined for another network?" Details of the routing table will be examined, including connected, static, and dynamic routes.

Because the router can route packets between networks, devices on different networks can communicate. This chapter will introduce the router, its role in networks, its main hardware and software components, and the routing process. Exercises which demonstrate how to access the router, configure basic router settings, and verify settings will be provided.

Refer to
Online Course
for Illustration

1.0.1.2 Activity – Do We Really Need a Map?

This modeling activity asks you to research travel directions from source to destination. Its purpose is to compare those types of directions to network routing directions.

Scenario

Using the Internet and Google Maps, located at http://maps.google.com, find a route between the capital city of your country and some other distant town or between two places within your own city. Pay close attention to the driving or walking directions Google Maps suggests.

Notice that in many cases, Google Maps suggests more than one route between the two locations you chose. It also allows you to put additional constraints on the route, such as avoiding highways or tolls.

Copy at least two route instructions supplied by Google Maps for this activity. Place your copies into a word processing document and save it for use with the next step.

Open the .pdf accompanying this modeling activity and complete it with a fellow student. Discuss the reflection questions listed on the .pdf and record your answers.

Be prepared to present your answers to the class.

1.1   Router Initial Configuration

1.1.1   Router Functions

Refer to
Online Course
for Illustration

1.1.1.1   Characteristics of a Network

Networks have had a significant impact on our lives. They have changed the way we live, work, and play.

Networks allow us to communicate, collaborate, and interact in ways we never did before. We use the network in a variety of ways, including web applications, IP telephony, video conferencing, interactive gaming, electronic commerce, education, and more.

As shown in the figure, there are many key structures and performance-related characteristics referred to when discussing networks:

- **Topology** - There are physical and logical topologies. The physical topology is the arrangement of the cables, network devices, and end systems. It describes how the network devices are actually interconnected with wires and cables. The logical topology is the path over which the data is transferred in a network. It describes how the network devices appear connected to network users.

- **Speed** - Speed is a measure of the data rate in bits per second (b/s) of a given link in the network.

- **Cost** - Cost indicates the general expense for purchasing of network components, and installation and maintenance of the network.

- **Security** - Security indicates how protected the network is, including the information that is transmitted over the network. The subject of security is important, and techniques and practices are constantly evolving. Consider security whenever actions are taken that affect the network.

- **Availability** - Availability is the likelihood that the network is available for use when it is required.

- **Scalability** - Scalability indicates how easily the network can accommodate more users and data transmission requirements. If a network design is optimized to only meet current requirements, it can be very difficult and expensive to meet new needs when the network grows.

- **Reliability** - Reliability indicates the dependability of the components that make up the network, such as the routers, switches, PCs, and servers. Reliability is often measured as a probability of failure or as the mean time between failures (MTBF).

These characteristics and attributes provide a means to compare different networking solutions.

Note   While the term "speed" is commonly used when referring to the network bandwidth, it is not technically accurate. The actual speed that the bits are transmitted does not vary over the same medium. The difference in bandwidth is due to the number of bits transmitted per second, not how fast they travel over wire or wireless medium.

Refer to
Online Course
for Illustration

1.1.1.2   Why Routing?

How does clicking a link in a web browser return the desired information in mere seconds? Although there are many devices and technologies collaboratively working together to enable this, the primary device is the router. Stated simply, a router connects one network to another network.

Communication between networks would not be possible without a router determining the best path to the destination and forwarding traffic to the next router along that path. The router is responsible for the routing of traffic between networks.

In the topology in the figure, the routers interconnect the networks at the different sites. When a packet arrives on a router interface, the router uses its routing table to determine how to reach the destination network. The destination of the IP packet might be a web server in another country or an email server on the local area network. It is the responsibility of routers to deliver those packets efficiently. The effectiveness of inter-network communications depends, to a large degree, on the ability of routers to forward packets in the most efficient way possible.

Refer to
Interactive Graphic
in online course

1.1.1.3   Routers Are Computers

Most network capable devices (e.g., computers, tablets, and smartphones) require the following components to operate, as shown in Figure 1:

- Central processing unit (CPU)

- Operating system (OS)

- Memory and storage (RAM, ROM, NVRAM, Flash, hard drive)

A router is essentially a specialized computer. It requires a CPU and memory to temporarily and permanently store data to execute operating system instructions, such as system initialization, routing functions, and switching functions.

Note   Cisco devices use the Cisco Internetwork Operating System (IOS) as the system software.

Router memory is classified as volatile or non-volatile. Volatile memory loses its content when the power is turned off, while non-volatile memory does not lose its content when the power is turned off.

The table in Figure 2 summarizes the types of router memory, the volatility, and examples of what is stored in each.

Unlike a computer, a router does not have video adapters or sound card adapters. Instead, routers have specialized ports and network interface cards to interconnect devices to other networks. Figure 3 identifies some of these ports and interfaces.

Refer to
Interactive Graphic
in online course

1.1.1.4   Routers Interconnect Networks

Most users are unaware of the presence of numerous routers on their own network or on the Internet. Users expect to be able to access web pages, send emails, and download music, regardless of whether the server accessed is on their own network or on another network. Networking professionals know that it is the router that is responsible for forwarding packets from network to network, from the original source to the final destination.

A router connects multiple networks, which means that it has multiple interfaces that each belong to a different IP network. When a router receives an IP packet on one interface, it determines which interface to use to forward the packet to the destination. The interface that the router uses to forward the packet may be the final destination, or it may be a network connected to another router that is used to reach the destination network.

In the animation in Figure 1, R1 and R2 are responsible for receiving the packet on one network and forwarding the packet out another network toward the destination network.

Each network that a router connects to typically requires a separate interface. These interfaces are used to connect a combination of both local-area networks (LANs) and wide-area networks (WANs). LANs are commonly Ethernet networks that contain devices, such as PCs, printers, and servers. WANs are used to connect networks over a large geographical area. For example, a WAN connection is commonly used to connect a LAN to the Internet service provider (ISP) network.

Notice that each site in Figure 2 requires the use of a router to interconnect to other sites. Even the Home Office requires a router. In this topology, the router located at the Home Office is a specialized device that performs multiple services for the home network.

Refer to **Video**
in online course

1.1.1.5   Routers Choose Best Paths

The primary functions of a router are to:

- Determine the best path to send packets

- Forward packets toward their destination

The router uses its routing table to determine the best path to use to forward a packet. When the router receives a packet, it examines the destination address of the packet and uses the routing table to search for the best path to that network. The routing table also includes the interface to be used to forward packets for each known network. When a match is found, the router encapsulates the packet into the data link frame of the outgoing or exit interface, and the packet is forwarded toward its destination.

It is possible for a router to receive a packet that is encapsulated in one type of data link frame, and to forward the packet out of an interface that uses a different type of data link frame. For example, a router may receive a packet on an Ethernet interface, but must forward the packet out of an interface configured with the Point-to-Point Protocol (PPP). The data link encapsulation depends on the type of interface on the router and the type of medium to which it connects. The different data link technologies that a router can connect to include Ethernet, PPP, Frame Relay, DSL, cable, and wireless (802.11, Bluetooth, etc.).

The animation in the figure follows a packet from the source PC to the destination PC. Notice that it is the responsibility of the router to find the destination network in its routing table and forward the packet on toward its destination. In this example, router R1 receives the packet encapsulated in an Ethernet frame. After de-encapsulating the packet, R1 uses the destination IP address of the packet to search its routing table for a matching network address. After a destination network address is found in the routing table, R1 encapsulates the packet inside a PPP frame and forwards the packet to R2. A similar process is performed by R2.

Note   Routers use static routes and dynamic routing protocols to learn about remote networks and build their routing tables.

Refer to
Interactive Graphic
in online course

1.1.1.6   Packet Forwarding Mechanisms

Routers support three packet-forwarding mechanisms:

- **Process switching** - An older packet forwarding mechanism still available for Cisco routers. When a packet arrives on an interface, it is forwarded to the control plane where the CPU matches the destination address with an entry in its routing table, and then determines the exit interface and forwards the packet. It is important to understand that the router does this for every packet, even if the destination is the same for a stream of packets. This process-switching mechanism is very slow and rarely implemented in modern networks.

- **Fast switching** - This is a common packet forwarding mechanism which uses a fast-switching cache to store next-hop information. When a packet arrives on an interface, it is forwarded to the control plane where the CPU searches for a match in the fast-switching cache. If it is not there, it is process-switched and forwarded to the exit interface. The flow information for the packet is also stored in the fast-switching cache. If another packet going to the same destination arrives on an interface, the next-hop information in the cache is re-used without CPU intervention.

- **Cisco Express Forwarding (CEF)** - CEF is the most recent and preferred Cisco IOS packet-forwarding mechanism. Like fast switching, CEF builds a Forwarding Information Base (FIB), and an adjacency table. However, the table entries are not packet-triggered like fast switching but change-triggered such as when something changes in the network topology. Therefore, when a network has converged, the FIB and adjacency tables contain all the information a router would have to consider when forwarding a packet. The FIB contains pre-computed reverse lookups, next hop information for routes including the interface and Layer 2 information. Cisco Express Forwarding is the fastest forwarding mechanism and the preferred choice on Cisco routers.

Figures 1 to 3 illustrate the differences between the three packet-forwarding mechanisms. Assume that a traffic flow consisting of five packets are all going to the same destination. As shown in Figure 1, with process switching, each packet must be processed by the CPU individually. Contrast this with fast switching, as shown in Figure 2. With fast switching, notice how only the first packet of a flow is process-switched and added to the fast-switching cache. The next four packets are quickly processed based on the information in the fast-switching cache. Finally, in Figure 3, CEF builds the FIB and adjacency tables, after the network has converged. All five packets are quickly processed in the data plane.

A common analogy used to describe the three packet-forwarding mechanisms is as follows:

- Process switching solves a problem by doing math long hand, even if it is the identical problem.

- Fast switching solves a problem by doing math long hand one time and remembering the answer for subsequent identical problems.

- CEF solves every possible problem ahead of time in a spreadsheet.

Refer to **Interactive Graphic** in online course

1.1.1.7 Activity – Identify Router Components

Refer to **Packet Tracer Activity** for this chapter

1.1.1.8 Packet Tracer – Using Traceroute to Discover the Network

The company you work for has acquired a new branch location. You asked for a topology map of the new location, but apparently one does not exist. However, you have username and password information for the new branch's networking devices and you know the web address for the new branch's server. Therefore, you will verify connectivity and use the **tracert** command to determine the path to the location. You will connect to the edge router of the new location to determine the devices and networks attached. As a part of this process, you will use various **show** commands to gather the necessary information to finish documenting the IP addressing scheme and create a diagram of the topology.

Refer to **Lab Activity** for this chapter

1.1.1.9 Lab – Mapping the Internet

In this lab, you will complete the following objectives:

- Part 1: Determine Network Connectivity to a Destination Host

- Part 2: Trace a Route to a Remote Server Using Tracert

1.1.2 Connect Devices

Refer to **Online Course** for Illustration

1.1.2.1 Connect to a Network

Network devices and end users typically connect to a network using a wired Ethernet or wireless connection. Refer to the figure as a sample reference topology. The LANs in the figure serve as an example of how users and network devices could connect to networks.

Home Office devices can connect as follows:

- Laptops and tablets connect wirelessly to a home router.

- A network printer connects using an Ethernet cable to the switch port on the home router.

- The home router connects to the service provider cable modem using an Ethernet cable.

- The cable modem connects to the Internet service provider (ISP) network.

The Branch site devices connect as follows:

- Corporate resources (i.e., file servers and printers) connect to Layer 2 switches using Ethernet cables.

- Desktop PCs and voice over IP (VoIP) phones connect to Layer 2 switches using Ethernet cables.

- Laptops and smartphones connect wirelessly to wireless access points (WAPs).

- The WAPs connect to switches using Ethernet cables.

- Layer 2 switches connect to an Ethernet interface on the edge router using Ethernet cables. An edge router is a device that sits at the edge or boundary of a network and routes between that network and another, such as between a LAN and a WAN.

- The edge router connects to a WAN service provider (SP).

- The edge router also connects to an ISP for backup purposes.

The Central site devices connect as follows:

- Desktop PCs and VoIP phones connect to Layer 2 switches using Ethernet cables.

- Layer 2 switches connect redundantly to multilayer Layer 3 switches using Ethernet fiber-optic cables (orange connections).

- Layer 3 multilayer switches connect to an Ethernet interface on the edge router using Ethernet cables.

- The corporate website server is connected using an Ethernet cable to the edge router interface.

- The edge router connects to a WAN SP.

- The edge router also connects to an ISP for backup purposes.

In the Branch and Central LANs, hosts are connected either directly or indirectly (via WAPs) to the network infrastructure using a Layer 2 switch.

Refer to
Online Course
for Illustration

1.1.2.2   Default Gateways

To enable network access, devices must be configured with IP address information to identify the appropriate:

- **IP address** - Identifies a unique host on a local network.

- **Subnet mask** - Identifies with which network subnet the host can communicate.

- **Default gateway** - Identifies the IP address of the router to send a packet to when the destination is not on the same local network subnet.

When a host sends a packet to a device that is on the same IP network, the packet is simply forwarded out of the host interface to the destination device.

When a host sends a packet to a device on a different IP network, then the packet is forwarded to the default gateway, because a host device cannot communicate directly with devices outside of the local network. The default gateway is the destination that routes traffic from the local network to devices on remote networks. It is often used to connect a local network to the Internet.

The default gateway is usually the address of the interface on the router connected to the local network. The router maintains routing table entries of all connected networks as well as entries of remote networks, and determines the best path to reach those destinations.

For example, if PC1 sends a packet to the Web Server located at 176.16.1.99, it would discover that the Web Server is not on the local network and it, therefore, must send the packet to the Media Access Control (MAC) address of its default gateway. The Packet protocol data unit (PDU) in the figure identifies the source and destination IP and MAC addresses.

Note   A router is also usually configured with its own default gateway. This is known as the Gateway of Last Resort.

Refer to
Online Course
for Illustration

1.1.2.3   Document Network Addressing

When designing a new network or mapping an existing network, document the network. At a minimum, the documentation should identify:

- Device names

- Interfaces used in the design

- IP addresses and subnet masks

- Default gateway addresses

As the figure shows, this information is captured by creating two useful network documents:

- **Topology diagram** - Provides a visual reference that indicates the physical connectivity and logical Layer 3 addressing. Often created using software, such as Microsoft Visio.

- **An addressing table** - A table that captures device names, interfaces, IPv4 addresses, subnet masks, and default gateway addresses.

Refer to
Interactive Graphic
in online course

1.1.2.4   Enable IP on a Host

A host can be assigned IP address information either:

- **Statically** - The host is manually assigned the correct IP address, subnet mask, and default gateway. The DNS server IP address can also be configured.

- **Dynamically** - IP address information is provided by a server using the Dynamic Host Configuration Protocol (DHCP). The DHCP server provides a valid IP address, subnet mask, and default gateway for end devices. Other information may be provided by the server.

Figure 1 and Figure 2 provide static and dynamic IPv4 address configuration examples.

Statically assigned addresses are commonly used to identify specific network resources, such as network servers and printers. They can also be used in smaller networks with few hosts. However, most host devices acquire their IPv4 address information by accessing a DHCPv4 server. In large enterprises, dedicated DHCPv4 servers providing services to many LANs are implemented. In a smaller branch or small office setting, DHCPv4 services can be provided by a Cisco Catalyst switch or a Cisco ISR.

Refer to
Interactive Graphic
in online course

1.1.2.5   Device LEDs

Host computers connect to a wired network using a network interface and RJ-45 Ethernet cable. Most network interfaces have one or two LED link indicators next to the interface. Typically, a green LED means a good connection while a blinking green LED indicates network activity.

If the link light is not on, then there may be a problem with either the network cable or the network itself. The switch port where the connection terminates would also have an LED indicator lit. If one or both ends are not lit, try a different network cable.

Note   The actual function of the LEDs varies between computer manufacturers.

Similarly, network infrastructure devices commonly use multiple LED indicators to provide a quick status view. For example, a Cisco Catalyst 2960 switch has several status LEDs to help monitor system activity and performance. These LEDs are generally lit green when the switch is functioning normally and lit amber when there is a malfunction.

Cisco ISRs use various LED indicators to provide status information. A Cisco 1941 router is shown in the figure. The LEDs on the router help the network administrator conduct some basic troubleshooting. Each device has a unique set of LEDs. Consult the device-specific documentation for an accurate description of the LEDs.

Refer to
Interactive Graphic
in online course

1.1.2.6   Console Access

In a production environment, infrastructure devices are commonly accessed remotely using Secure Shell (SSH) or HyperText Transfer Protocol Secure (HTTPS). Console access is really only required when initially configuring a device, or if remote access fails.

Console access requires:

- **Console cable** - RJ-45-to-DB-9 serial cable or a USB serial cable
- **Terminal emulation software** - Tera Term, PuTTY, HyperTerminal

The cable is connected between the serial port of the host and the console port on the device. Most computers and notebooks no longer include built-in serial ports. If the host does not have a serial port, the USB port can be used to establish a console connection. A special USB-to-RS-232 compatible serial port adapter is required when using the USB port.

The Cisco ISR G2 supports a USB serial console connection. To establish connectivity, a USB Type-A to USB Type-B (mini-B USB) is required, as well as an operating system device driver. This device driver is available from www.cisco.com. Although these routers have two console ports, only one console port can be active at a time. When a cable is plugged into the USB console port, the RJ-45 port becomes inactive. When the USB cable is removed from the USB port, the RJ-45 port becomes active.

The table in Figure 1 summarizes the console connection requirements. Figure 2 displays the various ports and cables required.

Refer to
Interactive Graphic
in online course

1.1.2.7   Enable IP on a Switch

Network infrastructure devices require IP addresses to enable remote management. Using the device IP address, the network administrator can remotely connect to the device using Telnet, SSH, HTTP, or HTTPS.

A switch does not have a dedicated interface to which an IP address can be assigned. Instead, the IP address information is configured on a virtual interface called a switched virtual interface (SVI).

For example, in Figure 1, the SVI on the Layer 2 switch S1 is assigned the IP address 192.168.10.2/24 and a default gateway of 192.168.10.1.

Use the Syntax Checker in Figure 2 to configure the Layer 2 switch S2.

Refer to
Interactive Graphic
in online course

1.1.2.8   Activity – Document an Addressing Scheme

Refer to **Packet
Tracer Activity**
for this chapter

1.1.2.9   Packet Tracer – Documenting the Network

Background/Scenario

Your job is to document the addressing scheme and connections used in the Central portion of the network. You will need to use a variety of commands to gather the required information.

1.1.3   Router Basic Settings

Refer to
Interactive Graphic
in online course

1.1.3.1   Configure Basic Router Settings

Cisco routers and Cisco switches have many similarities. They support a similar modal operating system, similar command structures, and many of the same commands. In addition, both devices have similar initial configuration steps.

For instance, the following configuration tasks should always be performed:

- **Name the device** – (Figure 1) Distinguishes it from other routers.

- **Secure management access** – (Figure 2) Secures privileged EXEC, user EXEC, and remote access.

- **Configure a banner** – (Figure 3) Provides legal notification of unauthorized access.

Always save the changes on a router as shown in Figure 4 and verify the basic configuration and router operations.

Use the Syntax Checker in Figure 5 to configure router R2.

Refer to
Interactive Graphic
in online course

1.1.3.2   Configure an IPv4 Router Interface

One distinguishing feature between switches and routers is the type of interfaces supported by each. For example, Layer 2 switches support LANs and, therefore, have multiple FastEthernet or Gigabit Ethernet ports.

Routers support LANs and WANs and can interconnect different types of networks; therefore, they support many types of interfaces. For example, G2 ISRs have one or two integrated Gigabit Ethernet interfaces and High-Speed WAN Interface Card (HWIC) slots to accommodate other types of network interfaces, including serial, DSL, and cable interfaces.

To be available, an interface must be:

- **Configured with an IP address and a subnet mask** - Use the **ip address** *ip-address subnet-mask* interface configuration command.

- **Activated** - By default, LAN and WAN interfaces are not activated (**shutdown**). To enable an interface, it must be activated using the **no shutdown** command. (This is similar to powering on the interface.) The interface must also be connected to another device (a hub, a switch, or another router) for the physical layer to be active.

Optionally, the interface could also be configured with a short description of up to 240 characters. It is good practice to configure a description on each interface. On production networks, the benefits of interface descriptions are quickly realized as they are helpful in troubleshooting and to identify a third party connection and contact information.

Depending on the type of interface, additional parameters may be required. For example, in the lab environment, the serial interface connecting to the serial cable end labeled DCE must be configured with the **clock rate** command.

Note   Accidentally using the **clock rate** command on a DTE interface generates a "%Error: This command applies only to DCE interface" informational message.

Figures 1 through 3 provide examples of configuring the router interfaces of R1. In Figure 3, notice that the state of Serial0/0/0 is "down". The status will change to "up" when the Serial0/0/0 interface on R2 is configured and activated.

Use the Syntax Checker in Figure 4 to configure router R2.

Refer to
Interactive Graphic
in online course

1.1.3.3   Configure an IPv6 Router Interface

Configuring an IPv6 interface is similar to configuring an interface for IPv4. Most IPv6 configuration and verification commands in the Cisco IOS are very similar to their IPv4 counterparts. In many cases, the only difference is the use of **ipv6** in place of **ip** in commands.

An IPv6 interface must be:

- **Configured with IPv6 address and subnet mask** - Use the **ipv6 address** *ipv6-address/prefix-length* [**link-local** | **eui-64**] interface configuration command.

- **Activated** - The interface must be activated using the **no shutdown** command.

Note   An interface can generate its own IPv6 link-local address without having a global unicast address by using the **ipv6 enable** interface configuration command.

Unlike IPv4, IPv6 interfaces will typically have more than one IPv6 address. At a minimum, an IPv6 device must have an IPv6 link-local address but will most likely also have an IPv6 global unicast address. IPv6 also supports the ability for an interface to have multiple IPv6 global unicast addresses from the same subnet. The following commands can be used to statically create a global unicast or link-local IPv6 address:

- **ipv6 address** *ipv6-address/prefix-length* - Creates a global unicast IPv6 address as specified.

- **ipv6 address** *ipv6-address/prefix-length* **eui-64** - Configures a global unicast IPv6 address with an interface identifier (ID) in the low-order 64 bits of the IPv6 address using the EUI-64 process.

- **ipv6 address** *ipv6-address/prefix-length* **link-local** - Configures a static link-local address on the interface that is used instead of the link-local address that is automatically configured when the global unicast IPv6 address is assigned to the interface or enabled using the **ipv6 enable** interface command. Recall, the **ipv6 enable** interface command is used to automatically create an IPv6 link-local address whether or not an IPv6 global unicast address has been assigned.

In the example topology shown in Figure 1, R1 must be configured to support the following IPv6 network addresses:

- 2001:0DB8:ACAD:0001::/64 or equivalently 2001:DB8:ACAD:1::/64

- 2001:0DB8:ACAD:0002::/64 or equivalently 2001:DB8:ACAD:2::/64

- 2001:0DB8:ACAD:0003::/64 or equivalently 2001:DB8:ACAD:3::/64

When the router is configured using the **ipv6 unicast-routing** global configuration command, the router begins sending ICMPv6 Router Advertisement messages out the interface. This enables a PC connected to the interface to automatically configure an IPv6 address and to set a default gateway without needing the services of a DHCPv6 server. Alternatively, a PC connected to the IPv6 network can have an IPv6 address manually configured, as shown in Figure 2. Notice that the default gateway address configured for PC1 is the IPv6 global unicast address of the R1 GigabitEthernet 0/0 interface.

The router interfaces in the example topology must be configured and enabled as shown in Figures 3 through 5.

Use the Syntax Checker in Figure 6 to configure the IPv6 global unicast addresses on router R2.

<table>
<tr><td>Refer to
Online Course
for Illustration</td></tr>
</table>

1.1.3.4   Configure an IPv4 Loopback Interface

Another common configuration of Cisco IOS routers is enabling a loopback interface.

The loopback interface is a logical interface internal to the router. It is not assigned to a physical port and can therefore never be connected to any other device. It is considered a software interface that is automatically placed in an "up" state, as long as the router is functioning.

The loopback interface is useful in testing and managing a Cisco IOS device because it ensures that at least one interface will always be available. For example, it can be used for testing purposes, such as testing internal routing processes, by emulating networks behind the router.

Additionally, the IPv4 address assigned to the loopback interface can be significant to processes on the router that use an interface IPv4 address for identification purposes, such as the Open Shortest Path First (OSPF) routing process. By enabling a loopback interface, the router will use the always available loopback interface address for identification, rather than an IP address assigned to a physical port that may go down.

Enabling and assigning a loopback address is simple:

```
Router(config)# interface loopback number

Router(config-if)# ip address ip-address subnet-mask

Router(config-if)# exit
```

Multiple loopback interfaces can be enabled on a router. The IPv4 address for each loopback interface must be unique and unused by any other interface.

Refer to **Packet Tracer Activity** for this chapter

1.1.3.5 Packet Tracer – Configuring IPv4 and IPv6 Interfaces

Background/Scenario

Routers R1 and R2 each have two LANs. Your task is to configure the appropriate addressing on each device and verify connectivity between the LANs.

1.1.4 Verify Connectivity of Directly Connected Networks

Refer to **Interactive Graphic** in online course

1.1.4.1 Verify Interface Settings

There are several **show** commands that can be used to verify the operation and configuration of an interface. The following three commands are especially useful to quickly identify an interface status:

- **show ip interface brief** - Displays a summary for all interfaces including the IPv4 address of the interface and current operational status.

- **show ip route** - Displays the contents of the IPv4 routing table stored in RAM. In Cisco IOS 15, active interfaces should appear in the routing table with two related entries identified by the code 'C' (Connected) or 'L' (Local). In previous IOS versions, only a single entry with the code 'C' will appear.

- **show running-config interface** *interface-id* - Displays the commands configured on the specified interface.

Figure 1 displays the output of the **show ip interface brief** command. The output reveals that the LAN interfaces and the WAN link are all activated and operational as indicated by the Status of "up" and Protocol of "up". A different output would indicate a problem with either the configuration or the cabling.

Note In Figure 1, the Embedded-Service-Engine0/0 interface is displayed because Cisco ISRs G2 have dual core CPUs on the motherboard. The Embedded-Service-Engine0/0 interface is outside the scope of this course.

Figure 2 displays the output of the **show ip route** command. Notice the three directly connected network entries and the three local host route interface entries. A local host route has an administrative distance of 0. It also has a /32 mask for IPv4, and a /128 mask for IPv6. The local host route is for routes on the router owning the IP address. It is used to allow the router to process packets destined to that IP.

Figure 3 displays the output of the **show running-config interface** command. The output displays the current commands configured on the specified interface.

The following two commands are used to gather more detailed interface information:

- **show interfaces** - Displays interface information and packet flow count for all interfaces on the device.

- **show ip interface** - Displays the IPv4 related information for all interfaces on a router.

Use the Syntax Checker in Figures 4 and 5 to verify the interfaces on R1.

Refer to
Interactive Graphic
in online course

1.1.4.2   Verify IPv6 Interface Settings

The commands to verify the IPv6 interface configuration are similar to the commands used for IPv4.

The **show ipv6 interface brief** command in Figure 1 displays a summary for each of the interfaces. The "up/up" output on the same line as the interface name indicates the Layer 1/ Layer 2 interface state. This is the same as the Status and Protocol columns in the equivalent IPv4 command.

The output displays two configured IPv6 addresses per interface. One address is the IPv6 global unicast address that was manually entered. The other address, which begins with FE80, is the link-local unicast address for the interface. A link-local address is automatically added to an interface whenever a global unicast address is assigned. An IPv6 network interface is required to have a link-local address, but not necessarily a global unicast address.

The **show ipv6 interface gigabitethernet 0/0** command output shown in Figure 2 displays the interface status and all of the IPv6 addresses belonging to the interface. Along with the link local address and global unicast address, the output includes the multicast addresses assigned to the interface, beginning with prefix FF02.

The **show ipv6 route** command shown in Figure 3 can be used to verify that IPv6 networks and specific IPv6 interface addresses have been installed in the IPv6 routing table. The **showipv6route** command will only display IPv6 networks, not IPv4 networks.

Within the routing table, a 'C' next to a route indicates that this is a directly connected network. When the router interface is configured with a global unicast address and is in the "up/up" state, the IPv6 prefix and prefix length is added to the IPv6 routing table as a connected route.

The IPv6 global unicast address configured on the interface is also installed in the routing table as a local route. The local route has a /128 prefix. Local routes are used by the routing table to efficiently process packets with the interface address of the router as the destination.

The **ping** command for IPv6 is identical to the command used with IPv4 except that an IPv6 address is used. As shown in Figure 4, the **ping** command is used to verify Layer 3 connectivity between R1 and PC1.

Refer to
Interactive Graphic
in online course

1.1.4.3   Filter Show Command Output

Commands that generate multiple screens of output are, by default, paused after 24 lines. At the end of the paused output, the --More-- text displays. Pressing **Enter** displays the next line and pressing the spacebar displays the next set of lines. Use the **terminal length** command to specify the number of lines to be displayed. A value of 0 (zero) prevents the router from pausing between screens of output.

Another very useful feature that improves the user experience in the command-line interface (CLI) is the filtering of **show** output. Filtering commands can be used to display specific sections of output. To enable the filtering command, enter a pipe (I) character after the **show** command and then enter a filtering parameter and a filtering expression.

The filtering parameters that can be configured after the pipe include:

- **section** - Shows entire section that starts with the filtering expression

- **include** - Includes all output lines that match the filtering expression

- **exclude** - Excludes all output lines that match the filtering expression

- **begin** - Shows all the output lines from a certain point, starting with the line that matches the filtering expression

Note   Output filters can be used in combination with any **show** command.

Figures 1 to 4 provide examples of the various output filters.

Use the Syntax Checker in Figure 5 to filter output.

Refer to
Interactive Graphic
in online course

1.1.4.4   Command History Feature

The command history feature is useful, because it temporarily stores the list of executed commands to be recalled.

To recall commands in the history buffer, press **Ctrl+P** or the **Up Arrow** key. The command output begins with the most recent command. Repeat the key sequence to recall successively older commands. To return to more recent commands in the history buffer, press **Ctrl+N** or the **Down Arrow** key. Repeat the key sequence to recall successively more recent commands.

By default, command history is enabled and the system captures the last 10 command lines in its history buffer. Use the **show history** privileged EXEC command to display the contents of the buffer.

It is also practical to increase the number of command lines that the history buffer records during the current terminal session only. Use the **terminal history size** user EXEC command to increase or decrease the size of the buffer.

Figure 1 displays a sample of the **terminal history size** and **show history** commands.

Use the Syntax Checker in Figure 2 to practice the two EXEC commands.

Refer to **Packet Tracer Activity** for this chapter

1.1.4.5   Packet Tracer – Configuring and Verifying a Small Network

Background/Scenario

In this activity, you will configure a router with basic settings including IP addressing. You will also configure a switch for remote management and configure the PCs. After you have successfully verified connectivity, you will use **show** commands to gather information about the network.

Refer to **Lab Activity** for this chapter

1.1.4.6   Lab – Configuring Basic Router Settings with IOS CLI

In this lab, you will complete the following objectives:

- Part 1: Set Up the Topology and Initialize Devices
- Part 2: Configure Devices and Verify Connectivity
- Part 3: Display Router Information
- Part 4: Configure IPv6 and Verify Connectivity

1.2   Routing Decisions

1.2.1   Switching Packets Between Networks

Refer to **Online Course** for Illustration

1.2.1.1   Router Switching Function

A primary function of a router is to forward packets toward their destination. This is accomplished by using a switching function, which is the process used by a router to accept a packet on one interface and forward it out of another interface. A key responsibility of the switching function is to encapsulate packets in the appropriate data link frame type for the outgoing data link.

Note   In this context, the term "switching" literally means moving packets from source to destination and should not be confused with the function of a Layer 2 switch.

After the router has determined the exit interface using the path determination function, the router must encapsulate the packet into the data link frame of the outgoing interface.

What does a router do with a packet received from one network and destined for another network? The router performs the following three major steps:

Step 1.   De-encapsulates the Layer 2 frame header and trailer to expose the Layer 3 packet.

Step 2.   Examines the destination IP address of the IP packet to find the best path in the routing table.

Step 3.   If the router finds a path to the destination, it encapsulates the Layer 3 packet into a new Layer 2 frame and forwards the frame out the exit interface.

As shown in the figure, devices have Layer 3 IPv4 addresses and Ethernet interfaces have Layer 2 data link addresses. For example, PC1 is configured with IPv4 address 192.168.1.10 and an example MAC address of 0A-10. As a packet travels from the source device to the final destination device, the Layer 3 IP addresses do not change. This is because the Layer 3 PDU does not change. However, the Layer 2 data link addresses change at every hop as the packet is de-encapsulated and re-encapsulated in a new Layer 2 frame by each router.

It is common for packets to require encapsulation into a different type of Layer 2 frame than the one which was received. For example, a router might receive an Ethernet encapsulated frame on a FastEthernet interface, and then process that frame to be forwarded out of a serial interface.

Notice in the figure that the ports between R2 and R3 do not have associated MAC addresses. This is because this is a serial link. MAC addresses are only required on multi-access networks, such as Ethernet. A serial link is a point-to-point connection and uses a different Layer 2 frame that does not require the use of a MAC address. In this example, when Ethernet frames are received on R2 from the Fa0/0 interface, destined for PC2, it is de-encapsulated and then re-encapsulated for the serial interface, such as a Point-to-Point Protocol (PPP) encapsulated frame. When R3 receives the PPP frame, it is de-encapsulated again and then re-encapsulated into an Ethernet frame with a destination MAC address of 0B-20, prior to being forwarded out the Fa0/0 interface.

Refer to **Video** in online course

1.2.1.2   Send a Packet

In the animation in the figure, PC1 is sending a packet to PC2. PC1 must determine if the destination IPv4 address is on the same network. PC1 determines its own subnet by doing an **AND** operation on its own IPv4 address and subnet mask. This produces the network address that PC1 belongs to. Next, PC1 does this same **AND** operation using the packet destination IPv4 address and the PC1 subnet mask.

If the destination network address is the same network as PC1, then PC1 does not use the default gateway. Instead, PC1 refers to its ARP cache for the MAC address of the device with that destination IPv4 address. If the MAC address is not in the cache, then PC1 generates an ARP request to acquire the address to complete the packet and send it to the destination. If the destination network address is on a different network, then PC1 forwards the packet to its default gateway.

To determine the MAC address of the default gateway, PC1 checks its ARP table for the IPv4 address of the default gateway and its associated MAC address.

If an ARP entry does not exist in the ARP table for the default gateway, PC1 sends an ARP request. Router R1 sends back an ARP reply. PC1 can then forward the packet to the MAC address of the default gateway, the Fa0/0 interface of router R1.

A similar process is used for IPv6 packets. Instead of the ARP process, IPv6 address resolution uses ICMPv6 Neighbor Solicitation and Neighbor Advertisement messages. IPv6-to-MAC address mapping are kept in a table similar to the ARP cache, called the neighbor cache.

Refer to **Video** in online course

1.2.1.3   Forward to the Next Hop

The following processes take place when R1 receives the Ethernet frame from PC1:

1. R1 examines the destination MAC address, which matches the MAC address of the receiving interface, FastEthernet 0/0. R1, therefore, copies the frame into its buffer.

2. R1 identifies the Ethernet Type field as 0x800, which means that the Ethernet frame contains an IPv4 packet in the data portion of the frame.

3. R1 de-encapsulates the Ethernet frame.

4. Because the destination IPv4 address of the packet does not match any of the directly connected networks of R1, R1 consults its routing table to route this packet. R1 searches the routing table for a network address that would include the destination IPv4 address of the packet as a host address within that network. In this example, the routing table has a route for the 192.168.4.0/24 network. The destination IPv4 address of the packet is 192.168.4.10, which is a host IPv4 address on that network.

The route that R1 finds to the 192.168.4.0/24 network has a next-hop IPv4 address of 192.168.2.2 and an exit interface of FastEthernet 0/1. This means that the IPv4 packet is encapsulated in a new Ethernet frame with the destination MAC address of the IPv4 address of the next-hop router.

Because the exit interface is on an Ethernet network, R1 must resolve the next-hop IPv4 address with a destination MAC address using ARP:

1. R1 looks up the next-hop IPv4 address of 192.168.2.2 in its ARP cache. If the entry is not in the ARP cache, R1 would send an ARP request out of its FastEthernet 0/1 interface and R2 would send back an ARP reply. R1 would then update its ARP cache with an entry for 192.168.2.2 and the associated MAC address.

2. The IPv4 packet is now encapsulated into a new Ethernet frame and forwarded out the FastEthernet 0/1 interface of R1.

The animation in the figure illustrates how R1 forwards the packet to R2.

Refer to **Video** in online course

1.2.1.4   Packet Routing

The following processes take place when R2 receives the frame on its Fa0/0 interface:

1. R2 examines the destination MAC address, which matches the MAC address of the receiving interface, FastEthernet 0/0. R2, therefore, copies the frame into its buffer.

2. R2 identifies the Ethernet Type field as 0x800, which means that the Ethernet frame contains an IPv4 packet in the data portion of the frame.

3. R2 de-encapsulates the Ethernet frame.

4. Because the destination IPv4 address of the packet does not match any of the interface addresses of R2, R2 consults its routing table to route this packet. R2 searches the routing table for the destination IPv4 address of the packet using the same process R1 used.

   The routing table of R2 has a route to the 192.168.4.0/24 network, with a next-hop IPv4 address of 192.168.3.2 and an exit interface of Serial 0/0/0. Because the exit interface is not an Ethernet network, R2 does not have to resolve the next-hop IPv4 address with a destination MAC address.

5. The IPv4 packet is now encapsulated into a new data link frame and sent out the Serial 0/0/0 exit interface.

When the interface is a point-to-point (P2P) serial connection, the router encapsulates the IPv4 packet into the proper data link frame format used by the exit interface (HDLC, PPP, etc.). Because there are no MAC addresses on serial interfaces, R2 sets the data link destination address to an equivalent of a broadcast.

The animation in the figure illustrates how R2 forwards the packet to R3.

Refer to **Video** in online course

1.2.1.5 Reach the Destination

The following processes take place when the frame arrives at R3:

1. R3 copies the data link PPP frame into its buffer.

2. R3 de-encapsulates the data link PPP frame.

3. R3 searches the routing table for the destination IPv4 address of the packet. The routing table has a route to a directly connected network on R3. This means that the packet can be sent directly to the destination device and does not need to be sent to another router.

Because the exit interface is a directly connected Ethernet network, R3 must resolve the destination IPv4 address of the packet with a destination MAC address:

1. R3 searches for the destination IPv4 address of the packet in its Address Resolution Protocol (ARP) cache. If the entry is not in the ARP cache, R3 sends an ARP request out of its FastEthernet 0/0 interface. PC2 sends back an ARP reply with its MAC address. R3 then updates its ARP cache with an entry for 192.168.4.10 and the MAC address that is returned in the ARP reply.

2. The IPv4 packet is encapsulated into a new Ethernet data link frame and sent out the FastEthernet 0/0 interface of R3.

3. When PC2 receives the frame, it examines the destination MAC address, which matches the MAC address of the receiving interface, its Ethernet network interface card (NIC). PC2, therefore, copies the rest of the frame into its buffer.

4. PC2 identifies the Ethernet Type field as 0x800, which means that the Ethernet frame contains an IPv4 packet in the data portion of the frame.

5. PC2 de-encapsulates the Ethernet frame and passes the IPv4 packet to the IPv4 process of its operating system.

The animation in the figure illustrates how R3 forwards the packet to PC2.

Refer to **Interactive Graphic** in online course

1.2.1.6 Activity – Match Layer 2 and Layer 3 Addressing

1.2.2 Path Determination

Refer to **Online Course** for Illustration

1.2.2.1 Routing Decisions

A primary function of a router is to determine the best path to use to send packets. To determine the best path, the router searches its routing table for a network address that matches the destination IP address of the packet.

The routing table search results in one of three path determinations:

- **Directly connected network** - If the destination IP address of the packet belongs to a device on a network that is directly connected to one of the interfaces of the router, that packet is forwarded directly to the destination device. This means that the destination IP address of the packet is a host address on the same network as the interface of the router.

- **Remote network** - If the destination IP address of the packet belongs to a remote network, then the packet is forwarded to another router. Remote networks can only be reached by forwarding packets to another router.

- **No route determined** - If the destination IP address of the packet does not belong to either a connected or remote network, the router determines if there is a Gateway of Last Resort available. A Gateway of Last Resort is set when a default route is configured or learned on a router. If there is a default route, the packet is forwarded to the Gateway of Last Resort. If the router does not have a default route, then the packet is discarded.

The logic flowchart in the figure illustrates the router packet forwarding decision process.

Refer to Video
in online course

1.2.2.2   Best Path

Determining the best path involves the evaluation of multiple paths to the same destination network and selecting the optimum or shortest path to reach that network. Whenever multiple paths to the same network exist, each path uses a different exit interface on the router to reach that network.

The best path is selected by a routing protocol based on the value or metric it uses to determine the distance to reach a network. A metric is the quantitative value used to measure the distance to a given network. The best path to a network is the path with the lowest metric.

Dynamic routing protocols typically use their own rules and metrics to build and update routing tables. The routing algorithm generates a value, or a metric, for each path through the network. Metrics can be based on either a single characteristic or several characteristics of a path. Some routing protocols can base route selection on multiple metrics, combining them into a single metric.

The following lists some dynamic protocols and the metrics they use:

- **Routing Information Protocol (RIP)** - Hop count

- **Open Shortest Path First (OSPF)** - Cisco's cost based on cumulative bandwidth from source to destination

- **Enhanced Interior Gateway Routing Protocol (EIGRP)** - Bandwidth, delay, load, reliability

The animation in the figure highlights how the path may be different depending on the metric being used.

Refer to Video
in online course

1.2.2.3   Load Balancing

What happens if a routing table has two or more paths with identical metrics to the same destination network?

When a router has two or more paths to a destination with equal cost metrics, then the router forwards the packets using both paths equally. This is called equal cost load balancing. The routing table contains the single destination network, but has multiple exit interfaces, one for each equal cost path. The router forwards packets using the multiple exit interfaces listed in the routing table.

If configured correctly, load balancing can increase the effectiveness and performance of the network. Equal cost load balancing can be configured to use both dynamic routing protocols and static routes.

Note   Only EIGRP supports unequal cost load balancing.

The animation in the figure provides an example of equal cost load balancing.

Refer to
Interactive Graphic
in online course

1.2.2.4   Administrative Distance

It is possible for a router to be configured with multiple routing protocols and static routes. If this occurs, the routing table may have more than one route source for the same destination network. For example, if both RIP and EIGRP are configured on a router, both routing protocols may learn of the same destination network. However, each routing protocol may decide on a different path to reach the destination based on that routing protocol's metrics. RIP chooses a path based on hop count, whereas EIGRP chooses a path based on its composite metric. How does the router know which route to use?

Cisco IOS uses what is known as the administrative distance (AD) to determine the route to install into the IP routing table. The AD represents the "trustworthiness" of the route; the lower the AD, the more trustworthy the route source. For example, a static route has an AD of 1, whereas an EIGRP-discovered route has an AD of 90. Given two separate routes to the same destination, the router chooses the route with the lowest AD. When a router has the choice of a static route and an EIGRP route, the static route takes precedence. Similarly, a directly connected route with an AD of 0 takes precedence over a static route with an AD of 1.

The figure lists various routing protocols and their associated ADs.

Refer to
Interactive Graphic
in online course

1.2.2.5   Activity – Order the Steps in the Packet Forwarding Process

Refer to
Interactive Graphic
in online course

1.2.2.6   Activity – Match the Administrative Distance to the Route Source

1.3   Router Operation

1.3.1   Analyze the Routing Table

Refer to
Online Course
for Illustration

1.3.1.1   The Routing Table

The routing table of a router stores information about:

- **Directly connected routes** - These routes come from the active router interfaces. Routers add a directly connected route when an interface is configured with an IP address and is activated.

■ **Remote routes** - These are remote networks connected to other routers. Routes to these networks can either be statically configured or dynamically learned through dynamic routing protocols.

Specifically, a routing table is a data file in RAM that is used to store route information about directly connected and remote networks. The routing table contains network or next hop associations. These associations tell a router that a particular destination can be optimally reached by sending the packet to a specific router that represents the next hop on the way to the final destination. The next hop association can also be the outgoing or exit interface to the next destination.

The figure identifies the directly connected networks and remote networks of router R1.

Refer to
Interactive Graphic
in online course

1.3.1.2   Routing Table Sources

On a Cisco router, the **show ip route** command can be used to display the IPv4 routing table of a router. A router provides additional route information, including how the route was learned, how long the route has been in the table, and which specific interface to use to get to a predefined destination.

Entries in the routing table can be added as:

■ **Local Route interfaces** - Added when an interface is configured and active. This entry is only displayed in IOS 15 or newer for IPv4 routes and all IOS releases for IPv6 routes.

■ **Directly connected interfaces** - Added to the routing table when an interface is configured and active.

■ **Static routes** - Added when a route is manually configured and the exit interface is active.

■ **Dynamic routing protocol** - Added when routing protocols that dynamically learn about the network, such as EIGRP or OSPF, are implemented and networks are identified.

The sources of the routing table entries are identified by a code. The code identifies how the route was learned. For instance, common codes include:

■ **L** - Identifies the address assigned to a router's interface. This allows the router to efficiently determine when it receives a packet for the interface instead of being forwarded.

■ **C** - Identifies a directly connected network.

■ **S** - Identifies a static route created to reach a specific network.

■ **D** - Identifies a dynamically learned network from another router using EIGRP.

■ **O** - Identifies a dynamically learned network from another router using the OSPF routing protocol.

The figure shows the routing table of R1 in a simple network.

Refer to
Online Course
for Illustration

1.3.1.3   Remote Network Routing Entries

As a network administrator, it is imperative to know how to interpret the content of IPv4 and IPv6 routing tables. The figure displays an IPv4 routing table entry on R1 for the route to remote network 10.1.1.0.

The entry identifies the following information:

- **Route source** - Identifies how the route was learned.

- **Destination network** - Identifies the address of the remote network.

- **Administrative distance** - Identifies the trustworthiness of the route source. Lower values indicate preferred route source.

- **Metric** - Identifies the value assigned to reach the remote network. Lower values indicate preferred routes.

- **Next-hop** - Identifies the IPv4 address of the next router to forward the packet to.

- **Route timestamp** - Identifies how much time has passed since the route was learned.

- **Outgoing interface** - Identifies the exit interface to use to forward a packet toward the final destination.

Refer to
Interactive Graphic
in online course

1.3.1.4   Activity – Interpret the Content of a Routing Table Entry

1.3.2   Directly Connected Routes

Refer to
Online Course
for Illustration

1.3.2.1   Directly Connected Interfaces

A newly deployed router, without any configured interfaces, has an empty routing table, as shown in the figure.

Before the interface state is considered up/up and added to the IPv4 routing table, the interface must:

- Be assigned a valid IPv4 or IPv6 address

- Be activated with the **no shutdown** command

- Receive a carrier signal from another device (router, switch, host, etc.)

When the interface is up, the network of that interface is added to the routing table as a directly connected network.

Refer to
Online Course
for Illustration

1.3.2.2   Directly Connected Routing Table Entries

An active, properly configured, directly connected interface actually creates two routing table entries. The figure displays the IPv4 routing table entries on R1 for the directly connected network 192.168.10.0.

The routing table entry for directly connected interfaces is simpler than the entries for remote networks. The entries contain the following information:

- **Route source** - Identifies how the route was learned. Directly connected interfaces have two route source codes. 'C' identifies a directly connected network. 'L' identifies the IPv4 address assigned to the router's interface.

■ **Destination network** - The address of the remote network.

■ **Outgoing interface** - Identifies the exit interface to use when forwarding packets to the destination network.

Note   Prior to IOS 15, local route routing table entries (L) were not displayed in the IPv4 routing table. Local route (L) entries have always been a part of the IPv6 routing table.

Refer to
Online Course
for Illustration

1.3.2.3   Directly Connected Examples

The examples in Figures 1 to 3 show the steps to configure and activate the interfaces attached to R1. Notice the Layer 1 and 2 informational messages generated as each interface is activated.

As each interface is added, the routing table automatically adds the connected ('C') and local ('L') entries. Figure 4 provides an example of the routing table with the directly connected interfaces of R1 configured and activated.

Use the Syntax Checker in Figure 5 to configure and activate the interfaces connected to R2.

Refer to
Interactive Graphic
in online course

1.3.2.4   Directly Connected IPv6 Example

The example in Figure 1 shows the configuration steps for the directly connected interfaces of R1 with the indicated IPv6 addresses. Notice the Layer 1 and Layer 2 informational messages generated as each interface is configured and activated.

The **show ipv6 route** command shown in Figure 2 is used to verify that IPv6 networks and specific IPv6 interface addresses have been installed in the IPv6 routing table. Like IPv4, a 'C' next to a route indicates that this is a directly connected network. An 'L' indicates the local route. In an IPv6 network, the local route has a /128 prefix. Local routes are used by the routing table to efficiently process packets with a destination address of the interface of the router.

Notice that there is also a route installed to the FF00::/8 network. This route is required for multicast routing.

Figure 3 displays how the **show ipv6 route** command can be combined with a specific network destination to display the details of how that route was learned by the router.

Figure 4 displays how connectivity to R2 can be verified using the **ping** command.

In Figure 5, notice what happens when the G0/0 LAN interface of R2 is the target of the **ping** command. The pings are unsuccessful. This is because R1 does not have an entry in the routing table to reach the 2001:DB8:ACAD:4::/64 network.

R1 requires additional information to reach a remote network. Remote network route entries can be added to the routing table using either:

■ Static routing

■ Dynamic routing protocols

Refer to **Packet Tracer Activity** for this chapter

1.3.2.5   Packet Tracer – Investigating Directly Connected Routes

Background

The network in the activity is already configured. You will log in to the routers and use **show** commands to discover and answer the questions below about the directly connected routes.

1.3.3   Statically Learned Routes

Refer to **Online Course** for Illustration

1.3.3.1   Static Routes

After directly connected interfaces are configured and added to the routing table, then static or dynamic routing can be implemented.

Static routes are manually configured. They define an explicit path between two networking devices. Unlike a dynamic routing protocol, static routes are not automatically updated and must be manually reconfigured if the network topology changes. The benefits of using static routes include improved security and resource efficiency. Static routes use less bandwidth than dynamic routing protocols, and no CPU cycles are used to calculate and communicate routes. The main disadvantage to using static routes is the lack of automatic reconfiguration if the network topology changes.

There are two common types of static routes in the routing table:

- Static route to a specific network

- Default static route

A static route can be configured to reach a specific remote network. IPv4 static routes are configured using the following command:

```
Router(config)#  ip route network mask { next-hop-ip | exit-intf }
```

A static route is identified in the routing table with the code 'S'.

A default static route is similar to a default gateway on a host. The default static route specifies the exit point to use when the routing table does not contain a path for the destination network. A default static route is useful when a router has only one exit point to another router, such as when the router connects to a central router or service provider.

To configure an IPv4 default static route, use the following command:

```
Router(config)#  ip route 0.0.0.0 0.0.0.0 { exit-intf | next-hop-ip }
```

The figure provides a simple scenario of how default and static routes can be applied.

Refer to **Interactive Graphic** in online course

1.3.3.2   Static Route Examples

Figure 1 shows the configuration of an IPv4 default static route on R1 to the Serial 0/0/0 interface. Notice that the configuration of the route generated an 'S*' entry in the routing table. The 'S' signifies that the route source is a static route while the asterisk (*) identifies this route as a possible candidate to be the default route. In fact, it has been chosen as the default route as evidenced by the line that reads, "Gateway of Last Resort is 0.0.0.0 to network 0.0.0.0."

Figure 2 shows the configuration of two static routes from R2 to reach the two LANs on R1. The route to 192.168.10.0/24 has been configured using the exit interface while the route to 192.168.11.0/24 has been configured using the next hop IPv4 address. Although both are acceptable, there are some differences in how they operate. For instance, notice how different they look in the routing table. Also notice that because these static routes were to specific networks, the output indicates that the Gateway of Last Resort is not set.

Note   Static and default static routes are discussed in detail in the next chapter.

Use the Syntax Checker in Figure 3 to configure a default static route on router R1 going to R2.

Use the Syntax Checker in Figure 4 to configure static routes on router R2 to reach the R1 LANs.

Refer to
Interactive Graphic
in online course

1.3.3.3   Static IPv6 Route Examples

Like IPv4, IPv6 supports static and default static routes. They are used and configured like IPv4 static routes.

To configure a default static IPv6 route, use the **ipv6 route ::/0** {*ipv6-address | interface-type interface-number*} global configuration command.

Figure 1 shows the configuration of a default static route on R1 to the Serial 0/0/0 interface.

Notice in the output shown in Figure 2 that the default static route configuration generated an 'S' entry in the routing table. The 'S' signifies that the route source is a static route. Unlike the IPv4 static route, there is no asterisk (*) or Gateway of Last Resort explicitly identified.

Like IPv4, static routes are routes explicitly configured to reach a specific remote network. Static IPv6 routes are configured using the **ipv6 route** *ipv6-prefix/prefix-length* {*ipv6-address\interface-type interface-number*} global configuration command.

The example in Figure 3 shows the configuration of two static routes from R2 to reach the two LANs on R1. The route to the 2001:0DB8:ACAD:2::/64 LAN is configured with an exit interface, while the route to the 2001:0DB8:ACAD:1::/64 LAN is configured with the next hop IPv6 address. The next hop IPv6 address can be either an IPv6 global unicast or link-local address.

Figure 4 shows the routing table with the new static routes installed.

Figure 5 confirms remote network connectivity to the 2001:0DB8:ACAD:4::/64 LAN on R2 from R1.

1.3.4   Dynamic Routing Protocols

Refer to
Online Course
for Illustration

1.3.4.1   Dynamic Routing

Dynamic routing protocols are used by routers to share information about the reachability and status of remote networks. Dynamic routing protocols perform several activities, including network discovery and maintaining routing tables.

Network discovery is the ability of a routing protocol to share information about the networks that it knows about with other routers that are also using the same routing protocol. Instead of depending on manually configured static routes to remote networks on every router, a dynamic routing protocol allows the routers to automatically learn about these networks from other routers. These networks, and the best path to each, are added to the routing table of the router, and identified as a network learned by a specific dynamic routing protocol.

During network discovery, routers exchange routes and update their routing tables. Routers have converged after they have finished exchanging and updating their routing tables. Routers then maintain the networks in their routing tables.

The figure provides a simple scenario of how two neighboring routers would initially exchange routing information. In this simplified exchange, R1 introduces itself and the networks it can reach. R2 responds with its list of networks.

Refer to
Online Course
for Illustration

1.3.4.2   IPv4 Routing Protocols

A router running a dynamic routing protocol does not only make a best path determination to a network, it also determines a new best path if the initial path becomes unusable (or if the topology changes). For these reasons, dynamic routing protocols have an advantage over static routes. Routers that use dynamic routing protocols automatically share routing information with other routers and compensate for any topology changes without involving the network administrator.

Cisco routers can support a variety of dynamic IPv4 routing protocols including:

- **EIGRP** - Enhanced Interior Gateway Routing Protocol
- **OSPF** - Open Shortest Path First
- **IS-IS** - Intermediate System-to-Intermediate System
- **RIP** - Routing Information Protocol

To determine which routing protocols are supported by the IOS, use the **router ?** command in global configuration mode as shown in the figure.

Refer to
Interactive Graphic
in online course

1.3.4.3   IPv4 Dynamic Routing Examples

In this dynamic routing example, assume that R1 and R2 have been configured to support the dynamic routing protocol EIGRP. The routers also advertise directly connected networks. R2 advertises that it is the default gateway to other networks.

The output in the figure displays the routing table of R1 after the routers have exchanged updates and converged. Along with the connected and link local interfaces, there are three 'D' entries in the routing table.

- The entry beginning with 'D*EX' identifies that the source of this entry was EIGRP ('D'). The route is a candidate to be a default route ('*'), and the route is an external route ('*EX') forwarded by EIGRP.

- The other two 'D' entries are routes installed in the routing table based on the update from R2 advertising its LANs.

Refer to
Interactive Graphic
in online course

1.3.4.4   IPv6 Routing Protocols

As shown in the figure, ISR devices support dynamic IPv6 routing protocols including:

- RIPng (RIP next generation)

- OSPFv3

- EIGRP for IPv6

Support for dynamic IPv6 routing protocols is dependent on hardware and IOS version. Most of the modifications in the routing protocols are to support the longer IPv6 addresses and different header structures.

To enable IPv6 routers to forward traffic, you must configure the **ipv6 unicast-routing** global configuration command.

Refer to
Interactive Graphic
in online course

1.3.4.5   IPv6 Dynamic Routing Examples

Routers R1 and R2 have been configured with the dynamic routing protocol EIGRP for IPv6. (This is the IPv6 equivalent of EIGRP for IPv4.)

To view the routing table on R1, enter the **show ipv6 route** command, as shown in the figure. The output in the figure displays the routing table of R1 after the routers have exchanged updates and converged. Along with the connected and local routes, there are two 'D' entries (EIGRP routes) in the routing table.

1.4   Summary

Refer to
Online Course
for Illustration

1.4.1.1   Activity – We Really Could Use a Map!

Scenario

Use the Ashland and Richmond routing tables shown in the file provided with this activity.

With the help of a classmate, draw a network topology using the information from the tables.

To assist you with this activity, follow these guidelines:

- **Start with the Ashland router** - use its routing table to identify ports and IP addresses/networks.

- **Add the Richmond router** - use its routing table to identify ports and IP addresses/networks.

- Add any other intermediary and end devices as specified by the tables.

In addition, record answers from your group to the reflection questions provided with this activity.

Be prepared to share your work with another group and/or the class.

Refer to **Online Course** for Illustration

1.4.1.2 Routing Concepts

There are many key structures and performance-related characteristics referred to when discussing networks: topology, speed, cost, security, availability, scalability, and reliability.

Cisco routers and Cisco switches have many similarities. They support a similar modal operating system, similar command structures, and many of the same commands. One distinguishing feature between switches and routers is the type of interfaces supported by each. Once an interface is configured on both devices, the appropriate **show** commands need to be used to verify a working interface.

The main purpose of a router is to connect multiple networks and forward packets from one network to the next. This means that a router typically has multiple interfaces. Each interface is a member or host on a different IP network.

Cisco IOS uses what is known as the administrative distance (AD) to determine the route to install into the IP routing table. The routing table is a list of networks known by the router. The routing table includes network addresses for its own interfaces, which are the directly connected networks, as well as network addresses for remote networks. A remote network is a network that can only be reached by forwarding the packet to another router.

Remote networks are added to the routing table in two ways: either by the network administrator manually configuring static routes or by implementing a dynamic routing protocol. Static routes do not have as much overhead as dynamic routing protocols; however, static routes can require more maintenance if the topology is constantly changing or is unstable.

Dynamic routing protocols automatically adjust to changes without any intervention from the network administrator. Dynamic routing protocols require more CPU processing and also use a certain amount of link capacity for routing updates and messages. In many cases, a routing table will contain both static and dynamic routes.

Routers make their primary forwarding decision at Layer 3, the Network layer. However, router interfaces participate in Layers 1, 2, and 3. Layer 3 IP packets are encapsulated into a Layer 2 data link frame and encoded into bits at Layer 1. Router interfaces participate in Layer 2 processes associated with their encapsulation. For example, an Ethernet interface on a router participates in the ARP process like other hosts on that LAN.

The Cisco IP routing table is not a flat database. The routing table is actually a hierarchical structure that is used to speed up the lookup process when locating routes and forwarding packets.

Components of the IPv6 routing table are very similar to the IPv4 routing table. For instance, it is populated using directly connected interfaces, static routes and dynamically learned routes.

Go to the online course to take the quiz and exam.

Chapter 1 Quiz

This quiz is designed to provide an additional opportunity to practice the skills and knowledge presented in the chapter and to prepare for the chapter exam. You will be allowed multiple attempts and the grade does not appear in the gradebook.

Chapter 1 Exam

The chapter exam assesses your knowledge of the chapter content.

Your Chapter Notes

Static Routing

2.0 Introduction

Refer to
Online Course
for Illustration

2.0.1.1 Static Routing

Routing is at the core of every data network, moving information across an internetwork from source to destination. Routers are the devices responsible for the transfer of packets from one network to the next.

Routers learn about remote networks either dynamically, using routing protocols, or manually, or using static routes. In many cases, routers use a combination of both dynamic routing protocols and static routes. This chapter focuses on static routing.

Static routes are very common and do not require the same amount of processing and overhead as dynamic routing protocols.

In this chapter, sample topologies will be used to configure IPv4 and IPv6 static routes and to present troubleshooting techniques. In the process, several important IOS commands and the resulting output will be examined. An introduction to the routing table using both directly connected networks and static routes will be included.

Refer to
Online Course
for Illustration

2.0.1.2 Activity – Which Way Should We Go

A huge sporting event is about to take place in your city. To attend the event, you make concise plans to arrive at the sports arena on time to see the entire game.

There are two routes you can take to drive to the event:

- **Highway route** - It is easy to follow and fast driving speeds are allowed.

- **Alternate, direct route** - You found this route using a city map. Depending on conditions, such as the amount of traffic or congestion, this just may be the way to get to the arena on time.

With a partner, discuss these options. Choose a preferred route to arrive at the arena in time to see every second of the huge sporting event.

Compare your optional preferences to network traffic, which route would you choose to deliver data communications for your small- to medium-sized business? Would it be the fastest, easiest route or the alternative, direct route? Justify your choice.

Complete the modeling activity .pdf and be prepared to justify your answers to the class or with another group.

2.1   Implement Static Routes

2.1.1   Static Routing

Refer to
Interactive Graphic
in online course

2.1.1.1   Reach Remote Networks

A router can learn about remote networks in one of two ways:

- **Manually** - Remote networks are manually entered into the route table using static routes.

- **Dynamically** - Remote routes are automatically learned using a dynamic routing protocol.

Figure 1 provides a sample scenario of static routing. Figure 2 provides a sample scenario of dynamic routing using EIGRP.

A network administrator can manually configure a static route to reach a specific network. Unlike a dynamic routing protocol, static routes are not automatically updated and must be manually reconfigured any time the network topology changes.

Refer to
Online Course
for Illustration

2.1.1.2   Why Use Static Routing?

Static routing provides some advantages over dynamic routing, including:

- Static routes are not advertised over the network, resulting in better security.

- Static routes use less bandwidth than dynamic routing protocols, no CPU cycles are used to calculate and communicate routes.

- The path a static route uses to send data is known.

Static routing has the following disadvantages:

- Initial configuration and maintenance is time-consuming.

- Configuration is error-prone, especially in large networks.

- Administrator intervention is required to maintain changing route information.

- Does not scale well with growing networks; maintenance becomes cumbersome.

- Requires complete knowledge of the whole network for proper implementation.

In the figure, dynamic and static routing features are compared. Notice that the advantages of one method are the disadvantages of the other.

Static routes are useful for smaller networks with only one path to an outside network. They also provide security in a larger network for certain types of traffic or links to other networks that need more control. It is important to understand that static and dynamic routing are not mutually exclusive. Rather, most networks use a combination of dynamic routing protocols and static routes. This may result in the router having multiple paths to a destination network via static routes and dynamically learned routes. However, recall that the administrative distance (AD) value is a measure of the preference of route sources. Route sources with low AD values are preferred over routes sources with higher AD values. The AD value for a static route is 1. Therefore, a static route will take precedence over all dynamically learned routes, which will have higher AD values.

Refer to
Online Course
for Illustration

2.1.1.3   When to Use Static Routes

Static routing has three primary uses:

- Providing ease of routing table maintenance in smaller networks that are not expected to grow significantly.

- Routing to and from stub networks. A stub network is a network accessed by a single route, and the router has only one neighbor.

- Using a single default route to represent a path to any network that does not have a more specific match with another route in the routing table. Default routes are used to send traffic to any destination beyond the next upstream router.

The figure shows an example of a stub network connection and a default route connection. Notice in the figure that any network attached to R1 would only have one way to reach other destinations, whether to networks attached to R2, or to destinations beyond R2. This means that network 172.16.3.0 is a stub network and R1 is a stub router.

In this example, a static route can be configured on R2 to reach the R1 LAN. Additionally, because R1 has only one way to send out non-local traffic, a default static route can be configured on R1 to point to R2 as the next hop for all other networks.

Refer to
Interactive Graphic
in online course

2.1.1.4   Activity – Identify the Advantages and Disadvantages of Static Routing

2.1.2   Types of Static Routes

Refer to
Online Course
for Illustration

2.1.2.1   Static Route Applications

As shown in the figure, static routes are most often used to connect to a specific network or to provide a Gateway of Last Resort for a stub network. They can also be used to:

- Reduce the number of routes advertised by summarizing several contiguous networks as one static route

- Create a backup route in case a primary route link fails

The following types of IPv4 and IPv6 static routes will be discussed:

- Standard static route

- Default static route

- Summary static route

- Floating static route

Refer to
Online Course
for Illustration

2.1.2.2   Standard Static Route

Both IPv4 and IPv6 support the configuration of static routes. Static routes are useful when connecting to a specific remote network.

The figure shows that R2 can be configured with a static route to reach the stub network 172.16.3.0/24.

Note   The example is highlighting a stub network, but in fact, a static route can be used to connect to any network.

Refer to
Online Course
for Illustration

2.1.2.3   Default Static Route

A default route is a route that matches all packets and is used by the router if a packet does not match any other, more specific route in the routing table. A default route can be dynamically learned or statically configured. A default static route is simply a static route with 0.0.0.0/0 as the destination IPv4 address. Configuring a default static route creates a Gateway of Last Resort.

Default static routes are used:

- When no other routes in the routing table match the packet destination IP address. In other words, when a more specific match does not exist. A common use is when connecting a company's edge router to the ISP network.

- When a router has only one other router to which it is connected. In this situation, the router is known as a stub router.

Refer to the figure for a stub network default route scenario.

Refer to
Online Course
for Illustration

2.1.2.4   Summary Static Route

To reduce the number of routing table entries, multiple static routes can be summarized into a single static route if:

- The destination networks are contiguous and can be summarized into a single network address.

- The multiple static routes all use the same exit interface or next-hop IP address.

In the figure, R1 would require four separate static routes to reach the 172.20.0.0/16 to 172.23.0.0/16 networks. Instead, one summary static route can be configured and still provide connectivity to those networks.

Note   Refer to the Chapter Appendix for more information on calculating and configuring summary static routes.

Refer to
Online Course
for Illustration

2.1.2.5   Floating Static Route

Another type of static route is a floating static route. Floating static routes are static routes that are used to provide a backup path to a primary static or dynamic route, in the event of a link failure. The floating static route is only used when the primary route is not available.

To accomplish this, the floating static route is configured with a higher administrative distance than the primary route. The administrative distance represents the trustworthiness of a route. If multiple paths to the destination exist, the router will choose the path with the lowest administrative distance.

For example, assume that an administrator wants to create a floating static route as a backup to an EIGRP-learned route. The floating static route must be configured with a higher administrative distance than EIGRP. EIGRP has an administrative distance of 90. If the floating static route is configured with an administrative distance of 95, the dynamic route learned through EIGRP is preferred to the floating static route. If the EIGRP-learned route is lost, the floating static route is used in its place.

In the figure, the Branch router typically forwards all traffic to the HQ router over the private WAN link. In this example, the routers exchange route information using EIGRP. A floating static route, with an administrative distance of 91 or higher, could be configured to serve as a backup route. If the private WAN link fails and the EIGRP route disappears from the routing table, the router selects the floating static route as the best path to reach the HQ LAN.

Refer to
Interactive Graphic
in online course

2.1.2.6   Activity – Identify the Type of Static Route

2.2   Configure Static and Default Routes

2.2.1   Configure IPv4 Static Routes

Refer to
Interactive Graphic
in online course

2.2.1.1   ip route Command

Static routes are configured using the **ip route** global configuration command. The basic syntax for the command is shown in the figure.

The following parameters are required to configure static routing:

- *network-address* - Destination network address of the remote network to be added to the routing table, often this is referred to as the prefix.

- *subnet-mask* - Subnet mask, or just mask, of the remote network to be added to the routing table. The subnet mask can be modified to summarize a group of networks.

One or both of the following parameters must also be used:

- *ip-address* - The IP address of the connecting router to use to forward the packet to the remote destination network. Commonly referred to as the next hop.

- *exit-intf* - The outgoing interface to use to forward the packet to the next hop.

The *distance* parameter is used to create a floating static route by setting an administrative distance that is higher than a dynamically learned route.

Refer to
Interactive Graphic
in online course

2.2.1.2 Next-Hop Options

In this example, Figures 1 to 3 display the routing tables of R1, R2, and R3. Notice that each router has entries only for directly connected networks and their associated local addresses. None of the routers have any knowledge of any networks beyond their directly connected interfaces.

For example, R1 has no knowledge of networks:

- 172.16.1.0/24 - LAN on R2

- 192.168.1.0/24 - Serial network between R2 and R3

- 192.168.2.0/24 - LAN on R3

Figure 4 displays a successful ping from R1 to R2. Figure 5 displays an unsuccessful ping to the R3 LAN. This is because R1 does not have an entry in its routing table for the R3 LAN network.

The next hop can be identified by an IP address, exit interface, or both. How the destination is specified creates one of the three following route types:

- **Next-hop route** - Only the next-hop IP address is specified

- **Directly connected static route** - Only the router exit interface is specified

- **Fully specified static route** - The next-hop IP address and exit interface are specified

Refer to
Interactive Graphic
in online course

2.2.1.3 Configure a Next-Hop Static Route

In a next-hop static route, only the next-hop IP address is specified. The exit interface is derived from the next hop. For example, in Figure 1, three next-hop static routes are configured on R1 using the IP address of the next hop, R2.

Before any packet is forwarded by a router, the routing table process must determine the exit interface to use to forward the packet. This is known as route resolvability.

Figure 2 details the basic packet forwarding process in the routing table for R1. When a packet is destined for the 192.168.2.0/24 network, R1:

1. Looks for a match in the routing table and finds that it has to forward the packets to the next-hop IPv4 address 172.16.2.2, as indicated by the label 1 in the figure. Every route that references only a next-hop IPv4 address and does not reference an exit interface must have the next-hop IPv4 address resolved using another route in the routing table with an exit interface.

2. R1 must now determine how to reach 172.16.2.2; therefore, it searches a second time for a 172.16.2.2 match. In this case, the IPv4 address matches the route for the directly connected network 172.16.2.0/24 with the exit interface Serial 0/0/0, as indicated by the label 2 in the figure. This lookup tells the routing table process that this packet is forwarded out of that interface.

It actually takes two routing table lookup processes to forward any packet to the 192.168.2.0/24 network. When the router performs multiple lookups in the routing table before forwarding a packet, it is performing a process known as a recursive lookup. Because recursive lookups consume router resources, they should be avoided when possible.

A recursive static route is valid (that is, it is a candidate for insertion in the routing table) only when the specified next hop resolves, either directly or indirectly, to a valid exit interface. If the exit interface is "down" or "administratively down", then the static route will not be installed in the routing table.

Use the Syntax Checker in Figures 3 and 4 to configure and verify next-hop static routes on R2 and R3.

Refer to
Interactive Graphic
in online course

2.2.1.4   Configure a Directly Connected Static Route

When configuring a static route, another option is to use the exit interface to specify the next-hop address.

In Figure 1, three directly connected static routes are configured on R1 using the exit interface. The routing table for R1 in Figure 2 shows that when a packet is destined for the 192.168.2.0/24 network, R1 looks for a match in the routing table, and finds that it can forward the packet out of its Serial 0/0/0 interface. No other lookups are required.

Notice how the routing table looks different for the route configured with an exit interface than for the route configured with a recursive entry.

Configuring a directly connected static route with an exit interface allows the routing table to resolve the exit interface in a single search, instead of two searches. Although the routing table entry indicates "directly connected", the administrative distance of the static route is still 1. Only a directly connected interface can have an administrative distance of 0.

Note   For point-to-point interfaces, you can use static routes that point to the exit interface or to the next-hop address. For multipoint/broadcast interfaces, it is more suitable to use static routes that point to a next-hop address.

Use the Syntax Checker in Figures 3 and 4 to configure and verify directly connected static routes on R2 and R3.

Note   CEF (Cisco Express Forwarding) is the default behavior on most platforms running IOS 12.0 or later. CEF provides optimized lookup for efficient packet forwarding by using two main data structures stored in the data plane: a FIB (Forwarding Information Base), which is a copy of the routing table, and an adjacency table that includes Layer 2 addressing information. The information combined in both of these tables work together so there is no recursive lookup needed for next-hop IP address lookups. In other words, a static route using a next-hop IP requires only a single lookup when CEF is enabled on the router. Although static routes that use only an exit interface on point-to-point networks are common, the use of the default CEF forwarding mechanism makes this practice unnecessary. CEF is discussed in more detail later in the course.

Refer to
Interactive Graphic
in online course

2.2.1.5   Configure a Fully Specified Static Route

Fully Specified Static Route

In a fully specified static route, both the exit interface and the next-hop IP address are specified. This is another type of static route that is used in older IOSs, prior to CEF. This form of static route is used when the exit interface is a multi-access interface and it is necessary to explicitly identify the next hop. The next hop must be directly connected to the specified exit interface.

Suppose that the network link between R1 and R2 is an Ethernet link and that the GigabitEthernet 0/1 interface of R1 is connected to that network, as shown in Figure 1. CEF is not enabled. To eliminate the recursive lookup, a directly connected static route can be implemented using the following command:

```
R1(config)# ip route 192.168.2.0 255.255.255.0 GigabitEthernet 0/1
```

However, this may cause unexpected or inconsistent results. The difference between an Ethernet multi-access network and a point-to-point serial network is that a point-to-point serial network has only one other device on that network, the router at the other end of the link. With Ethernet networks, there may be many different devices sharing the same multi-access network, including hosts and even multiple routers. By only designating the Ethernet exit interface in the static route, the router will not have sufficient information to determine which device is the next-hop device.

R1 knows that the packet needs to be encapsulated in an Ethernet frame and sent out the GigabitEthernet 0/1 interface. However, R1 does not know the next-hop IPv4 address; therefore, it cannot determine the destination MAC address for the Ethernet frame.

Depending upon the topology and the configurations on other routers, this static route may or may not work. It is recommended that when the exit interface is an Ethernet network, that a fully specified static route is used, including both the exit interface and the next-hop address.

As shown in Figure 2, when forwarding packets to R2, the exit interface is GigabitEthernet 0/1 and the next-hop IPv4 address is 172.16.2.2.

Note   With the use of CEF, a fully specified static route is no longer necessary. A static route using a next-hop address should be used.

Use the Syntax Checker in Figure 3 and 4 to configure and verify fully specified static routes on R2 and R3.

Refer to
Interactive Graphic
in online course

2.2.1.6   Verify a Static Route

Along with **ping** and **traceroute**, useful commands to verify static routes include:

- show ip route
- show ip route static
- show ip route *network*

Figure 1 displays sample output of the **show ip route static** command. In the example, the output is filtered using the pipe and **begin** parameter. The output reflects the use of static routes using the next-hop address.

Figure 2 displays sample output of the **show ip route 192.168.2.1** command.

Figure 3 verifies the **ip route** configuration in the running configuration.

Use the Syntax Checker in Figure 4 to verify the routing settings of R2.

Use the Syntax Checker in Figure 5 to verify the routing settings of R3.

2.2.2 Configure IPv4 Default Routes

Refer to
Online Course
for Illustration

2.2.2.1 Default Static Route

Routers commonly use default routes that are either configured locally or learned from another router, using a dynamic routing protocol. A default route does not require any left-most bits to match between the default route and the destination IPv4 address. A default route is used when no other routes in the routing table match the destination IP address of the packet. In other words, if a more specific match does not exist, then the default route is used as the Gateway of Last Resort.

Default static routes are commonly used when connecting:

- An edge router to a service provider network

- A stub router (a router with only one upstream neighbor router)

As shown in the figure, the command syntax for a default static route is similar to any other static route, except that the network address is **0.0.0.0** and the subnet mask is **0.0.0.0**.

Note   An IPv4 default static route is commonly referred to as a quad-zero route.

Refer to
Online Course
for Illustration

2.2.2.2 Configure a Default Static Route

R1 can be configured with three static routes to reach all of the remote networks in the example topology. However, R1 is a stub router because it is only connected to R2. Therefore, it would be more efficient to configure a default static route.

The example in the figure configures a default static route on R1. With the configuration shown in the example, any packets not matching more specific route entries are forwarded to 172.16.2.2.

Refer to
Interactive Graphic
in online course

2.2.2.3 Verify a Default Static Route

In the figure, the **show ip route static** command output displays the contents of the static routes in the routing table. Note the asterisk (*)next to the route with code 'S'. As displayed in the Codes table in the figure, the asterisk indicates that this static route is a candidate default route, which is why it is selected as the Gateway of Last Resort.

The key to this configuration is the /0 mask. The subnet mask in a routing table determines how many bits must match between the destination IP address of the packet and the route in the routing table. A binary 1 indicates that the bits must match. A binary 0 indicates that the bits do not have to match. A /0 mask in this route entry indicates that none of the bits are required to match. The default static route matches all packets for which a more specific match does not exist.

Refer to **Packet Tracer Activity** for this chapter

2.2.2.4   Packet Tracer – Configuring IPv4 Static and Default Routes

Background/Scenario

In this activity, you will configure static and default routes. A static route is a route that is entered manually by the network administrator to create a route that is reliable and safe. There are four different static routes that are used in this activity: a recursive static route, a directly connected static route, a fully specified static route, and a default route.

Refer to **Lab Activity** for this chapter

2.2.2.5   Lab – Configuring IPv4 Static and Default Routes

In this lab, you will complete the following objectives:

- Part 1: Set Up the Topology and Initialize Devices
- Part 2: Configure Basic Device Settings and Verify Connectivity
- Part 3: Configure Static Routes
- Part 4: Configure and Verify a Default Route

2.2.3   Configure IPv6 Static Routes

Refer to **Interactive Graphic** in online course

2.2.3.1   The ipv6 route Command

Static routes for IPv6 are configured using the **ipv6 route** global configuration command. Figure 1 shows the simplified version of the command syntax.

Most of parameters are identical to the IPv4 version of the command. An IPv6 static route can also be implemented as:

- Standard IPv6 static route
- Default IPv6 static route
- Summary IPv6 static route
- Floating IPv6 static route

As with IPv4, these routes can be configured as recursive, directly connected, or fully specified.

The **ipv6 unicast-routing** global configuration command must be configured to enable the router to forward IPv6 packets. Figure 2 displays the enabling of IPv6 unicast routing.

Use the Syntax Checker in Figures 3 and 4 to enable IPv6 unicast routing on R2 and R3.

Refer to **Interactive Graphic** in online course

2.2.3.2   Next-Hop Options

In this example, Figures 1 to 3 display the routing tables of R1, R2, and R3. Each router has entries only for directly connected networks and their associated local addresses. None of the routers have any knowledge of any networks beyond their directly connected interfaces.

For example, R1 has no knowledge of networks:

- 2001:DB8:ACAD:2::/64 - LAN on R2

- 2001:DB8:ACAD:5::/64 - Serial network between R2 and R3

- 2001:DB8:ACAD:3::/64 - LAN on R3

Figure 4 displays a successful ping from R1 to R2. Figure 5 displays an unsuccessful ping to the R3 LAN. This is because R1 does not have an entry in its routing table for that network.

The next hop can be identified by an IPv6 address, exit interface, or both. How the destination is specified creates one of three route types:

- **Next-hop static IPv6 route** - Only the next-hop IPv6 address is specified

- **Directly connected static IPv6 route** - Only the router exit interface is specified

- **Fully specified static IPv6 route** - The next-hop IPv6 address and exit interface are specified

Refer to **Interactive Graphic** in online course

2.2.3.3   Configure a Next-Hop Static IPv6 Route

In a next-hop static route, only the next-hop IPv6 address is specified. The exit interface is derived from the next hop. For instance, in Figure 1, three next-hop static routes are configured on R1.

As with IPv4, before any packet is forwarded by the router, the routing table process must resolve the route to determine the exit interface to use to forward the packet. The route resolvability process will vary depending upon the type of forwarding mechanism being used by the router. CEF (Cisco Express Forwarding) is the default behavior on most platforms running IOS 12.0 or later.

Figure 2 details the basic packet forwarding route resolvability process in the routing table for R1 without the use of CEF. When a packet is destined for the 2001:DB8:ACAD:3::/64 network, R1:

1. Looks for a match in the routing table and finds that it has to forward the packets to the next-hop IPv6 address 2001:DB8:ACAD:4::2. Every route that references only a next-hop IPv6 address and does not reference an exit interface must have the next-hop IPv6 address resolved using another route in the routing table with an exit interface.

2. R1 must now determine how to reach 2001:DB8:ACAD:4::2; therefore, it searches a second time looking for a match. In this case, the IPv6 address matches the route for the directly connected network 2001:DB8:ACAD:4::/64 with the exit interface Serial 0/0/0. This lookup tells the routing table process that this packet is forwarded out of that interface.

Therefore, it actually takes two routing table lookup processes to forward any packet to the 2001:DB8:ACAD:3::/64 network. When the router has to perform multiple lookups in the routing table before forwarding a packet, it is performing a process known as a recursive lookup.

A recursive static IPv6 route is valid (that is, it is a candidate for insertion in the routing table) only when the specified next hop resolves, either directly or indirectly, to a valid exit interface.

Use the Syntax Checker in Figure 3 and Figure 4 to configure next-hop static IPv6 routes.

Refer to
Interactive Graphic
in online course

2.2.3.4   Configure a Directly Connected Static IPv6 Route

When configuring a static route on point-to-point networks, an alternative to using the next-hop IPv6 address is to specify the exit interface. This is an alternative used in older IOSs or whenever CEF is disabled, to avoid the recursive lookup problem.

For instance, in Figure 1, three directly connected static routes are configured on R1 using the exit interface.

The IPv6 routing table for R1 in Figure 2 shows that when a packet is destined for the 2001:DB8:ACAD:3::/64 network, R1 looks for a match in the routing table and finds that it can forward the packet out of its Serial 0/0/0 interface. No other lookups are required.

Notice how the routing table looks different for the route configured with an exit interface than the route configured with a recursive entry.

Configuring a directly connected static route with an exit interface allows the routing table to resolve the exit interface in a single search instead of two searches. Recall that with the use of the CEF forwarding mechanism, static routes with an exit interface are considered unnecessary. A single lookup is performed using a combination of the FIB and adjacency table stored in the data plane.

Use the Syntax Checker in Figure 3 and Figure 4 to configure directly connected static IPv6 routes.

Refer to
Interactive Graphic
in online course

2.2.3.5   Configure a Fully Specified Static IPv6 Route

In a fully specified static route, both the exit interface and the next-hop IPv6 address are specified. Similar to fully specified static routes used with IPv4, this would be used if CEF were not enabled on the router and the exit interface was on a multi-access network. With CEF, a static route using only a next-hop IPv6 address would be the preferred method even when the exit interface is a multi-access network.

Unlike IPv4, there is a situation in IPv6 when a fully specified static route must be used. If the IPv6 static route uses an IPv6 link-local address as the next-hop address, a fully specified static route including the exit interface must be used. Figure 1 shows an example of a fully qualified IPv6 static route using an IPv6 link-local address as the next-hop address.

The reason a fully specified static route must be used is because IPv6 link-local addresses are not contained in the IPv6 routing table. Link-local addresses are only unique on a given link or network. The next-hop link-local address may be a valid address on multiple networks connected to the router. Therefore, it is necessary that the exit interface be included.

In Figure 1, a fully specified static route is configured using R2's link-local address as the next-hop address. Notice that IOS requires that an exit interface be specified.

Figure 2 shows the IPv6 routing table entry for this route. Notice that both the next-hop link-local address and the exit interface are included.

Use the Syntax Checker in Figure 3 to configure fully specified static IPv6 routes on R2 to reach R1's LAN using a link-local address.

Refer to
Interactive Graphic
in online course

2.2.3.6 Verify IPv6 Static Routes

Along with **ping** and **traceroute**, useful commands to verify static routes include:

- **show ipv6 route**
- **show ipv6 route static**
- **show ipv6 route network**

Figure 1 displays sample output of the **show ipv6 route static** command. The output reflects the use of static routes using next-hop global unicast addresses.

Figure 2 displays sample output from the **show ip route 2001:DB8:ACAD:3::** command.

Figure 3 verifies the **ipv6 route** configuration in the running configuration.

2.2.4 Configure IPv6 Default Routes

Refer to
Online Course
for Illustration

2.2.4.1 Default Static IPv6 Route

A default route is a static route that matches all packets. Instead of routers storing routes for all of the networks in the Internet, they can store a single default route to represent any network that is not in the routing table. A default route does not require any left-most bits to match between the default route and the destination IPv6 address.

Routers commonly use default routes that are either configured locally, or learned from another router using a dynamic routing protocol. They are used when no other routes match the packet's destination IP address in the routing table. In other words, if a more specific match does not exist, then use the default route as the Gateway of Last Resort.

Default static routes are commonly used when connecting:

- A company's edge router to a service provider network.
- A router with only an upstream neighbor router. The router has no other neighbors and is therefore, referred to as a stub router.

As shown in the figure, the command syntax for a default static route is similar to any other static route, except that the ipv6-prefix/prefix-length is ::/0, which matches all routes.

The basic command syntax of a default static route is:

- **ipv6 route ::/0** {*ipv6-address* | *exit-intf*}

Refer to
Online Course
for Illustration

2.2.4.2 Configure a Default Static IPv6 Route

R1 can be configured with three static routes to reach all of the remote networks in our topology. However, R1 is a stub router because it is only connected to R2. Therefore, it would be more efficient to configure a default static IPv6 route.

The example in the figure displays a configuration for a default static IPv6 route on R1.

Refer to
Interactive Graphic
in online course

2.2.4.3   Verify a Default Static Route

In Figure 1, the **show ipv6 route static** command output displays the contents of the routing table.

Unlike IPv4, IPv6 does not explicitly state that the default IPv6 is the Gateway of Last Resort.

The key to this configuration is the ::/0 mask. Remember that the IPv6 prefix-length in a routing table determines how many bits must match between the destination IP address of the packet and the route in the routing table. The ::/0 mask indicates that none of the bits are required to match. As long as a more specific match does not exist, the default static IPv6 route matches all packets.

Figure 2 displays a successful ping to the R3 LAN interface.

Refer to **Packet
Tracer Activity**
for this chapter

2.2.4.4   Packet Tracer – Configuring IPv6 Static and Default Routes

In this activity, you will configure IPv6 static and default routes. A static route is a route that is entered manually by the network administrator to create a route that is reliable and safe. There are four different static routes used in this activity: a recursive static route; a directly connected static route; a fully specified static route; and a default route.

Refer to
Lab Activity
for this chapter

2.2.4.5   Lab – Configuring IPv6 Static and Default Routes

In this lab, you will complete the following objectives:

■ Part 1: Build the Network and Configure Basic Device Settings

■ Part 2: Configure IPv6 Static and Default Routes

2.2.5   Configure Floating Static Routes

Refer to
Online Course
for Illustration

2.2.5.1   Floating Static Routes

Floating static routes are static routes that have an administrative distance greater than the administrative distance of another static route or dynamic routes. They are very useful when providing a backup to a primary link, as shown in the figure.

By default, static routes have an administrative distance of 1, making them preferable to routes learned from dynamic routing protocols. For example, the administrative distances of some common dynamic routing protocols are:

■ EIGRP = 90

■ IGRP = 100

■ OSPF = 110

■ IS-IS = 115

■ RIP = 120

The administrative distance of a static route can be increased to make the route less desirable than that of another static route or a route learned through a dynamic routing protocol. In this way, the static route "floats" and is not used when the route with the better administrative distance is active. However, if the preferred route is lost, the floating static route can take over, and traffic can be sent through this alternate route.

Refer to
Interactive Graphic
in online course

2.2.5.2 Configure an IPv4 Floating Static Route

IPv4 floating static routes are configured using the **ip route** global configuration command and specifying an administrative distance. If no administrative distance is configured, the default value (1) is used.

Refer to the topology in Figure 1. In this scenario, the preferred default route from R1 is to R2. The connection to R3 should be used for backup only.

R1 is configured with a default static route pointing to R2. Because no administrative distance is configured, the default value (1) is used for this static route. R1 is also configured with a floating static default pointing to R3 with an administrative distance of 5. This value is greater than the default value of 1 and therefore; this route floats and is not present in the routing table, unless the preferred route fails.

Figure 2 verifies that the default route to R2 is installed in the routing table. Note that the backup route to R3 is not present in the routing table.

Use the Syntax Checker in Figure 3 to configure R3 similarly to R1.

Refer to
Interactive Graphic
in online course

2.2.5.3 Test the IPv4 Floating Static Route

Because the default static route on R1 to R2 has an administrative distance of 1, traffic from R1 to R3 should go through R2. The output in Figure 1 confirms that traffic between R1 and R3 flows through R2.

What would happen if R2 failed? To simulate this failure both serial interfaces of R2 are shut down, as shown in Figure 2.

Notice in Figure 3 that R1 automatically generates messages indicating that the serial interface to R2 is down. A look at the routing table verifies that the default route is now pointing to R3 using the floating static default route configured with an AD value of 5 and a next-hop of 10.10.10.2.

The output in Figure 4 confirms that traffic now flows directly between R1 and R3.

Refer to
Interactive Graphic
in online course

2.2.5.4 Configure an IPv6 Floating Static Route

IPv6 floating static routes are configured using the **ipv6 route** global configuration command and specifying an administrative distance. If no administrative distance is configured, the default value (1) is used.

Refer to the topology in Figure 1. In this scenario, the preferred default route from R1 is to R2. The connection to R3 should be used for backup only.

R1 is configured with an IPv6 default static route pointing to R2. Because no administrative distance is configured, the default value (1) is used for this static route. R1 is also configured with an IPv6 floating static default pointing to R3 with an administrative distance of 5. This value is greater than the default value of 1 and therefore; this route floats and is not present in the routing table, unless the preferred route fails.

Figure 2 verifies that both IPv6 static default routes are in the running configuration. Figure 3 verifies that the IPv6 static default route to R2 is installed in the routing table. Note that the backup route to R3 is not present in the routing table.

The process for testing the IPv6 floating static route is the same as for the IPv4 floating static route. Shut down the interfaces on R2 to simulate a failure. R1 will install the route to R3 in the route table and use it to send default traffic.

Refer to **Packet Tracer Activity** for this chapter

2.2.5.5   Packet Tracer – Configuring Floating Static Routes

In this activity, you will configure IPv4 and IPv6 floating static routes. These routes are manually configured with an administrative distance greater than that of the primary route and, therefore, would not be in the routing table until the primary route fails. You will test failover to the backup routes, and then restore connectivity to the primary route.

2.2.6   Configure Static Host Routes

Refer to **Interactive Graphic** in online course

2.2.6.1   Automatically Installed Host Routes

A host route is an IPv4 address with a 32-bit mask or an IPv6 address with a 128-bit mask. There are three ways a host route can be added to the routing table:

■ Automatically installed when an IP address is configured on the router (as shown in Figures 1 and 2)

■ Configured as a static host route

■ Host route automatically obtained through other methods (discussed in later courses)

Cisco IOS automatically installs a host route, also known as a local host route, when an interface address is configured on the router. A host route allows for a more efficient process for packets that are directed to the router itself, rather than for packet forwarding. This is in addition to the connected route, designated with a C in the routing table for the network address of the interface.

When an active interface on a router is configured with an IP address, a local host route is automatically added to the routing table. The local routes are marked with "L" in the output of the routing table. The IP addresses assigned to the Branch Serial0/0/0 interface are 198.51.100.1/30 for IPv4 and 2001:DB8:ACAD:1::1/64 for IPv6. The local routes for the interface are installed by the IOS in the routing table as shown in the output in Figure 1 for IPv4 and Figure 2 for IPv6.

Note   For IPv4, the local routes marked with "L" were introduced with IOS version 15.

Refer to **Interactive Graphic** in online course

2.2.6.2   Configure IPv4 and IPv6 Static Host Routes

A host route can be a manually configured static route to direct traffic to a specific destination device, such as an authentication server. The static route uses a destination IP address and a 255.255.255.255 (/32) mask for IPv4 host routes and a /128 prefix length for IPv6 host routes. Static routes are marked with "S" in the output of the routing table. An IPv4 and an IPv6 host route is configured on the BRANCH router to access the server in the topology in Figure 1.

For IPv6 static routes, the next-hop address can be the link-local address of the adjacent router. However, you must specify an interface type and an interface number when using a link-local address as the next hop, as shown in Figure 2.

Use the Syntax Checker in Figure 3 to configure and verify IPv4 and IPv6 static host routes.

2.3   Troubleshoot Static and Default Route

2.3.1   Packet Processing with Static Routes

2.3.1.1   Static Routes and Packet Forwarding

Refer to **Video** in online course

The following example describes the packet forwarding process with static routes.

In the figure, click the Play button to see the animation, where PC1 is sending a packet to PC3:

1. The packet arrives on the GigabitEthernet 0/0 interface of R1.

2. R1 does not have a specific route to the destination network, 192.168.2.0/24; therefore, R1 uses the default static route.

3. R1 encapsulates the packet in a new frame. Because the link to R2 is a point-to-point link, R1 adds an "all 1s" address for the Layer 2 destination address.

4. The frame is forwarded out of the Serial 0/0/0 interface. The packet arrives on the Serial 0/0/0 interface on R2.

5. R2 de-encapsulates the frame and looks for a route to the destination. R2 has a static route to 192.168.2.0/24 out of the Serial 0/0/1 interface.

6. R2 encapsulates the packet in a new frame. Because the link to R3 is a point-to-point link, R2 adds an "all 1s" address for the Layer 2 destination address.

7. The frame is forwarded out of the Serial 0/0/1 interface. The packet arrives on the Serial 0/0/1 interface on R3.

8. R3 de-encapsulates the frame and looks for a route to the destination. R3 has a connected route to 192.168.2.0/24 out of the GigabitEthernet 0/0 interface.

9. R3 looks up the ARP table entry for 192.168.2.10 to find the Layer 2 Media Access Control (MAC) address for PC3. If no entry exists, R3 sends an Address Resolution Protocol (ARP) request out of the GigabitEthernet 0/0 interface, and PC3 responds with an ARP reply, which includes the PC3 MAC address.

10. R3 encapsulates the packet in a new frame with the MAC address of the GigabitEthernet 0/0 interface as the source Layer 2 address and the MAC address of PC3 as the destination MAC address.

11. The frame is forwarded out of GigabitEthernet 0/0 interface. The packet arrives on the network interface card (NIC) interface of PC3.

2.3.2   Troubleshoot IPv4 Static and Default Route Configuration

Refer to **Interactive Graphic** in online course

2.3.2.1   Troubleshoot a Missing Route

Networks are subject to forces that can cause their status to change quite often:

■ An interface fails

■ A service provider drops a connection

- Links become oversaturated

- An administrator enters a wrong configuration

When there is a change in the network, connectivity may be lost. Network administrators are responsible for pinpointing and solving the problem. To find and solve these issues, a network administrator must be familiar with tools to help isolate routing problems quickly.

Common IOS troubleshooting commands include:

- **ping**

- **traceroute**

- **show ip route**

- **show ip interface brief**

- **show cdp neighbors detail**

Figure 1 displays the result of an extended ping from the source interface of R1 to the LAN interface of R3. An extended ping is an enhanced version of the ping utility. Extended ping enables you to specify the source IP address for the ping packets.

Figure 2 displays the result of a traceroute from R1 to the R3 LAN.

Figure 3 displays the routing table of R1.

Figure 4 provides a quick status of all interfaces on the router.

Figure 5 provides a list of directly connected Cisco devices. This command validates Layer 2 (and therefore Layer 1) connectivity. For example, if a neighbor device is listed in the command output, but it cannot be pinged, then Layer 3 addressing should be investigated.

Refer to
Interactive Graphic
in online course

2.3.2.2   Solve a Connectivity Problem

Finding a missing (or misconfigured) route is a relatively straightforward process, if the right tools are used in a methodical manner.

For instance, in this example, the user at PC1 reports that he cannot access resources on the R3 LAN. This can be confirmed by pinging the LAN interface of R3 using the LAN interface of R1 as the source (see Figure 1). The results show that there is no connectivity between these LANs.

A traceroute in Figure 2 reveals that R2 is not responding as expected. For some reason, R2 forwards the traceroute back to R1. R1 returns it to R2. This loop would continue until the time to live (TTL) value decrements to zero, in which case, the router would then send an Internet Control Message Protocol (ICMP) destination unreachable message to R1.

The next step is to investigate the routing table of R2, because it is the router displaying a strange forwarding pattern. The routing table in Figure 3 reveals that the 192.168.2.0/24 network is configured incorrectly. A static route to the 192.168.2.0/24 network has been configured using the next-hop address 172.16.2.1. Using the configured next-hop address, packets destined for the 192.168.2.0/24 network are sent back to R1. It is clear from the topology that the 192.168.2.0/24 network is connected to R3, not R1. Therefore, the static route to the 192.168.2.0/24 network on R2 must use next-hop 192.168.1.1, not 172.16.2.1.

Figure 4 shows output from the running configuration that reveals the incorrect **ip route** statement. The incorrect route is removed and the correct route is then entered.

Figure 5 verifies that R1 can now reach the LAN interface of R3. As a last step in confirmation, the user on PC1 should also test connectivity to the 192.168.2.0/24 LAN.

Refer to **Packet Tracer Activity** for this chapter

2.3.2.3   Packet Tracer – Troubleshooting Static Routes

In this activity, PC1 reports that they cannot access resources at the Server. Locate the problem, decide on an appropriate solution and resolve the issue.

Refer to **Lab Activity** for this chapter

2.3.2.4   Lab – Troubleshooting Static Routes

In this lab, you will complete the following objectives:

- Part 1: Build the Network and Configure Basic Device Settings

- Part 2: Troubleshoot Static Routes in an IPv4 Network

- Part 3: Troubleshoot Static Routes in an IPv6 Network

2.4   Summary

Refer to **Online Course** for Illustration

2.4.1.1   Activity – Make It Static

As the use of IPv6 addressing becomes more prevalent, it is important for network administrators to be able to direct network traffic between routers.

To prove that you are able to direct IPv6 traffic correctly and review the IPv6 default static route curriculum concepts, use the topology as shown in the .pdf file provided, specifically for this activity.

Work with a partner to write an IPv6 statement for each of the three scenarios. Try to write the route statements without the assistance of completed labs, Packet Tracer files, etc.

Scenario 1

IPv6 default static route from R2 directing all data through your S0/0/0 interface to the next hop address on R1.

Scenario 2

IPv6 default static route from R3 directing all data through your S0/0/1 interface to the next hop address on R2.

Scenario 3

IPv6 default static route from R2 directing all data through your S0/0/1 interface to the next hop address on R3.

When complete, get together with another group and compare your written answers. Discuss any differences found in your comparisons.

Refer to
Online Course
for Illustration

2.4.1.2   Static Routing

In this chapter, you learned how IPv4 and IPv6 static routes can be used to reach remote networks. Remote networks are networks that can only be reached by forwarding the packet to another router. Static routes are easily configured. However, in large networks, this manual operation can become quite cumbersome. Static routes are still used, even when a dynamic routing protocol is implemented.

Static routes can be configured with a next-hop IP address, which is commonly the IP address of the next-hop router. When a next-hop IP address is used, the routing table process must resolve this address to an exit interface. On point-to-point serial links, it is usually more efficient to configure the static route with an exit interface. On multi-access networks, such as Ethernet, both a next-hop IP address and an exit interface can be configured on the static route.

Static routes have a default administrative distance of 1. This administrative distance also applies to static routes configured with a next-hop address, as well as an exit interface.

A static route is only entered in the routing table if the next-hop IP address can be resolved through an exit interface. Whether the static route is configured with a next-hop IP address or exit interface, if the exit interface that is used to forward that packet is not in the routing table, the static route is not included in the routing table.

A default route is configured with a 0.0.0.0 network address and a 0.0.0.0 subnet mask for IPv4, and the prefix/prefix-length ::/0 for IPv6. If there is not a more specific match in the routing table, the routing table uses the default route to forward the packet to another router.

A floating static route can be configured to back up a main link by manipulating its administrative value.

Go to the online course to take the quiz and exam.

Chapter 2 Quiz

This quiz is designed to provide an additional opportunity to practice the skills and knowledge presented in the chapter and to prepare for the chapter exam. You will be allowed multiple attempts and the grade does not appear in the gradebook.

Chapter 2 Exam

The chapter exam assesses your knowledge of the chapter content.

Your Chapter Notes

Dynamic Routing

3.0 Introduction

Refer to
Online Course
for Illustration

3.0.1.1 Dynamic Routing

The data networks that we use in our everyday lives to learn, play, and work range from small, local networks to large, global internetworks. At home, a user may have a router and two or more computers. At work, an organization may have multiple routers and switches servicing the data communication needs of hundreds or even thousands of PCs.

Routers forward packets by using information in the routing table. Routes to remote networks can be learned by the router in two ways: static routes and dynamic routes.

In a large network with numerous networks and subnets, configuring and maintaining static routes between these networks requires a great deal of administrative and operational overhead. This operational overhead is especially cumbersome when changes to the network occur, such as a down link or implementing a new subnet. Implementing dynamic routing protocols can ease the burden of configuration and maintenance tasks and give the network scalability.

This chapter introduces dynamic routing protocols. It compares the use of static and dynamic routing. Then the implementation of dynamic routing using the Routing Information Protocol version 1 (RIPv1) and version 2 (RIPv2) is discussed. The chapter concludes with an in-depth look at the routing table.

Refer to
Online Course
for Illustration

3.0.1.2 How Much Does This Cost

This modeling activity illustrates the network concept of routing cost.

You will be a member of a team of five students who travel routes to complete the activity scenarios. One digital camera or bring your own device (BYOD) with camera, a stopwatch, and the student file for this activity will be required per group. One person will function as the photographer and event recorder, as selected by each group. The remaining four team members will actively participate in the scenarios below.

A school or university classroom, hallway, outdoor track area, school parking lot, or any other location can serve as the venue for these activities.

Activity 1

The tallest person in the group establishes a start and finish line by marking 15 steps from start to finish, indicating the distance of the team route. Each student will take 15 steps from the start line toward the finish line and then stop on the 15th step—no further steps are allowed.

Note   Not all of the students may reach the same distance from the start line due to their height and stride differences. The photographer will take a group picture of the entire team's final location after taking the 15 steps required.

Activity 2

A new start and finish line will be established; however, this time, a longer distance for the route will be established than the distance specified in Activity 1. No maximum steps are to be used as a basis for creating this particular route. One at a time, students will "walk the new route from beginning to end twice".

Each team member will count the steps taken to complete the route. The recorder will time each student and at the end of each team member's route, record the time that it took to complete the full route and how many steps were taken, as recounted by each team member and recorded on the team's student file.

After both activities have been completed, teams will use the digital picture taken for Activity 1 and their recorded data from Activity 2 file to answer the reflection questions.

Group answers can be discussed as a class, time permitting.

3.1   Dynamic Routing Protocols

3.1.1   Dynamic Routing Protocol Overview

Refer to
Interactive Graphic
in online course

3.1.1.1   Dynamic Routing Protocol Evolution

Dynamic routing protocols have been used in networks since the late 1980s. One of the first routing protocols was RIP. RIPv1 was released in 1988, but some of the basic algorithms within the protocol were used on the Advanced Research Projects Agency Network (ARPANET) as early as 1969.

As networks evolved and became more complex, new routing protocols emerged. The RIP protocol was updated to RIPv2 to accommodate growth in the network environment. However, RIPv2 still does not scale to the larger network implementations of today. To address the needs of larger networks, two advanced routing protocols were developed: Open Shortest Path First (OSPF) and Intermediate System-to-Intermediate System (IS-IS). Cisco developed the Interior Gateway Routing Protocol (IGRP) and Enhanced IGRP (EIGRP), which also scales well in larger network implementations.

Additionally, there was the need to connect different internetworks and provide routing between them. The Border Gateway Protocol (BGP) is now used between Internet service providers (ISPs). BGP is also used between ISPs and their larger private clients to exchange routing information.

Figure 1 displays the timeline of when the various protocols were introduced.

Figure 2 classifies the protocols.

With the advent of numerous consumer devices using IP, the IPv4 addressing space is nearly exhausted; thus, IPv6 has emerged. To support the communication based on IPv6, newer versions of the IP routing protocols have been developed, as shown in the IPv6 row in the Figure 2.

Refer to **Video** in online course

3.1.1.2   Dynamic Routing Protocol Components

Routing protocols are used to facilitate the exchange of routing information between routers. A routing protocol is a set of processes, algorithms, and messages that are used to exchange routing information and populate the routing table with the routing protocol's choice of best paths. The purpose of dynamic routing protocols includes:

■ Discovery of remote networks

■ Maintaining up-to-date routing information

■ Choosing the best path to destination networks

■ Ability to find a new best path if the current path is no longer available

The main components of dynamic routing protocols include:

■ **Data structures** - Routing protocols typically use tables or databases for its operations. This information is kept in RAM.

■ **Routing protocol messages** - Routing protocols use various types of messages to discover neighboring routers, exchange routing information, and other tasks to learn and maintain accurate information about the network.

■ **Algorithm** - An algorithm is a finite list of steps used to accomplish a task. Routing protocols use algorithms for facilitating routing information and for best path determination.

Routing protocols allow routers to dynamically share information about remote networks and automatically offer this information to their own routing tables. Click Play in the figure to see an animation of this process.

Routing protocols determine the best path, or route, to each network. That route is then offered to the routing table. The route will be installed in the routing table is there is not another routing source with a lower administrative distance. For example, a static route with an administrative distance of 1 will have precedence over the same network learned by a dynamic routing protocol. A primary benefit of dynamic routing protocols is that routers exchange routing information when there is a topology change. This exchange allows routers to automatically learn about new networks and also to find alternate paths when there is a link failure to a current network.

3.1.2   Dynamic versus Static Routing

Refer to **Online Course** for Illustration

3.1.2.1   Static Routing Uses

Before identifying the benefits of dynamic routing protocols, consider the reasons why network professionals use static routing. Dynamic routing certainly has several advantages over static routing; however, static routing is still used in networks today. In fact, networks typically use a combination of both static and dynamic routing.

Static routing has several primary uses, including:

■ Providing ease of routing table maintenance in smaller networks that are not expected to grow significantly.

■ Routing to and from a stub network, which is a network with only one default route out and no knowledge of any remote networks.

■ Accessing a single default route (which is used to represent a path to any network that does not have a more specific match with another route in the routing table).

The figure provides a sample scenario of static routing.

Refer to
Online Course
for Illustration

3.1.2.2 Static Routing Advantages and Disadvantages

The table in the figure highlights the advantages and disadvantages of static routing. Static routing is easy to implement in a small network. Static routes stay the same, which makes them fairly easy to troubleshoot. Static routes do not send update messages; therefore, they require very little overhead.

The disadvantages of static routing include:

■ They are not easy to implement in a large network.

■ Managing the static configurations can become time consuming.

■ If a link fails, a static route cannot reroute traffic.

Refer to
Interactive Graphic
in online course

3.1.2.3 Dynamic Routing Protocols Uses

Dynamic routing protocols help the network administrator manage the time-consuming and exacting process of configuring and maintaining static routes.

Imagine maintaining the static routing configurations for the seven routers in Figure 1.

What if the company grew and now had four regions and 28 routers to manage, as shown in Figure 2? What happens when a link goes down? How do you ensure that redundant paths are available?

Dynamic routing is the best choice for large networks like the one shown.

Refer to
Online Course
for Illustration

3.1.2.4 Dynamic Routing Advantages and Disadvantages

The table in the figure highlights the advantages and disadvantages of dynamic routing. Dynamic routing protocols work well in any type of network consisting of several routers. They are scalable and automatically determine better routes if there is a change in the topology. Although there is more to the configuration of dynamic routing protocols, they are simpler to configure than static routing in a large network.

There are disadvantages to dynamic routing. Dynamic routing requires knowledge of additional commands. It is also less secure than static routing because the interfaces identified by the routing protocol send routing updates out. Routes taken may differ between packets. The routing algorithm uses additional CPU, RAM, and link bandwidth.

Notice how dynamic routing addresses the disadvantages of static routing.

Refer to
Interactive Graphic
in online course

3.1.2.5 Activity – Compare Static and Dynamic Routing

3.2 RIPv2

3.2.1 Configuring the RIP Protocol

Refer to
Interactive Graphic
in online course

3.2.1.1 Router RIP Configuration Mode

Although RIP is rarely used in modern networks, it is useful as a foundation for understanding basic network routing. This section provides a brief overview of how to configure basic RIP settings and how to verify RIPv2.

Refer to the reference topology in Figure 1 and the addressing table in Figure 2. In this scenario, all routers have been configured with basic management features and all interfaces identified in the reference topology are configured and enabled. There are no static routes configured and no routing protocols enabled; therefore, remote network access is currently impossible. RIPv1 is used as the dynamic routing protocol. To enable RIP, use the **router rip** command, as shown in Figure 3. This command does not directly start the RIP process. Instead, it provides access to the router configuration mode where the RIP routing settings are configured. When enabling RIP, the default version is RIPv1.

To disable and eliminate RIP, use the **no router rip** global configuration command. This command stops the RIP process and erases all existing RIP configurations.

Figure 4 displays the various RIP commands that can be configured. The highlighted keywords are covered in this section.

Refer to
Interactive Graphic
in online course

3.2.1.2 Advertise Networks

By entering the RIP router configuration mode, the router is instructed to run RIPv1. But the router still needs to know which local interfaces it should use for communication with other routers, as well as which locally connected networks it should advertise to those routers.

To enable RIP routing for a network, use the **network** *network-address* router configuration mode command. Enter the classful network address for each directly connected network. This command:

- Enables RIP on all interfaces that belong to a specific network. Associated interfaces now both send and receive RIP updates.

- Advertises the specified network in RIP routing updates sent to other routers every 30 seconds.

Note   RIPv1 is a classful routing protocol for IPv4. Therefore, if a subnet address is entered, the IOS automatically converts it to the classful network address. For example, entering the **network 192.168.1.32** command would automatically be converted to **network 192.168.1.0** in the running configuration file. The IOS does not give an error message, but instead corrects the input and enters the classful network address.

In Figure 1, the **network** command is used to advertise the R1 directly connected networks.

Use the Syntax Checker in Figure 2 to configure a similar configuration on R2 and R3.

Refer to
Interactive Graphic
in online course

3.2.1.3   Verify RIP Routing

The **show ip protocols** command displays the IPv4 routing protocol settings currently configured on the router. This output displayed in Figure 1 confirms most RIP parameters including:

1. RIP routing is configured and running on router R1.

2. The values of various timers; for example, the next routing update, is sent by R1 in 16 seconds.

3. The version of RIP configured is currently RIPv1.

4. R1 is currently summarizing at the classful network boundary.

5. The classful networks are advertised by R1. These are the networks that R1 includes in its RIP updates.

6. The RIP neighbors are listed, including their next-hop IP address, the associated AD that R2 uses for updates sent by this neighbor, and when the last update was received from this neighbor.

Note   This command is also very useful when verifying the operations of other routing protocols (i.e., EIGRP and OSPF).

The **show ip route** command displays the RIP routes installed in the routing table. In Figure 2, R1 now knows about the highlighted networks.

Use the Syntax Checker in Figure 3 to verify the R2 and R3 RIP settings and routes.

Refer to
Interactive Graphic
in online course

3.2.1.4   Enable and Verify RIPv2

By default, when a RIP process is configured on a Cisco router, it is running RIPv1, as shown in Figure 1. However, even though the router only sends RIPv1 messages, it can interpret both RIPv1 and RIPv2 messages. A RIPv1 router ignores the RIPv2 fields in the route entry.

Use the **version 2** router configuration mode command to enable RIPv2, as shown in Figure 2. Notice how the **show ip protocols** command verifies that R2 is now configured to send and receive version 2 messages only. The RIP process now includes the subnet mask in all updates, making RIPv2 a classless routing protocol.

Note   Configuring **version 1** enables RIPv1 only, while configuring **no version** returns the router to the default setting of sending version 1 updates but listening for version 1 and version 2 updates.

Figure 3 verifies that there are no longer any RIP routes in the routing table. This is because R1 is now only listening for RIPv2 updates. R2 and R3 are still sending RIPv1 updates. Therefore, the **version 2** command must be configured on all routers in the routing domain.

Use the Syntax Checker in Figure 4 to enable RIPv2 on R2 and R3.

Refer to
Interactive Graphic
in online course

3.2.1.5   Disable Auto Summarization

As shown in Figure 1, RIPv2 automatically summarizes networks at major network boundaries by default, just like RIPv1.

To modify the default RIPv2 behavior of automatic summarization, use the **no auto-summary** router configuration mode command as shown in Figure 2. This command has no effect when using RIPv1. When automatic summarization has been disabled, RIPv2 no longer summarizes networks to their classful address at boundary routers. RIPv2 now includes all subnets and their appropriate masks in its routing updates. The **show ip protocols** now states that "automatic network summarization is not in effect".

Note   RIPv2 must be enabled before automatic summarization is disabled.

Use the Syntax Checker in Figure 3 to disable automatic summarization on R2 and R3.

Refer to
Interactive Graphic
in online course

3.2.1.6   Configure Passive Interfaces

By default, RIP updates are forwarded out all RIP-enabled interfaces. However, RIP updates really only need to be sent out interfaces that are connected to other RIPenabled routers.

For instance, refer to the topology in Figure 1. RIP sends updates out of its G0/0 interface even though no RIP device exists on that LAN. R1 has no way of knowing this and, as a result, sends an update every 30 seconds. Sending out unneeded updates on a LAN impacts the network in three ways:

- **Wasted Bandwidth** - Bandwidth is used to transport unnecessary updates. Because RIP updates are either broadcasted or multicasted, switches also forward the updates out all ports.

- **Wasted Resources** - All devices on the LAN must process the update up to the transport layers, at which point the devices will discard the update.

- **Security Risk** - Advertising updates on a broadcast network is a security risk. RIP updates can be intercepted with packet sniffing software. Routing updates can be modified and sent back to the router, corrupting the routing table with false metrics that misdirect traffic.

Use the **passive-interface** router configuration command to prevent the transmission of routing updates through a router interface, but still allow that network to be advertised to other routers. The command stops routing updates out the specified interface. However, the network that the specified interface belongs to is still advertised in routing updates that are sent out other interfaces.

There is no need for R1, R2, and R3 to forward RIP updates out of their LAN interfaces. The configuration in Figure 2 identifies the R1 G0/0 interface as passive. The **show ip protocols** command is then used to verify that the Gigabit Ethernet interface was passive. Notice that the G0/0 interface is no longer listed as sending or receiving version 2 updates, but instead is now listed under the Passive Interface(s) section. Also notice that the network 192.168.1.0 is still listed under Routing for Networks, which means that this network is still included as a route entry in RIP updates that are sent to R2.

Note   All routing protocols support the **passive-interface** command.

Use the Syntax Checker in Figure 3 to configure the LAN interface as a passive interface on R2 and R3.

As an alternative, all interfaces can be made passive using the **passive-interface default** command. Interfaces that should not be passive can be re-enabled using the **no passive-interface** command.

Refer to
Interactive Graphic
in online course

3.2.1.7   Propagate a Default Route

Refer to Figure 1. In this scenario, R1 is the edge router, single-homed to a service provider. Therefore, all that is required for R1 to reach the Internet is a default static route going out of the Serial 0/0/1 interface.

Similar default static routes could be configured on R2 and R3, but it is much more scalable to enter it one time on the edge router R1 and then have R1 propagate it to all other routers using RIP. To provide Internet connectivity to all other networks in the RIP routing domain, the default static route needs to be advertised to all other routers that use the dynamic routing protocol.

To propagate a default route in RIP, the edge router must be configured with:

■ A default static route using the **ip route 0.0.0.0 0.0.0.0** command.

■ The **default-information originate** router configuration command. This instructs R1 to originate default information, by propagating the static default route in RIP updates.

The example in Figure 2 configures a fully-specified default static route to the service provider and then the route is propagated by RIP. Notice that R1 now has a Gateway of Last Resort and default route installed in its routing table.

Use the Syntax Checker in Figure 3 to verify that the default route has been propagated to R2 and R3.

Refer to Packet
Tracer Activity
for this chapter

3.2.1.8   Packet Tracer – Configuring RIPv2

Although RIP is rarely used in modern networks, it is useful as a foundation for understanding basic network routing. In this activity, you will configure a default route, RIPv2 with appropriate network statements and passive interfaces, and verify full connectivity.

Refer to
Lab Activity
for this chapter

3.2.1.9   Lab – Configuring Basic RIPv2

In this lab you will complete the following objectives:

■ Part 1: Build the Network and Configure Basic Device Settings

■ Part 2: Configure and Verify RIPv2 Routing

3.3   The Routing Table

3.3.1   Parts of an IPv4 Route Entry

Refer to
Interactive Graphic
in online course

3.3.1.1   Routing Table Entries

The topology displayed in Figure 1 is used as the reference topology for this section. Notice that in the topology:

- R1 is the edge router that connects to the Internet; therefore, it is propagating a default static route to R2 and R3.

- R1, R2, and R3 contain discontiguous networks separated by another classful network.

- R3 is also introducing a 192.168.0.0/16 supernet route.

Figure 2 displays the IPv4 routing table of R1 with directly connected, static, and dynamic routes.

Note   The routing table hierarchy in Cisco IOS was originally implemented with the classful routing scheme. Although the routing table incorporates both classful and classless addressing, the overall structure is still built around this classful scheme.

Refer to
Interactive Graphic
in online course

3.3.1.2   Directly Connected Entries

As highlighted in Figure 1, the routing table of R1 contains three directly connected networks. Notice that two routing table entries are automatically created when an active router interface is configured with an IP address and subnet mask.

Figure 2 displays one of the routing table entries on R1 for the directly connected network 172.16.1.0. These entries were automatically added to the routing table when the GigabitEthernet 0/0 interface was configured and activated. The entries contain the following information:

- **Route source** - Identifies how the route was learned. Directly connected interfaces have two route source codes. C identifies a directly connected network. Directly connected networks are automatically created whenever an interface is configured with an IP address and activated. L identifies that this is a local route. Local routes are automatically created whenever an interface is configured with an IP address and activated.

- **Destination network** - The address of the remote network and how that network is connected.

- **Outgoing interface** - Identifies the exit interface to use when forwarding packets to the destination network.

A router typically has multiple interfaces configured. The routing table stores information about both directly connected and remote routes. As with directly connected networks, the route source identifies how the route was learned. For instance, common codes for remote networks include:

- **S** - Identifies that the route was manually created by an administrator to reach a specific network. This is known as a static route.

- **D** - Identifies that the route was learned dynamically from another router using the EIGRP routing protocol.

- **O** - Identifies that the route was learned dynamically from another router using the OSPF routing protocol.

- **R** - Identifies that the route was learned dynamically from another router using the RIP routing protocol.

Refer to
Online Course
for Illustration

3.3.1.3   Remote Network Entries

The figure displays an IPv4 routing table entry on R1 for the route to remote network 172.16.4.0 on R3. The entry identifies the following information:

- **Route source** - Identifies how the route was learned.

- **Destination network** - Identifies the address of the remote network.

- **Administrative distance (AD)** - Identifies the trustworthiness of the route source. The AD for static routes is 1 and the AD for connected routes is 0. Dynamic routing protocols have an AD higher than 1 depending upon the protocol.

- **Metric** - Identifies the value assigned to reach the remote network. Lower values indicate preferred routes. The metric for static and connected routes is 0.

- **Next hop** - Identifies the IPv4 address of the next router to forward the packet to.

- **Route timestamp** - Identifies from when the route was last heard.

- **Outgoing interface** - Identifies the exit interface to use to forward a packet toward the final destination.

Refer to
Interactive Graphic
in online course

3.3.1.4   Activity – Identify Parts of an IPv4 Routing Table Entry

3.3.2   Dynamically Learned IPv4 Routes

Refer to
Online Course
for Illustration

3.3.2.1   Routing Table Terms

A dynamically built routing table provides a great deal of information, as shown in the figure. Therefore, it is crucial to understand the output generated by the routing table. Special terms are applied when discussing the contents of a routing table.

The Cisco IP routing table is not a flat database. The routing table is actually a hierarchical structure that is used to speed up the lookup process when locating routes and forwarding packets. Within this structure, the hierarchy includes several levels.

Routes are discussed in terms of:

- Ultimate route

- Level 1 route

- Level 1 parent route

- Level 2 child routes

Refer to
Online Course
for Illustration

3.3.2.2   Ultimate Route

An ultimate route is a routing table entry that contains either a next-hop IPv4 address or an exit interface. Directly connected, dynamically learned, and local routes are ultimate routes.

In the figure, the highlighted areas are examples of ultimate routes. Notice that all of these routes specify either a next-hop IPv4 address or an exit interface.

Refer to
Interactive Graphic
in online course

3.3.2.3   Level 1 Route

A level 1 route is a route with a subnet mask equal to or less than the classful mask of the network address. Therefore, a level 1 route can be a:

- **Network route** - A network route that has a subnet mask equal to that of the classful mask.

- **Supernet route** - A supernet route is a network address with a mask less than the classful mask, for example, a summary address.

- **Default route** - A default route is a static route with the address 0.0.0.0/0.

The source of the level 1 route can be a directly connected network, static route, or a dynamic routing protocol.

Figure 1 highlights how level 1 routes are also ultimate routes.

Figure 2 highlights level 1 routes.

Refer to
Interactive Graphic
in online course

3.3.2.4   Level 1 Parent Route

As illustrated in Figure 1, the 172.16.0.0 and 209.165.200.0 routes are level 1 parent routes. A parent route is a level 1 network route that is subnetted. A parent route can never be an ultimate route.

Figure 2 highlights the level 1 parent routes in the routing table of R1. In the routing table, it basically provides a heading for the specific subnets it contains. Each entry displays the classful network address, the number of subnets and the number of different subnet masks into which the classful address has been subdivided.

Refer to
Interactive Graphic
in online course

3.3.2.5   Level 2 Child Route

A level 2 child route is a route that is a subnet of a classful network address. As illustrated in Figure 1, a level 1 parent route is a level 1 network route that is subnetted. Level 1 parent routes contain level 2 child routes, as shown in Figure 2.

Like a level 1 route, the source of a level 2 route can be a directly connected network, a static route, or a dynamically learned route. Level 2 child routes are also ultimate routes.

Note   The routing table hierarchy in Cisco IOS has a classful routing scheme. A level 1 parent route is the classful network address of the subnet route. This is the case even if a classless routing protocol is the source of the subnet route.

Figure 3 highlights the child routes in the routing table of R1.

Refer to
Interactive Graphic
in online course

3.3.2.6   Activity – Identify Parent and Child IPv4 Routes

3.3.3   The IPv4 Route Lookup Process

Refer to
Interactive Graphic
in online course

3.3.3.1   Route Lookup Process

When a packet arrives on a router interface, the router examines the IPv4 header, identifies the destination IPv4 address, and proceeds through the router lookup process.

In Figure 1, the router examines level 1 network routes for the best match with the destination address of the IPv4 packet:

1. If the best match is a level 1 ultimate route, then this route is used to forward the packet.

2. If the best match is a level 1 parent route, proceed to the next step.

In Figure 2, the router examines child routes (the subnet routes) of the parent route for a best match:

3. If there is a match with a level 2 child route, that subnet is used to forward the packet.

4. If there is not a match with any of the level 2 child routes, proceed to the next step.

In Figure 3, the router continues searching level 1 supernet routes in the routing table for a match, including the default route, if there is one:

5. If there is now a lesser match with a level 1 supernet or default routes, the router uses that route to forward the packet.

6. If there is not a match with any route in the routing table, the router drops the packet.

Note   A route referencing only a next-hop IP address and not an exit interface, must be resolved to a route with an exit interface, if Cisco Express Forwarding (CEF) is not being used. Without CEF, a recursive lookup is performed on the next-hop IP address until the route is resolved to an exit interface. CEF is enabled by default.

Refer to
Online Course
for Illustration

3.3.3.2   Best Route = Longest Match

What is meant by the router must find the best match in the routing table? Best match is equal to the longest match.

For there to be a match between the destination IPv4 address of a packet and a route in the routing table, a minimum number of far left bits must match between the IPv4 address of the packet and the route in the routing table. The subnet mask of the route in the routing table is used to determine the minimum number of far left bits that must match. Remember that an IPv4 packet only contains the IPv4 address and not the subnet mask.

The best match is the route in the routing table that has the most number of far left matching bits with the destination IPv4 address of the packet. The route with the greatest number of equivalent far left bits, or the longest match, is always the preferred route.

In the figure, a packet is destined for 172.16.0.10. The router has three possible routes that match this packet: 172.16.0.0/12, 172.16.0.0/18, and 172.16.0.0/26. Of the three routes, 172.16.0.0/26 has the longest match and is chosen to forward the packet. Remember, for any of these routes to be considered a match there must be at least the number of matching bits indicated by the subnet mask of the route.

Refer to
Interactive Graphic
in online course

3.3.3.3 Activity – Determine the Longest Match Route

3.3.4 Analyze an IPv6 Routing Table

Refer to
Online Course
for Illustration

3.3.4.1 IPv6 Routing Table Entries

Components of the IPv6 routing table are very similar to the IPv4 routing table. For instance, it is populated using directly connected interfaces, static routes, and dynamically learned routes.

Because IPv6 is classless by design, all routes are effectively level 1 ultimate routes. There is no level 1 parent of level 2 child routes.

The topology displayed in the figure is used as the reference topology for this section. Notice that in the topology:

- R1, R2, and R3 are configured in a full mesh topology. All routers have redundant paths to various networks.

- R2 is the edge router and connects to the ISP; however, a default static route is not being advertised.

- EIGRP for IPv6 has been configured on all three routers.

Note   Although EIGRP for IPv6 is used to populate the routing tables, the operation and configuration of EIGRP is beyond the scope of this course.

Refer to
Interactive Graphic
in online course

3.3.4.2 Directly Connected Entries

The routing table of R1 is displayed in Figure 1 using the **show ipv6 route** command. Although, the command output is displayed slightly differently than in the IPv4 version, it still contains the relevant route information.

Figure 2 highlights the connected network and local routing table entries of the directly connected interfaces. The three entries were added when the interfaces were configured and activated.

As shown in Figure 3, directly connected route entries display the following information:

- **Route source** - Identifies how the route was learned. Directly connected interfaces have two route source codes (C identifies a directly connected network while L identifies that this is a local route.)

- **Directly connected network** - The IPv6 address of the directly connected network.

- **Administrative distance** - Identifies the trustworthiness of the route source. IPv6 uses the same distances as IPv4. A value of 0 indicates the best, most trustworthy source.

- **Metric** - Identifies the value assigned to reach the remote network. Lower values indicate preferred routes.

- **Outgoing interface** - Identifies the exit interface to use when forwarding packets to the destination network.

Note The serial links have reference bandwidths configured to observe how EIGRP metrics select the best route. The reference bandwidth is not a realistic representation of modern networks. It is used only to provide a visual depiction of link speed.

Refer to
Interactive Graphic
in online course

3.3.4.3 Remote IPv6 Network Entries

Figure 1 highlights the routing table entries for the three remote networks (i.e., R2 LAN, R3 LAN, and the link between R2 and R3). The three entries were added by the EIGRP.

Figure 2 displays a routing table entry on R1 for the route to remote network 2001:DB8:CAFE:3::/64 on R3. The entry identifies the following information:

- **Route source** - Identifies how the route was learned. Common codes include O (OSPF), D (EIGRP), R (RIP), and S (Static route).

- **Destination network** - Identifies the address of the remote IPv6 network.

- **Administrative distance** - Identifies how trustworthiness of the route source. IPv6 uses the same distances as IPv4.

- **Metric** - Identifies the value assigned to reach the remote network. Lower values indicate preferred routes.

- **Next hop** - Identifies the IPv6 address of the next router to forward the packet to.

- **Outgoing interface** - Identifies the exit interface to use to forward a packet toward the final destination.

When an IPv6 packet arrives on a router interface, the router examines the IPv6 header and identifies the destination IPv6 address. The router then proceeds through the following router lookup process.

The router examines level 1 network routes for the best match with the destination address of the IPv6 packet. Just like IPv4, the longest match is the best match. For example, if there are multiple matches in the routing table, the router chooses the route with the longest match. A match is made by matching the far left bits of the packet's destination IPv6 address with the IPv6 prefix and prefix-length in the IPv6 routing table.

Refer to
Interactive Graphic
in online course

3.3.4.4 Activity – Identify Parts of an IPv6 Routing Table Entry

3.4 Summary

Refer to
Online Course
for Illustration

3.4.1.1 IPv6 – Details, Details...

After studying the concepts presented in this chapter concerning IPv6, you should be able to read a routing table easily and interpret the IPv6 routing information listed within it.

With a partner, use the IPv6 routing table diagram and the .pdf provided with this activity.

Record your answers to the Reflection questions.

Then compare your answers with, at least, one other group from the class.

Refer to
Online Course
for Illustration

3.4.1.2 Dynamic Routing

Dynamic routing protocols are used by routers to facilitate the exchange of routing information between routers. The purpose of dynamic routing protocols includes: discovering remote networks, maintaining up-to-date routing information, choosing the best path to destination networks, and finding a new best path if the current path is no longer available. While dynamic routing protocols require less administrative overhead than static routing, they do require dedicating part of a router's resources for protocol operation, including CPU time and network link bandwidth.

Networks typically use a combination of both static and dynamic routing. Dynamic routing is the best choice for large networks and static routing is better for stub networks.

Routing protocols are responsible for discovering remote networks, as well as maintaining accurate network information. When there is a change in the topology routing protocols propagate that information throughout the routing domain. The process of bringing all routing tables to a state of consistency, where all of the routers in the same routing domain, or area, have complete and accurate information about the network, is called convergence. Some routing protocols converge faster than others.

Routers sometimes learn about multiple routes to the same network from both static routes and dynamic routing protocols. When a router learns about a destination network from more than one routing source, Cisco routers use the administrative distance value to determine which source to use. Each dynamic routing protocol has a unique administrative value, along with static routes and directly connected networks. The lower the administrative value, the more preferred the route source. A directly connected network is always the preferred source, followed by static routes and then various dynamic routing protocols.

Routing table entries contain a route source, a destination network, and an outgoing interface. Route sources can be either connected, local, static, or from a dynamic routing protocol.

IPv4 routing tables can contain four types of routes: ultimate routes, level 1 routes, level 1 parent routes, and level 2 child routes. Because IPv6 is classless by design, all routes are effectively level 1 ultimate routes. There is no level 1 parent of level 2 child routes.

Go to the online course to take the quiz and exam.

Chapter 3 Quiz

This quiz is designed to provide an additional opportunity to practice the skills and knowledge presented in the chapter and to prepare for the chapter exam. You will be allowed multiple attempts and the grade does not appear in the gradebook.

Chapter 3 Exam

The chapter exam assesses your knowledge of the chapter content.

Your Chapter Notes

Switched Networks

4.0 Introduction

Refer to
Online Course
for Illustration

4.0.1.1 Switched Networks

Modern networks continue to evolve to keep pace with the changing way organizations carry out their daily business. Users now expect instant access to company resources from anywhere and at any time. These resources not only include traditional data, but also video and voice. There is also an increasing need for collaboration technologies. These technologies allow real-time sharing of resources between multiple remote individuals, as though they were at the same physical location.

Different devices must seamlessly work together to provide a fast, secure, and reliable connection between hosts. LAN switches provide the connection point for end users into the enterprise network and are also primarily responsible for the control of information within the LAN environment. Routers facilitate the movement of information between LANs, and are generally unaware of individual hosts. All advanced services depend on the availability of a robust routing and switching infrastructure on which they can build. This infrastructure must be carefully designed, deployed, and managed, to provide a stable platform.

This chapter begins an examination of the flow of traffic in a modern network. It examines some of the current network design models and the way LAN switches build forwarding tables and use the MAC address information to efficiently switch data between hosts.

Refer to
Online Course
for Illustration

4.0.1.2 Sent or Received Instructions

Individually, or in groups (per the instructor's decision), discuss various ways hosts send and receive data, voice, and streaming video.

Develop a matrix (table) listing network data types that can be sent and received. Provide five examples.

Note For an example of the matrix, see the document prepared for this modeling activity.

Save your work in either hard- or soft-copy format. Be prepared to discuss your matrix and statements in a class discussion.

4.1 LAN Design

4.1.1 Converged Networks

Refer to
Interactive Graphic
in online course

4.1.1.1 Growing Complexity of Networks

Our digital world is changing. The ability to access the Internet and the corporate network is no longer confined to physical offices, geographical locations, or time zones. In today's globalized workplace, employees can access resources from anywhere in the world and information must be available at any time, and on any device, as shown in Figure 1. These requirements drive the need to build next-generation networks that are secure, reliable, and highly available.

These next generation networks must not only support current expectations and equipment, but must also be able to integrate legacy platforms. Figure 2 shows some common legacy devices that must often be incorporated into network design. Figure 3 illustrates some of the newer platforms (converged networks) that help to provide access to the network anytime, anywhere, and on any device.

Refer to
Interactive Graphic
in online course

4.1.1.2 Elements of a Converged Network

To support collaboration, business networks employ converged solutions using voice systems, IP phones, voice gateways, video support, and video conferencing (Figure 1). Including data services, a converged network with collaboration support may include the following features:

- **Call control** - Telephone call processing, caller ID, call transfer, hold, and conference

- **Voice messaging** - Voicemail

- **Mobility** - Receive important calls wherever you are

- **Automated attendant** - Serve customers faster by routing calls directly to the right department or individual

One of the primary benefits of transitioning to the converged network is that there is just one physical network to install and manage. This results in substantial savings over the installation and management of separate voice, video, and data networks. Such a converged network solution integrates IT management so that any moves, additions, and changes are completed with an intuitive management interface. A converged network solution also provides PC softphone application support, as well as point-to-point video, so that users can enjoy personal communications with the same ease of administration and use as a voice call.

The convergence of services onto the network has resulted in an evolution in networks from a traditional data transport role, to a super-highway for data, voice, and video communication. This one physical network must be properly designed and implemented to allow the reliable handling of the various types of information that it must carry. A structured design is required to allow management of this complex environment.

Click Play in Figure 2 to see a video of a few of the collaboration services in action.

Refer to
Interactive Graphic
in online course

4.1.1.3 Cisco Borderless Networks

With the increasing demands of the converged network, the network must be developed with an architectural approach that embeds intelligence, simplifies operations, and is scalable to meet future demands. One of the more recent developments in network design is the Cisco Borderless Network.

The Cisco Borderless Network is a network architecture that combines innovation and design. It allows organizations to support a borderless network that can connect anyone, anywhere, anytime, on any device; securely, reliably, and seamlessly. This architecture is designed to address IT and business challenges, such as supporting the converged network and changing work patterns.

The Cisco Borderless Network provides the framework to unify wired and wireless access, including policy, access control, and performance management across many different device types. Using this architecture, the borderless network is built on a hierarchical infrastructure of hardware that is scalable and resilient, as shown in Figure 1. By combining this hardware infrastructure with policy-based software solutions, the Cisco Borderless Network provides two primary sets of services: network services, and user and endpoint services that are all managed by an integrated management solution. It enables different network elements to work together, and allows users to access resources from any place, at any time, while providing optimization, scalability, and security.

Click Play in Figure 2 to see a video about the evolution of the borderless network.

Refer to
Interactive Graphic
in online course

4.1.1.4 Hierarchy in the Borderless Switched Network

Creating a borderless switched network requires that sound network design principles are used to ensure maximum availability, flexibility, security, and manageability. The borderless switched network must deliver on current requirements and future required services and technologies. Borderless switched network design guidelines are built upon the following principles:

- **Hierarchical** - Facilitates understanding the role of each device at every tier, simplifies deployment, operation, and management, and reduces fault domains at every tier

- **Modularity** - Allows seamless network expansion and integrated service enablement on an on-demand basis

- **Resiliency** - Satisfies user expectations for keeping the network always on

- **Flexibility** - Allows intelligent traffic load sharing by using all network resources

These are not independent principles. Understanding how each principle fits in the context of the others is critical. Designing a borderless switched network in a hierarchical fashion creates a foundation that allows network designers to overlay security, mobility, and unified communication features. Two time-tested and proven hierarchical design frameworks for campus networks are the three-tier layer and the two-tier layer models, as illustrated in Figures 1 and 2.

The three critical layers within these tiered designs are the access, distribution, and core layers. Each layer can be seen as a well-defined, structured module with specific roles and functions in the campus network. Introducing modularity into the campus hierarchical design further ensures that the campus network remains resilient and flexible enough to provide critical network services. Modularity also helps to allow for growth and changes that occur over time.

Refer to
Interactive Graphic
in online course

4.1.1.5   Access, Distribution, and Core Layers

Access Layer

The access layer represents the network edge, where traffic enters or exits the campus network. Traditionally, the primary function of an access layer switch is to provide network access to the user. Access layer switches connect to distribution layer switches, which implement network foundation technologies such as routing, quality of service, and security.

To meet network application and end-user demand, the next-generation switching platforms now provide more converged, integrated, and intelligent services to various types of endpoints at the network edge. Building intelligence into access layer switches allows applications to operate on the network more efficiently and securely.

Distribution Layer

The distribution layer interfaces between the access layer and the core layer to provide many important functions, including:

- Aggregating large-scale wiring closet networks

- Aggregating Layer 2 broadcast domains and Layer 3 routing boundaries

- Providing intelligent switching, routing, and network access policy functions to access the rest of the network

- Providing high availability through redundant distribution layer switches to the end-user and equal cost paths to the core

- Providing differentiated services to various classes of service applications at the edge of the network

Core Layer

The core layer is the network backbone. It connects several layers of the campus network. The core layer serves as the aggregator for all of the other campus blocks and ties the campus together with the rest of the network. The primary purpose of the core layer is to provide fault isolation and high-speed backbone connectivity.

Figure 1 shows a three-tier campus network design for organizations where the access, distribution, and core are each separate layers. To build a simplified, scalable, cost-effective, and efficient physical cable layout design, the recommendation is to build an extended-star physical network topology from a centralized building location to all other buildings on the same campus.

In some cases where extensive physical or network scalability does not exist, maintaining separate distribution and core layers is not required. In smaller campus locations where there are fewer users accessing the network or in campus sites consisting of a single building, separate core and distribution layers may not be needed. In this scenario, the recommendation is the alternate two-tier campus network design, also known as the collapsed core network design.

Figure 2 shows a two-tier campus network design example for an enterprise campus where the distribution and core layers are collapsed into a single layer.

Refer to
Interactive Graphic
in online course

4.1.1.6   Activity - Identify Switched Network Terminology

4.1.2   Switched Networks

Refer to
Interactive Graphic
in online course

4.1.2.1   Role of Switched Networks

The role of switched networks has evolved dramatically in the last two decades. It was not long ago that flat Layer 2 switched networks were the norm. Flat Layer 2 switched networks relied on the Ethernet and the widespread use of hub repeaters to propagate LAN traffic throughout an organization. As shown in Figure 1, networks have fundamentally changed to switched LANs in a hierarchical network. A switched LAN allows more flexibility, traffic management, and additional features:

- Quality of service

- Additional security

- Support for wireless networking and connectivity

- Support for new technologies, such as IP telephony and mobility services

Figure 2 shows the hierarchical design used in the borderless switched network.

Refer to
Interactive Graphic
in online course

4.1.2.2   Form Factors

There are various types of switches used in business networks. It is important to deploy the appropriate types of switches based on network requirements. Figure 1 highlights some common business considerations when selecting switch equipment.

When selecting the type of switch, the network designer must choose between a fixed configuration or a modular configuration, and stackable or non-stackable. Another consideration is the thickness of the switch, which is expressed in number of rack units. This is important for switches that are mounted in a rack. For example, the fixed configuration switches shown in Figure 2 are all 1 rack unit (1U). These options are sometimes referred to as switch form factors.

Fixed Configuration Switches

Fixed configuration switches do not support features or options beyond those that originally came with the switch (Figure 2). The particular model determines the features and options available. For example, a 24-port gigabit fixed switch cannot support additional ports. There are typically different configuration choices that vary in how many and what types of ports are included with a fixed configuration switch.

Modular Configuration Switches

Modular configuration switches offer more flexibility in their configuration. Modular configuration switches typically come with different sized chassis that allow for the installation of different numbers of modular line cards (Figure 3). The line cards actually contain the ports. The line card fits into the switch chassis the way that expansion cards fit into a PC. The larger the chassis, the more modules it can support. There are many different chassis sizes. A modular switch with a single 24-port line card could have an additional 24-port line card installed to bring the total number of ports up to 48.

Stackable Configuration Switches

Stackable configuration switches can be interconnected using a special cable that provides high-bandwidth throughput between the switches (Figure 4). Cisco StackWise technology allows the interconnection of up to nine switches. Switches can be stacked one on top of the other with cables connecting the switches in a daisy chain fashion. The stacked switches effectively operate as a single larger switch. Stackable switches are desirable where fault tolerance and bandwidth availability are critical and a modular switch is too costly to implement. By cross-connecting these stacked switches, the network can recover quickly if a single switch fails. Stackable switches use a special port for interconnections. Many Cisco stackable switches also support StackPower technology, which enables power sharing among stack members.

Refer to **Interactive Graphic** in online course

4.1.2.3 Activity - Identify Switch Hardware

4.2 The Switched Environment

4.2.1 Frame Forwarding

Refer to **Video** in online course

4.2.1.1 Switching as a General Concept in Networking and Telecommunications

The concept of switching and forwarding frames is universal in networking and telecommunications. Various types of switches are used in LANs, WANs, and the public switched telephone network (PSTN). The fundamental concept of switching refers to a device making a decision based on two criteria:

- Ingress port

- Destination address

The decision on how a switch forwards traffic is made in relation to the flow of that traffic. The term ingress is used to describe where a frame enters the device on a port. The term egress is used to describe frames leaving the device from a particular port.

A LAN switch maintains a table that it uses to determine how to forward traffic through the switch. Click Play in the figure to see an animation of the switching process. In this example:

- If a message enters switch port 1 and has a destination address of EA, then the switch forwards the traffic out port 4.

- If a message enters switch port 5 and has a destination address of EE, then the switch forwards the traffic out port 1.

- If a message enters switch port 3 and has a destination address of AB, then the switch forwards the traffic out port 6.

The only intelligence of the LAN switch is its ability to use its table to forward traffic based on the ingress port and the destination address of a message. With a LAN switch, there is only one master switching table that describes a strict association between addresses and ports; therefore, a message with a given destination address always exits the same egress port, regardless of the ingress port it enters.

Layer 2 Ethernet switches forward Ethernet frames based on the destination MAC address of the frames.

Refer to
Online Course
for Illustration

4.2.1.2 Dynamically Populating a Switch MAC Address Table

Switches use MAC addresses to direct network communications through the switch, to the appropriate port, toward the destination. A switch is made up of integrated circuits and the accompanying software that controls the data paths through the switch. For a switch to know which port to use to transmit a frame, it must first learn which devices exist on each port. As the switch learns the relationship of ports to devices, it builds a table called a MAC address, or content addressable memory (CAM) table. CAM is a special type of memory used in high-speed searching applications.

LAN switches determine how to handle incoming data frames by maintaining the MAC address table. A switch builds its MAC address table by recording the MAC address of each device connected to each of its ports. The switch uses the information in the MAC address table to send frames destined for a specific device out the port which has been assigned to that device.

The following two-step process is performed on every Ethernet frame that enters a switch.

Step 1. Learn – Examining the Source MAC Address
Every frame that enters a switch is checked for new information to learn. It does this by examining the frame's source MAC address and port number where the frame entered the switch:

- If the source MAC address does not exist, it is added to the table along with the incoming port number.

- If the source MAC address does exist, the switch updates the refresh timer for that entry. By default, most Ethernet switches keep an entry in the table for five minutes.

Note   If the source MAC address does exist in the table but on a different port, the switch treats this as a new entry. The entry is replaced using the same MAC address, but with the more current port number.

Step 2. Forward – Examining the Destination MAC Address
If the destination MAC address is a unicast address, the switch will look for a match between the destination MAC address of the frame and an entry in its MAC address table:

- If the destination MAC address is in the table, it will forward the frame out the specified port.

- If the destination MAC address is not in the table, the switch will forward the frame out all ports except the incoming port. This is called an unknown unicast.

Note   If the destination MAC address is a broadcast or a multicast, the frame is also flooded out all ports except the incoming port.

Refer to **Video**
in online course

Click Play in the figure to view a demonstration of how two connected switches build MAC address tables.

Click here to download video slides from the demonstration.

Click here to read the transcript of this video.

Refer to
Interactive Graphic
in online course

4.2.1.3   Switch Forwarding Methods

As networks grew and enterprises began to experience slower network performance, Ethernet bridges (an early version of a switch) were added to networks to limit the size of the collision domains. In the 1990s, advancements in integrated circuit technologies allowed for Ethernet LAN switches to replace Ethernet bridges. These switches were able to move the Layer 2 forwarding decisions from software to application-specific-integrated circuits (ASICs). ASICs reduce the packet-handling time within the device, and allow the device to handle an increased number of ports without degrading performance. This method of forwarding data frames at Layer 2 was referred to as store-and-forward switching. This term distinguished it from cut-through switching.

As shown in Figure 1, the store-and-forward method makes a forwarding decision on a frame after it has received the entire frame and checked the frame for errors using a mathematical error-checking mechanism known as a cyclic redundancy check (CRC).

By contrast, the cut-through method, as shown in Figure 2 begins the forwarding process after the destination MAC address of an incoming frame and the egress port has been determined.

Refer to
Online Course
for Illustration

4.2.1.4   Store-and-Forward Switching

Store-and-forward switching has two primary characteristics that distinguish it from cut-through: error checking and automatic buffering.

Error Checking

A switch using store-and-forward switching performs an error check on an incoming frame. After receiving the entire frame on the ingress port, as shown in the figure, the switch compares the frame-check-sequence (FCS) value in the last field of the datagram against its own FCS calculations. The FCS is an error checking process that helps to ensure that the frame is free of physical and data-link errors. If the frame is error-free, the switch forwards the frame. Otherwise the frame is dropped.

Automatic Buffering

The ingress port buffering process used by store-and-forward switches provides the flexibility to support any mix of Ethernet speeds. For example, handling an incoming frame traveling into a 100 Mb/s Ethernet port that must be sent out a 1 Gb/s interface would require using the store-and-forward method. With any mismatch in speeds between the ingress and egress ports, the switch stores the entire frame in a buffer, computes the FCS check, forwards it to the egress port buffer and then sends it.

Store-and-forward switching is Cisco's primary LAN switching method.

A store-and-forward switch drops frames that do not pass the FCS check; therefore, it does not forward invalid frames. By contrast, a cut-through switch may forward invalid frames because no FCS check is performed.

Refer to
Online Course
for Illustration

4.2.1.5   Cut-Through Switching

An advantage to cut-through switching is the ability of the switch to start forwarding a frame earlier than store-and-forward switching. There are two primary characteristics of cut-through switching: rapid frame forwarding and fragment free.

Rapid Frame Forwarding

As indicated in the figure, a switch using the cut-through method can make a forwarding decision as soon as it has looked up the destination MAC address of the frame in its MAC address table. The switch does not have to wait for the rest of the frame to enter the ingress port before making its forwarding decision.

With today's MAC controllers and ASICs, a switch using the cut-through method can quickly decide whether it needs to examine a larger portion of a frame's headers for additional filtering purposes. For example, the switch can analyze past the first 14 bytes (the source MAC address, destination MAC, and the EtherType fields), and examine an additional 40 bytes in order to perform more sophisticated functions relative to IPv4 Layers 3 and 4.

The cut-through switching method does not drop most invalid frames. Frames with errors are forwarded to other segments of the network. If there is a high error rate (invalid frames) in the network, cut-through switching can have a negative impact on bandwidth; thus, clogging up bandwidth with damaged and invalid frames.

Fragment Free

Fragment free switching is a modified form of cut-through switching in which the switch waits for the collision window (64 bytes) to pass before forwarding the frame. This means each frame will be checked into the data field to make sure no fragmentation has occurred. Fragment free switching provides better error checking than cut-through, with practically no increase in latency.

The lower latency speed of cut-through switching makes it more appropriate for extremely demanding, high-performance computing (HPC) applications that require process-to-process latencies of 10 microseconds or less.

Refer to
Interactive Graphic
in online course

4.2.1.6   Activity – Frame Forwarding Methods

Refer to
Interactive Graphic
in online course

4.2.1.7   Activity – Switch It!

4.2.2   Switching Domains

Refer to
Online Course
for Illustration

4.2.2.1   Collision Domains

In hub-based Ethernet segments, network devices compete for the medium, because devices must take turns when transmitting. The network segments that share the same bandwidth between devices are known as collision domains. When two or more devices within that the same collision domain try to communicate at the same time, a collision will occur.

If an Ethernet switch port is operating in half duplex, each segment is in its own collision domain. However, Ethernet switch ports operating in full duplex eliminate collisions;

therefore, there is no collision domain. By default, Ethernet switch ports will autonegotiate full duplex when the adjacent device can also operate in full duplex. If the switch port is connected to a device operating in half-duplex, such as a legacy hub, then the switch port will operate in half duplex. In the case of half duplex, the switch port will be part of a collision domain.

As shown in the figure, full-duplex is chosen if both devices have the capability along with their highest common bandwidth.

Refer to **Video** in online course

4.2.2.2   Broadcast Domains

A collection of interconnected switches forms a single broadcast domain. Only a network layer device, such as a router, can divide a Layer 2 broadcast domain. Routers are used to segment broadcast domains, but will also segment a collision domain.

When a device sends a Layer 2 broadcast, the destination MAC address in the frame is set to all binary ones.

The Layer 2 broadcast domain is referred to as the MAC broadcast domain. The MAC broadcast domain consists of all devices on the LAN that receive broadcast frames from a host.

Click Play in the figure to see this in the first half of the animation.

When a switch receives a broadcast frame, it forwards the frame out each of its ports, except the ingress port where the broadcast frame was received. Each device connected to the switch receives a copy of the broadcast frame and processes it. Broadcasts are sometimes necessary for initially locating other devices and network services, but they also reduce network efficiency. Network bandwidth is used to propagate the broadcast traffic. Too many broadcasts and a heavy traffic load on a network can result in congestion, which slows down network performance.

When two switches are connected together, the broadcast domain is increased, as seen in the second half of the animation. In this case, a broadcast frame is forwarded to all connected ports on switch S1. Switch S1 is connected to switch S2. The frame is then also propagated to all devices connected to switch S2.

Refer to **Online Course** for Illustration

4.2.2.3   Alleviating Network Congestion

LAN switches have special characteristics that make them effective at alleviating network congestion. By default, interconnected switch ports attempt to establish a link in full duplex, therefore eliminating collision domains. Each full duplex port of the switch provides the full bandwidth to the device or devices that are connected to that port. A full-duplex connection can carry transmitted and received signals at the same time. Full-duplex connections have dramatically increased LAN network performance, and are required for 1 Gb/s Ethernet speeds and higher.

Switches interconnect LAN segments, use a table of MAC addresses to determine the segment to which the frame is to be sent, and can lessen or eliminate collisions entirely. The following are some important characteristics of switches that contribute to alleviating network congestion:

- **High port density** - Switches have high-port densities: 24- and 48-port switches are often just a single rack unit and operate at speeds of 100 Mb/s, 1 Gb/s, and 10 Gb/s. Large enterprise switches may support many hundreds of ports.

- **Large frame buffers** - The ability to store more received frames before having to start dropping them is useful, particularly when there may be congested ports to servers or other parts of the network.

- **Port speed** - Depending on the cost of a switch, it may be possible to support a mixture of speeds. Ports of 100 Mb/s, and 1 or 10 Gb/s are common (100 Gb/s is also possible).

- **Fast internal switching** - Having fast internal forwarding capabilities allows high performance. The method that is used may be a fast internal bus or shared memory, which affects the overall performance of the switch.

- **Low per-port cost** - Switches provide high-port density at a lower cost.

Refer to
Interactive Graphic
in online course

4.2.2.4 Activity – Circle the Domain

4.3 Summary

Refer to
Online Course
for Illustration

4.3.1.1 It's Network Access Time

Use Packet Tracer for this activity. Internet connectivity is not required. Work with a classmate to create two network designs to accommodate the following scenarios:

Scenario 1 – Classroom Design (LAN)

- 15 student end devices represented by 1 or 2 PCs

- 1 instructor end device preferably represented by a server

- Stream video presentations over LAN connection

Scenario 2 – Administrative Design (WAN)

- All requirements as listed in Scenario 1

- Access to and from a remote administrative server for video presentations and pushed updates for network application software

Both the LAN and WAN designs should fit on one Packet Tracer file screen. All intermediary devices should be labeled with the switch model (or name) and the router model (or name).

Save your work and be ready to justify your device decisions and layout to your instructor and to the class.

Refer to
Interactive Graphic
in online course

4.3.1.2 Basic Switch Configurations

Refer to
Online Course
for Illustration

4.3.1.3 Switched Networks

We have seen that the trend in networks is towards convergence using a single set of wires and devices to handle voice, video, and data transmission. In addition, there has been a dramatic shift in the way businesses operate. No longer are employees constrained to physical offices or by geographic boundaries. Resources must now be seamlessly available anytime and anywhere. The Cisco Borderless Network architecture enables different elements, from access switches to wireless access points, to work together and allow users to access resources from any place at any time.

The traditional three-layer hierarchical design model divides the network into core, distribution, and access layers, and allows each portion of the network to be optimized for specific functionality. It provides modularity, resiliency, and flexibility, which creates a foundation that allows network designers to overlay security, mobility, and unified communication features. In some networks, having a separate core and distribution layer is not required. In these networks, the functionality of the core layer and the distribution layer are often collapsed together.

Cisco LAN switches use ASICs to forward frames based on the destination MAC address. Before this can be accomplished, it must first use the source MAC address of incoming frames to build up a MAC address table in content-addressable memory (CAM). If the destination MAC address is contained in this table, the frame is forwarded only to the specific destination port. In cases where the destination MAC address is not found in the MAC address table, the frames are flooded out all ports, except the one on which the frame was received.

Switches use either store-and-forward or cut-through switching. Store-and-forward reads the entire frame into a buffer and checks the CRC before forwarding the frame. Cut-through switching only reads the first portion of the frame and starts forwarding it as soon as the destination address is read. Although this is extremely fast, no error checking is done on the frame before forwarding.

Switches attempt to autonegotiate full-duplex communication by default. Switch ports do not block broadcasts and connecting switches together can extend the size of the broadcast domain, often resulting in degraded network performance.

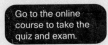
Go to the online course to take the quiz and exam.

Chapter 4 Quiz

This quiz is designed to provide an additional opportunity to practice the skills and knowledge presented in the chapter and to prepare for the chapter exam. You will be allowed multiple attempts and the grade does not appear in the gradebook.

Chapter 4 Exam

The chapter exam assesses your knowledge of the chapter content.

Your Chapter Notes

Switch Configuration

5.0 Introduction

Refer to **Online Course** for Illustration

5.0.1.1 Switch Configuration

Switches are used to connect multiple devices together on the same network. In a properly designed network, LAN switches are responsible for directing and controlling the data flow at the access layer to networked resources.

Cisco switches are self-configuring and no additional configurations are necessary for them to function out of the box. However, Cisco switches run Cisco IOS, and can be manually configured to better meet the needs of the network. This includes adjusting port speed, bandwidth, and security requirements.

Additionally, Cisco switches can be managed both locally and remotely. To remotely manage a switch, it needs to have an IP address and default gateway configured. These are just two of the configurations discussed in this chapter.

Switches operate at the access layer where client network devices connect directly to the network and IT departments want uncomplicated network access for the users. It is one of the most vulnerable areas of the network because it is so exposed to the user. Switches need to be configured to be resilient to attacks of all types while they are protecting user data and allowing for high speed connections. Port security is one of the security features that Cisco managed switches provide.

This chapter examines some of the basic switch configuration settings required to maintain a secure, available, switched LAN environment.

Refer to **Online Course** for Illustration

5.0.1.2 Activity – Stand By Me

Scenario

When you arrived to class today, you were given a number by your instructor to use for this introductory class activity.

When class begins, your instructor will ask certain students with specific numbers to stand. Your job is to record the standing students' numbers for each scenario.

Scenario 1

Students with numbers **starting** with the number **5** should stand. Record the numbers of the standing students.

Scenario 2

Students with numbers __ending__ in __B__ should stand. Record the numbers of the standing students.

Scenario 3

Students with the number __505C__ should stand. Record the number of the standing student.

At the end of this activity, divide into small groups and record answers to the Reflection questions on the .pdf file for this activity.

Save your work and be prepared to share it with another student or the entire class.

5.1 Basic Switch Configuration

5.1.1 Configure a Switch with Initial Settings

Refer to
Interactive Graphic
in online course

5.1.1.1 Switch Boot Sequence

After a Cisco switch is powered on, it goes through the following boot sequence:

1. First, the switch loads a power-on self-test (POST) program stored in ROM. POST checks the CPU subsystem. It tests the CPU, DRAM, and the portion of the flash device that makes up the flash file system.

2. Next, the switch loads the boot loader software. The boot loader is a small program stored in ROM that is run immediately after POST successfully completes.

3. The boot loader performs low-level CPU initialization. It initializes the CPU registers, which control where physical memory is mapped, the quantity of memory, and its speed.

4. The boot loader initializes the flash file system on the system board.

5. Finally, the boot loader locates and loads a default IOS operating system software image into memory and gives control of the switch over to the IOS.

The boot loader finds the Cisco IOS image on the switch as follows: the switch attempts to automatically boot by using information in the BOOT environment variable. If this variable is not set, the switch attempts to load and execute the first executable file it can by performing a recursive, depth-first search throughout the flash file system. In a depth-first search of a directory, each encountered subdirectory is completely searched before continuing the search in the original directory. On Catalyst 2960 Series switches, the image file is normally contained in a directory that has the same name as the image file (excluding the .bin file extension).

The IOS operating system then initializes the interfaces using the Cisco IOS commands found in the startup-config file, which is stored in NVRAM.

In the figure, the BOOT environment variable is set using the **boot system** global configuration mode command. Notice that the IOS is located in a distinct folder and the folder path is specified. Use the command **show boot** to see what the current IOS boot file is set to.

Refer to
Online Course
for Illustration

5.1.1.2   Recovering From a System Crash

The boot loader provides access into the switch if the operating system cannot be used because of missing or damaged system files. The boot loader has a command-line that provides access to the files stored in flash memory.

The boot loader can be accessed through a console connection following these steps:

Step 1.   Connect a PC by console cable to the switch console port. Configure terminal emulation software to connect to the switch.

Step 2.   Unplug the switch power cord.

Step 3.   Reconnect the power cord to the switch and, within 15 seconds, press and hold down the **Mode** button while the System LED is still flashing green.

Step 4.   Continue pressing the **Mode** button until the System LED turns briefly amber and then solid green; then release the **Mode** button.

Step 5.   The boot loader **switch:** prompt appears in the terminal emulation software on the PC.

The boot loader command line supports commands to format the flash file system, reinstall the operating system software, and recover a lost or forgotten password. For example, the **dir** command can be used to view a list of files within a specified directory, as shown in the figure.

Note   Notice that in this example, the IOS is located in the root of the flash folder.

Refer to
Online Course
for Illustration

5.1.1.3   Switch LED Indicators

Cisco Catalyst switches have several status LED indicator lights. You can use the switch LEDs to quickly monitor switch activity and performance. Switches of different models and feature sets will have different LEDs and their placement on the front panel of the switch may also vary.

The figure shows the switch LEDs and the Mode button for a Cisco Catalyst 2960 switch. The Mode button is used to toggle through port status, port duplex, port speed, and PoE (if supported) status of the port LEDs. The following describes the purpose of the LED indicators, and the meaning of their colors:

■ **System LED** - Shows whether the system is receiving power and is functioning properly. If the LED is off, it means the system is not powered on. If the LED is green, the system is operating normally. If the LED is amber, the system is receiving power but is not functioning properly.

■ **Redundant Power System (RPS) LED** - Shows the RPS status. If the LED is off, the RPS is off, or it is not properly connected. If the LED is green, the RPS is connected and ready to provide backup power. If the LED is blinking green, the RPS is connected but is unavailable because it is providing power to another device. If the LED is amber, the RPS is in standby mode, or in a fault condition. If the LED is blinking amber, the internal power supply in the switch has failed, and the RPS is providing power.

■ **Port Status LED** - Indicates that the port status mode is selected when the LED is green. This is the default mode. When selected, the port LEDs will display colors with different meanings. If the LED is off, there is no link, or the port was administratively shut down. If the LED is green, a link is present. If the LED is blinking green, there is activity and the port is sending or receiving data. If the LED is alternating green-amber, there is a link fault. If the LED is amber, the port is blocked to ensure that a loop does not exist in the forwarding domain and is not forwarding data (typically, ports will remain in this state for the first 30 seconds after being activated). If the LED is blinking amber, the port is blocked to prevent a possible loop in the forwarding domain.

■ **Port Duplex LED** - Indicates the port duplex mode is selected when the LED is green. When selected, port LEDs that are off are in half-duplex mode. If the port LED is green, the port is in full-duplex mode.

■ **Port Speed LED** - Indicates the port speed mode is selected. When selected, the port LEDs will display colors with different meanings. If the LED is off, the port is operating at 10 Mb/s. If the LED is green, the port is operating at 100 Mb/s. If the LED is blinking green, the port is operating at 1000 Mb/s.

■ **Power over Ethernet (PoE) Mode LED** - If PoE is supported; a PoE mode LED will be present. If the LED is off, it indicates the PoE mode is not selected and that none of the ports have been denied power or placed in a fault condition. If the LED is blinking amber, the PoE mode is not selected but at least one of the ports has been denied power, or has a PoE fault. If the LED is green, it indicates the PoE mode is selected and the port LEDs will display colors with different meanings. If the port LED is off, the PoE is off. If the port LED is green, the PoE is on. If the port LED is alternating green-amber, PoE is denied because providing power to the powered device will exceed the switch power capacity. If the LED is blinking amber, PoE is off due to a fault. If the LED is amber, PoE for the port has been disabled.

Refer to
Online Course
for Illustration

5.1.1.4 Preparing for Basic Switch Management

To prepare a switch for remote management access, the switch must be configured with an IP address and a subnet mask. Keep in mind, that to manage the switch from a remote network, the switch must be configured with a default gateway. This is very similar to configuring the IP address information on host devices. In the figure, the switch virtual interface (SVI) on S1 should be assigned an IP address. The SVI is a virtual interface, not a physical port on the switch.

SVI is a concept related to VLANs. VLANs are numbered logical groups to which physical ports can be assigned. Configurations and settings applied to a VLAN are also applied to all the ports assigned to that VLAN.

By default, the switch is configured to have the management of the switch controlled through VLAN 1. All ports are assigned to VLAN 1 by default. For security purposes, it is considered a best practice to use a VLAN other than VLAN 1 for the management VLAN.

Note that these IP settings are only for remote management access to the switch; the IP settings do not allow the switch to route Layer 3 packets.

Refer to
Interactive Graphic
in online course

5.1.1.5   Configuring Basic Switch Management Access with IPv4

Step 1.   Configure Management Interface
An IPv4 address and subnet mask is configured on the management SVI of the switch from VLAN interface configuration mode. As shown in Figure 1, the **interface vlan 99** command is used to enter interface configuration mode. The **ip address** command is used to configure the IPv4 address. The **no shutdown** command enables the interface. In this example, VLAN 99 is configured with IPv4 address 172.17.99.11.

The SVI for VLAN 99 will not appear as "up/up" until VLAN 99 is created and there is a device connected to a switch port associated with VLAN 99. To create a VLAN with the vlan_id of 99, and associate it to an interface, use the following commands:

```
S1(config)#   vlan vlan_id

S1(config-vlan)#   name vlan_name

S1(config-vlan)#   exit

S1(config)#   interface interface_id

S1(config-if)# switchport access vlan vlan_id
```

Step 2.   Configure Default Gateway
The switch should be configured with a default gateway if it will be managed remotely from networks that are not directly connected. The default gateway is the router to which the switch is connected. The switch will forward its IP packets with destination IP addresses outside the local network to the default gateway. As shown in Figure 2, R1 is the default gateway for S1. The interface on R1 connected to the switch has the IPv4 address 172.17.99.1. This address is the default gateway address for S1.

To configure the default gateway for the switch, use the **ip default-gateway** command. Enter the IPv4 address of the default gateway. The default gateway is the IPv4 address of the router interface to which the switch is connected. Use the **copy running-config startup-config** command to back up your configuration.

Step 3.   Verify Configuration
As shown in Figure 3, the **show ip interface brief** command is useful when determining the status of both physical and virtual interfaces. The output shown confirms that interface VLAN 99 has been configured with an IPv4 address and subnet mask.

Refer to
Lab Activity
for this chapter

5.1.1.6   Lab - Basic Switch Configuration

In this lab, you will complete the following objectives:

- Part 1: Cable the Network and Verify the Default Switch Configuration

- Part 2: Configure Basic Network Device Settings

- Part 3: Verify and Test Network Connectivity

- Part 4: Manage the MAC Address Table

5.1.2   Configure Switch Ports

Refer to
Online Course
for Illustration

5.1.2.1   Duplex Communication

The figure illustrates full-duplex and half-duplex communication.

Full-duplex communication improves the performance of a switched LAN. Full-duplex communication increases effective bandwidth by allowing both ends of a connection to transmit and receive data simultaneously. This is also known as bidirectional communication. This method of optimizing network performance requires micro-segmentation. A micro-segmented LAN is created when a switch port has only one device connected and is operating in full-duplex mode. When a switch port is operating in full-duplex mode, there is no collision domain associated with the port.

Unlike full-duplex communication, half-duplex communication is unidirectional. Sending and receiving data does not occur at the same time. Half-duplex communication creates performance issues because data can flow in only one direction at a time, often resulting in collisions. Half-duplex connections are typically seen in older hardware, such as hubs. Full-duplex communication has replaced half-duplex in most hardware.

Gigabit Ethernet and 10Gb NICs require full-duplex connections to operate. In full-duplex mode, the collision detection circuit on the NIC is disabled. Frames that are sent by the two connected devices cannot collide because the devices use two separate circuits in the network cable. Full-duplex connections require a switch that supports full-duplex configuration, or a direct connection using an Ethernet cable between two devices.

Standard, shared hub-based Ethernet configuration efficiency is typically rated at 50 to 60 percent of the stated bandwidth. Full-duplex offers 100 percent efficiency in both directions (transmitting and receiving). This results in a 200 percent potential use of the stated bandwidth.

Refer to
Interactive Graphic
in online course

5.1.2.2   Configure Switch Ports at the Physical Layer

Duplex and Speed

Switch ports can be manually configured with specific duplex and speed settings. Use the **duplex** interface configuration mode command to manually specify the duplex mode for a switch port. Use the **speed** interface configuration mode command to manually specify the speed for a switch port. In Figure 1, port F0/1 on switch S1 and S2 are manually configured with the **full** keyword for the **duplex** command, and the **100** keyword for the **speed** command.

The default setting for both duplex and speed for switch ports on Cisco Catalyst 2960 and 3560 switches is auto. The 10/100/1000 ports operate in either half- or full-duplex mode when they are set to 10 or 100 Mb/s, but when they are set to 1000 Mb/s (1 Gb/s), they operate only in full-duplex mode. Auto-negotiation is useful when the speed and duplex settings of the device connecting to the port are unknown or may change. When connecting to known devices, such as servers, dedicated workstations, or network devices, best practice is to manually set the speed and duplex settings.

When troubleshooting switch port issues, the duplex and speed settings should be checked.

Note   Mismatched settings for the duplex mode and speed of switch ports can cause connectivity issues. Auto-negotiation failure creates mismatched settings.

All fiber optic ports, such as 1000BASE-SX ports, operate only at one preset speed and are always full-duplex.

Use the Syntax Checker in Figure 2 to configure port F0/1 of switch S1.

Refer to
Interactive Graphic
in online course

5.1.2.3   Auto-MDIX

Until recently, certain cable types (straight-through or crossover) were required when connecting devices. Switch-to-switch or switch-to-router connections required using different Ethernet cables. Using the automatic medium-dependent interface crossover (auto-MDIX) feature on an interface eliminates this problem. When auto-MDIX is enabled, the interface automatically detects the required cable connection type (straight-through or crossover) and configures the connection appropriately. When connecting to switches without the auto-MDIX feature, straight-through cables must be used to connect to devices such as servers, workstations, or routers. Crossover cables must be used to connect to other switches or repeaters.

With auto-MDIX enabled, either type of cable can be used to connect to other devices, and the interface automatically adjusts to communicate successfully. On newer Cisco switches, the **mdix auto** interface configuration mode command enables the feature. When using auto-MDIX on an interface, the interface speed and duplex must be set to **auto** so that the feature operates correctly.

The commands to enable auto-MDIX are shown in Figure 1.

Note   The auto-MDIX feature is enabled by default on Catalyst 2960 and Catalyst 3560 switches, but is not available on the older Catalyst 2950 and Catalyst 3550 switches.

To examine the auto-MDIX setting for a specific interface, use the **show controllers ethernet-controller** command with the **phy** keyword. To limit the output to lines referencing auto-MDIX, use the **include Auto-MDIX** filter. As shown in Figure 2, the output indicates On or Off for the feature.

Use the Syntax Checker in Figure 3 to configure the FastEthernet 0/1 interface on S2 for auto-MDIX.

Refer to
Interactive Graphic
in online course

5.1.2.4   Verifying Switch Port Configuration

Figure 1 describes some of the options for the **show** command that are helpful in verifying common configurable switch features.

Figure 2 shows sample abbreviated output from the **show running-config** command. Use this command to verify that the switch has been correctly configured. As seen in the output for S1, some important information is shown:

- Fast Ethernet 0/18 interface configured with the management VLAN 99

- VLAN 99 configured with an IPv4 address of 172.17.99.11 255.255.255.0

- Default gateway set to 172.17.99.1

The **show interfaces** command is another commonly used command, which displays status and statistics information on the network interfaces of the switch. The **show interfaces** command is frequently used when configuring and monitoring network devices.

Figure 3 shows the output from the **show interfaces fastEthernet 0/18** command. The first line in the figure indicates that the FastEthernet 0/18 interface is up/up meaning that it is operational. Further down, the output shows that the duplex is full and the speed is 100 Mb/s.

Refer to
Interactive Graphic
in online course

5.1.2.5   Network Access Layer Issues

The output from the **show interfaces** command can be used to detect common media issues. One of the most important parts of this output is the display of the line and data link protocol status. Figure 1 indicates the summary line to check the status of an interface.

The first parameter (FastEthernet0/1 is up) refers to the hardware layer and indicates if the interface is receiving a carrier detect signal. The second parameter (line protocol is up) refers to the data link layer and indicates whether the data link layer protocol keepalives are being received.

Based on the output of the **show interfaces** command, possible problems can be fixed as follows:

- If the interface is up and the line protocol is down, a problem exists. There could be an encapsulation type mismatch, the interface on the other end could be error-disabled, or there could be a hardware problem.

- If the line protocol and the interface are both down, a cable is not attached or some other interface problem exists. For example, in a back-to-back connection, the other end of the connection may be administratively down.

- If the interface is administratively down, it has been manually disabled (the **shutdown** command has been issued) in the active configuration.

Figure 2 shows an example of **show interfaces** command output. The example shows counters and statistics for the FastEthernet0/1 interface.

Some media errors are not severe enough to cause the circuit to fail, but do cause network performance issues. Figure 3 explains some of these common errors which can be detected using the **show interfaces** command.

"Input errors" is the sum of all errors in datagrams that were received on the interface being examined. This includes runts, giants, CRC, no buffer, frame, overrun, and ignored counts. The reported input errors from the **show interfaces** command include the following:

- **Runt Frames** - Ethernet frames that are shorter than the 64-byte minimum allowed length are called runts. Malfunctioning NICs are the usual cause of excessive runt frames, but they can also be caused by collisions.

- **Giants** - Ethernet frames that are larger than the maximum allowed size are called giants.

- **CRC errors** - On Ethernet and serial interfaces, CRC errors usually indicate a media or cable error. Common causes include electrical interference, loose or damaged connections, or incorrect cabling. If you see many CRC errors, there is too much noise on the link and you should inspect the cable. You should also search for and eliminate noise sources.

"Output errors" is the sum of all errors that prevented the final transmission of datagrams out the interface that is being examined. The reported output errors from the **show interfaces** command include the following:

- **Collisions** - Collisions in half-duplex operations are normal. However, you should never see collisions on an interface configured for full-duplex communication.

- **Late collisions** - A late collision refers to a collision that occurs after 512 bits of the frame have been transmitted. Excessive cable lengths are the most common cause of late collisions. Another common cause is duplex misconfiguration. For example, you could have one end of a connection configured for full-duplex and the other for half-duplex. You would see late collisions on the interface that is configured for half-duplex. In that case, you must configure the same duplex setting on both ends. A properly designed and configured network should never have late collisions.

Refer to
Online Course
for Illustration

5.1.2.6 Troubleshooting Network Access Layer Issues

Most issues that affect a switched network are encountered during the original implementation. Theoretically, after it is installed, a network continues to operate without problems. However, cabling gets damaged, configurations change, and new devices are connected to the switch that require switch configuration changes. Ongoing maintenance and troubleshooting of the network infrastructure is required.

To troubleshoot scenarios involving no connection, or a bad connection, between a switch and another device, follow this general process:

Use the **show interfaces** command to check the interface status.

If the interface is down:

- Check to make sure that the proper cables are being used. Additionally, check the cable and connectors for damage. If a bad or incorrect cable is suspected, replace the cable.

- If the interface is still down, the problem may be due to a mismatch in speed setting. The speed of an interface is typically auto-negotiated; therefore, even if it is manually configured on one interface, the connecting interface should auto-negotiate accordingly. If a speed mismatch does occur through misconfiguration, or a hardware or software issue, then that may result in the interface going down. Manually set the same speed on both connection ends if a problem is suspected.

If the interface is up, but issues with connectivity are still present:

- Using the **show interfaces** command, check for indications of excessive noise. Indications may include an increase in the counters for runts, giants, and CRC errors. If there is excessive noise, first find and remove the source of the noise, if possible. Also, verify that the cable does not exceed the maximum cable length and check the type of cable that is used.

■ If noise is not an issue, check for excessive collisions. If there are collisions or late collisions, verify the duplex settings on both ends of the connection. Much like the speed setting, the duplex setting is usually auto-negotiated. If there does appear to be a duplex mismatch, manually set the duplex to full on both ends of the connection.

5.2   Switch Security

5.2.1   Secure Remote Access

Refer to
Interactive Graphic
in online course

5.2.1.1   SSH Operation

Secure Shell (SSH) is a protocol that provides a secure (encrypted) management connection to a remote device. SSH should replace Telnet for management connections. Telnet is an older protocol that uses unsecure plaintext transmission of both the login authentication (username and password) and the data transmitted between the communicating devices. SSH provides security for remote connections by providing strong encryption when a device is authenticated (username and password) and also for the transmitted data between the communicating devices. SSH is assigned to TCP port 22. Telnet is assigned to TCP port 23.

In Figure 1, an attacker can monitor packets using Wireshark. A Telnet stream can be targeted to capture the username and password.

In Figure 2, the attacker can capture the username and password of the administrator from the plaintext Telnet session.

Figure 3 shows the Wireshark view of an SSH session. The attacker can track the session using the IP address of the administrator device.

However, in Figure 4, the username and password are encrypted.

To enable SSH on a Catalyst 2960 switch, the switch must be using a version of the IOS software including cryptographic (encrypted) features and capabilities. In Figure 5, use the **show version** command on the switch to see which IOS the switch is currently running. An IOS filename that includes the combination "k9" supports cryptographic (encrypted) features and capabilities.

Refer to
Interactive Graphic
in online course

5.2.1.2   Configuring SSH

Before configuring SSH, the switch must be minimally configured with a unique hostname and the correct network connectivity settings.

Step 1.   Verify SSH support.
Use the **show ip ssh** command to verify that the switch supports SSH. If the switch is not running an IOS that supports cryptographic features, this command is unrecognized.

Step 2.   Configure the IP domain.
Configure the IP domain name of the network using the **ip domain-name** *domain-name* global configuration mode command. In Figure 1, the *domain-name* value is **cisco.com**.

Step 3.   Generate RSA key pairs.

Not all versions of the IOS default to SSH version 2, and SSH version 1 has known security flaws. To configure SSH version 2, issue the **ip ssh version 2** global configuration mode command. Generating an RSA key pair automatically enables SSH. Use the **crypto key generate rsa** global configuration mode command to enable the SSH server on the switch and generate an RSA key pair. When generating RSA keys, the administrator is prompted to enter a modulus length. The sample configuration in Figure 1 uses a modulus size of 1,024 bits. A longer modulus length is more secure, but it takes longer to generate and to use.

Note   To delete the RSA key pair, use the **crypto key zeroize rsa** global configuration mode command. After the RSA key pair is deleted, the SSH server is automatically disabled.

Step 4.   Configure user authentication.

The SSH server can authenticate users locally or using an authentication server. To use the local authentication method, create a username and password pair using the **username** *username* **secret** *password* global configuration mode command. In the example, the user **admin** is assigned the password **ccna**.

Step 5.   Configure the vty lines.

Enable the SSH protocol on the vty lines using the **transport input ssh** line configuration mode command. The Catalyst 2960 has vty lines ranging from 0 to 15. This configuration prevents non-SSH (such as Telnet) connections and limits the switch to accept only SSH connections. Use the **line vty** global configuration mode command and then the **login local** line configuration mode command to require local authentication for SSH connections from the local username database.

Step 6.   Enable SSH version 2.

By default, SSH supports both versions 1 and 2. When supporting both versions, this is shown in the **show ip ssh** output as supporting version 1.99. Version 1 has known vulnerabilities. For this reason, it is recommended to enable only version 2. Enable SSH version using the **ip ssh version 2** global configuration command.

Use the Syntax Checker in Figure 2 to configure SSH on switch S1.

Refer to **Interactive Graphic** in online course

5.2.1.3   Verifying SSH

On a PC, an SSH client such as PuTTY, is used to connect to an SSH server. For the examples in Figures 1 to 3, the following have been configured:

■ SSH enabled on switch S1

■ Interface VLAN 99 (SVI) with IPv4 address 172.17.99.11 on switch S1

■ PC1 with IPv4 address 172.17.99.21

In Figure 1, the PC initiates an SSH connection to the SVI VLAN IPv4 address of S1.

In Figure 2, the user has been prompted for a username and password. Using the configuration from the previous example, the username **admin** and password **ccna** are entered. After entering the correct combination, the user is connected via SSH to the CLI on the Catalyst 2960 switch.

To display the version and configuration data for SSH on the device that you configured as an SSH server, use the **show ip ssh** command. In the example, SSH version 2 is enabled. To check the SSH connections to the device, use the **show ssh** command (see Figure 3).

Refer to **Packet Tracer Activity** for this chapter

5.2.1.4   Packet Tracer - Configuring SSH

SSH should replace Telnet for management connections. Telnet uses insecure plaintext communications. SSH provides security for remote connections by providing strong encryption of all transmitted data between devices. In this activity, you will secure a remote switch with password encryption and SSH.

5.2.2   Switch Port Security

Refer to **Online Course** for Illustration

5.2.2.1   Secure Unused Ports

Disable Unused Ports

A simple method that many administrators use to help secure the network from unauthorized access is to disable all unused ports on a switch. For example, if a Catalyst 2960 switch has 24 ports and there are three Fast Ethernet connections in use, it is good practice to disable the 21 unused ports. Navigate to each unused port and issue the Cisco IOS **shutdown** command. If, later on, a port must be reactivated, it can be enabled with the **no shutdown** command. The figure shows partial output for this configuration.

It is simple to make configuration changes to multiple ports on a switch. If a range of ports must be configured, use the **interface range** command.

```
Switch(config)# interface range type module/first-number - last-number
```

The process of enabling and disabling ports can be time-consuming, but it enhances security on the network and is well worth the effort.

Refer to **Interactive Graphic** in online course

5.2.2.2   Port Security: Operation

Port Security

All switch ports (interfaces) should be secured before the switch is deployed for production use. One way to secure ports is by implementing a feature called port security. Port security limits the number of valid MAC addresses allowed on a port. The MAC addresses of legitimate devices are allowed access, while other MAC addresses are denied.

Port security can be configured to allow one or more MAC addresses. If the number of MAC addresses allowed on the port is limited to one, then only the device with that specific MAC address can successfully connect to the port.

If a port is configured as a secure port and the maximum number of MAC addresses is reached, any additional attempts to connect by unknown MAC addresses will generate a security violation. Figure 1 summarizes these points.

Secure MAC Address Types

There are a number of ways to configure port security. The type of secure address is based on the configuration and includes:

- **Static secure MAC addresses** - MAC addresses that are manually configured on a port by using the **switchport port-security mac-address** *mac-address* interface configuration mode command. MAC addresses configured in this way are stored in the address table and are added to the running configuration on the switch.

- **Dynamic secure MAC addresses** - MAC addresses that are dynamically learned and stored only in the address table. MAC addresses configured in this way are removed when the switch restarts.

- **Sticky secure MAC addresses** - MAC addresses that can be dynamically learned or manually configured, then stored in the address table and added to the running configuration.

Sticky Secure MAC addresses

To configure an interface to convert dynamically learned MAC addresses to sticky secure MAC addresses and add them to the running configuration, you must enable sticky learning. Sticky learning is enabled on an interface by using the **switchport port-security mac-address sticky** interface configuration mode command.

When this command is entered, the switch converts all dynamically learned MAC addresses, including those that were dynamically learned before sticky learning was enabled, into sticky secure MAC addresses. All sticky secure MAC addresses are added to the address table and to the running configuration.

Sticky secure MAC addresses can also be manually defined. When sticky secure MAC addresses are configured by using the **switchport port-security mac-address sticky** *mac-address* interface configuration mode command, all specified addresses are added to the address table and the running configuration.

If the sticky secure MAC addresses are saved to the startup configuration file, then when the switch restarts or the interface shuts down, the interface does not need to relearn the addresses. If the sticky secure addresses are not saved, they will be lost.

If sticky learning is disabled by using the **no switchport port-security mac-address sticky** interface configuration mode command, the sticky secure MAC addresses remain part of the address table, but are removed from the running configuration.

Figure 2 shows the characteristics of sticky secure MAC addresses.

Note   The port security feature will not work until port security is enabled on the interface using the **switchport port-security** command.

Refer to
Online Course
for Illustration

5.2.2.3 Port Security: Violation Modes

An interface can be configured for one of three violation modes, specifying the action to be taken if a violation occurs. The figure presents which kinds of data traffic are forwarded when one of the following security violation modes are configured on a port:

- **Protect** - When the number of secure MAC addresses reaches the limit allowed on the port, packets with unknown source addresses are dropped until a sufficient number of secure MAC addresses are removed, or the number of maximum allowable addresses is increased. There is no notification that a security violation has occurred.

- **Restrict** - When the number of secure MAC addresses reaches the limit allowed on the port, packets with unknown source addresses are dropped until a sufficient number of secure MAC addresses are removed, or the number of maximum allowable addresses is increased. In this mode, there is a notification that a security violation has occurred.

- **Shutdown** - In this (default) mode, a port security violation causes the interface to immediately become error-disabled and turns off the port LED. It increments the violation counter. When a secure port is in the error-disabled state, it can be brought out of this state by entering the **shutdown** interface configuration mode command followed by the **no shutdown** command.

To change the violation mode on a switch port, use the **switchport port-security violation** {**protect** | **restrict** | **shutdown**} interface configuration mode command.

Refer to
Interactive Graphic
in online course

5.2.2.4 Port Security: Configuring

Figure 1 summarizes the default port security settings on a Cisco Catalyst switch.

Figure 2 shows the Cisco IOS CLI commands needed to configure port security on the Fast Ethernet F0/18 port on the S1 switch. Notice that the example does not specify a violation mode. In this example, the violation mode is shutdown (the default mode).

Figure 3 shows how to enable sticky secure MAC addresses for port security on Fast Ethernet port 0/19 of switch S1. As stated earlier, the maximum number of secure MAC addresses can be manually configured. In this example, the Cisco IOS command syntax is used to set the maximum number of MAC addresses to 10 for port 0/19. The violation mode is set to shutdown, by default.

Refer to
Interactive Graphic
in online course

5.2.2.5 Port Security: Verifying

Verify Port Security

After configuring port security on a switch, check each interface to verify that the port security is set correctly, and check to ensure that the static MAC addresses have been configured correctly.

Verify Port Security Settings

To display port security settings for the switch, or for the specified interface, use the **show port-security interface** [*interface-id*] command. The output for the dynamic port security configuration is shown in Figure 1. By default, there is one MAC address allowed on this port.

The output shown in Figure 2 shows the values for the sticky port security settings. The maximum number of addresses is set to 10, as configured.

Note   The MAC address is identified as a sticky MAC.

Sticky MAC addresses are added to the MAC address table and to the running configuration. As shown in Figure 3, the sticky MAC for PC2 has been added to the running configuration for S1.

Verify Secure MAC Addresses

To display all secure MAC addresses configured on all switch interfaces, or on a specified interface with aging information for each, use the **show port-security address** command. As shown in Figure 4, the secure MAC addresses are listed along with the types.

Refer to **Interactive Graphic** in online course

5.2.2.6   Ports in Error Disabled State

When a port is configured with port security, a violation can cause the port to become error disabled. When a port is error disabled, it is effectively shut down and no traffic is sent or received on that port. A series of port security related messages display on the console (Figure 1).

Note   The port protocol and link status is changed to down.

The port LED will turn off. The **show interfaces** command identifies the port status as **err-disabled** (Figure 2). The output of the **show port-security interface** command now shows the port status as **secure-shutdown**. Because the port security violation mode is set to shutdown, the port with the security violation goes to the error disabled state.

The administrator should determine what caused the security violation before re-enabling the port. If an unauthorized device is connected to a secure port, the port should not be re-enabled until the security threat is eliminated. To re-enable the port, use the **shutdown** interface configuration mode command (Figure 3). Then, use the **no shutdown** interface configuration command to make the port operational.

Refer to **Packet Tracer Activity** for this chapter

5.2.2.7   Packet Tracer - Configuring Switch Port Security

In this activity, you will configure and verify port security on a switch. Port security allows you to restrict a port's ingress traffic by limiting the MAC addresses that are allowed to send traffic into the port.

Refer to **Packet Tracer Activity** for this chapter

5.2.2.8   Packet Tracer - Troubleshooting Switch Port Security

The employee who normally uses PC1 brought his laptop from home, disconnected PC1 and connected the laptop to the telecommunication outlet. After reminding him of the security policy that does not allow personal devices on the network, you now must reconnect PC1 and re-enable the port.

Refer to
Lab Activity
for this chapter

5.2.2.9   Lab - Configuring Switch Security Features

In this lab, you will complete the following objectives:

- Part 1: Set Up the Topology and Initialize Devices
- Part 2: Configure Basic Device Settings and Verify Connectivity
- Part 3: Configure and Verify SSH Access on S1
- Part 4: Configure and Verify Security Features on S1

5.3   Summary

Refer to
Online Course
for Illustration

5.3.1.1   Activity – Switch Trio

Scenario

You are the network administrator for a small- to medium-sized business. Corporate headquarters for your business has mandated that on all switches in all offices, security must be implemented. The memorandum delivered to you this morning states:

"By Monday, April 18, 20xx, the first three ports of all configurable switches located in all offices must be secured with MAC addresses – one address will be reserved for the printer, one address will be reserved for the laptop in the office, and one address will be reserved for the office server.

If a port's security is breached, we ask you to shut it down until the reason for the breach can be certified.

Please implement this policy no later than the date stated in this memorandum. For questions, call 1.800.555.1212. Thank you. The Network Management Team"

Work with a partner in the class and create a Packet Tracer example to test this new security policy. After you have created your file, test it with, at least, one device to ensure it is operational or validated.

Save your work and be prepared to share it with the entire class.

Refer to **Packet
Tracer Activity**
for this chapter

5.3.1.2   Packet Tracer - Skills Integration Challenge

The network administrator asked you to configure a new switch. In this activity, you will use a list of requirements to configure the new switch with initial settings, SSH, and port security.

Refer to
Online Course
for Illustration

5.3.1.3   Switch Configuration

When a Cisco LAN switch is first powered on it goes through the following boot sequence:

1. First, the switch loads a power-on self-test (POST) program stored in ROM. POST checks the CPU subsystem. It tests the CPU, DRAM, and the portion of the flash device that makes up the flash file system.

2. Next, the switch loads the boot loader software. The boot loader is a small program stored in ROM and is run immediately after POST successfully completes.

3. The boot loader performs low-level CPU initialization. It initializes the CPU registers, which control where physical memory is mapped, the quantity of memory, and its speed.

4. The boot loader initializes the flash file system on the system board.

5. Finally, the boot loader locates and loads a default IOS operating system software image into memory and gives control of the switch over to the IOS.

The specific Cisco IOS file that is loaded is specified by the BOOT environmental variable. After the Cisco IOS is loaded it uses the commands found in the startup-config file to initialize and configure the interfaces. If the Cisco IOS files are missing or damaged, the boot loader program can be used to reload or recover from the problem.

The operational status of the switch is displayed by a series of LEDs on the front panel. These LEDs display such things as port status, duplex, and speed.

An IP address is configured on the SVI of the management VLAN to allow for remote configuration of the device. A default gateway belonging to the management VLAN must be configured on the switch using the **ip default-gateway** command. If the default gateway is not properly configured, remote management is not possible. It is recommended that Secure Shell (SSH) be used to provide a secure (encrypted) management connection to a remote device to prevent the sniffing of unencrypted user names and passwords, which is possible when using protocols such as Telnet.

One of the advantages of a switch is that it allows full-duplex communication between devices, effectively doubling the communication rate. Although it is possible to specify the speed and duplex settings of a switch interface, it is recommended that the switch be allowed to set these parameters automatically to avoid errors.

Switch port security is a requirement to prevent such attacks as MAC Address Flooding and DHCP Spoofing. Switch ports should be configured to allow only frames with specific source MAC addresses to enter. Frames from unknown source MAC addresses should be denied and cause the port to shut down to prevent further attacks.

Port security is only one defense against network compromise. There are 10 best practices that represent the best insurance for a network:

- Develop a written security policy for the organization.

- Shut down unused services and ports.

- Use strong passwords and change them often.

- Control physical access to devices.

- Avoid using standard insecure HTTP websites, especially for login screens. Instead use the more secure HTTPS.

- Perform backups and test the backed up files on a regular basis.

- Educate employees about social engineering attacks, and develop policies to validate identities over the phone, via email, and in person.

- Encrypt sensitive data and protect it with a strong password.

- Implement security hardware and software, such as firewalls.

- Keep IOS software up-to-date by installing security patches weekly or daily, if possible.

These methods are only a starting point for security management. Organizations must remain vigilant at all times to defend against continually evolving threats.

Go to the online course to take the quiz and exam.

Chapter 5 Quiz

This quiz is designed to provide an additional opportunity to practice the skills and knowledge presented in the chapter and to prepare for the chapter exam. You will be allowed multiple attempts and the grade does not appear in the gradebook.

Chapter 5 Exam

The chapter exam assesses your knowledge of the chapter content.

Your Chapter Notes

VLANs

6.0 Introduction

6.0.1.1 VLANs

Network performance is an important factor in the productivity of an organization. One of the technologies used to improve network performance is the separation of large broadcast domains into smaller ones. By design, routers will block broadcast traffic at an interface. However, routers normally have a limited number of LAN interfaces. A router's primary role is to move information between networks, not to provide network access to end devices.

The role of providing access into a LAN is normally reserved for an access layer switch. A virtual local area network (VLAN) can be created on a Layer 2 switch to reduce the size of broadcast domains, similar to a Layer 3 device. VLANs are commonly incorporated into network design making it easier for a network to support the goals of an organization. While VLANs are primarily used within switched local area networks, modern implementations of VLANs allow them to span MANs and WANs.

Because VLANs segment the network, a Layer 3 process is required to allow traffic to move from one network segment to another.

This Layer 3 routing process can either be implemented using a router or a Layer 3 switch interface. The use of a Layer 3 device provides a method for controlling the flow of traffic between network segments, including network segments created by VLANs.

The first part of this chapter will cover how to configure, manage, and troubleshoot VLANs and VLAN trunks. The second part of this chapter focuses on implementing inter-VLAN routing using a router. Inter-VLAN routing on a Layer 3 switch is covered in a later course.

6.0.1.2 Class Activity – Vacation Station

Scenario

You have purchased a three floor vacation home at the beach for rental purposes. The floor plan is identical on each floor. Each floor offers one digital television for renters to use.

According to the local Internet service provider, only three stations may be offered within a television package. It is your job to decide which television packages you offer your guests.

- Divide the class into groups of three students per group.
- Choose three different stations to make one subscription package for each floor of your rental home.
- Complete the PDF for this activity.
- Share your completed group-reflection answers with the class.

6.1   VLAN Segmentation

6.1.1   Overview of VLANs

Refer to
Online Course
for Illustration

6.1.1.1   VLAN Definitions

Within a switched internetwork, VLANs provide segmentation and organizational flexibility. VLANs provide a way to group devices within a LAN. A group of devices within a VLAN communicate as if they were attached to the same cable. VLANs are based on logical connections, instead of physical connections.

VLANs allow an administrator to segment networks based on factors such as function, project team, or application, without regard for the physical location of the user or device. Devices within a VLAN act as if they are in their own independent network, even if they share a common infrastructure with other VLANs. Any switch port can belong to a VLAN, and unicast, broadcast, and multicast packets are forwarded and flooded only to end stations within the VLAN where the packets are sourced. Each VLAN is considered a separate logical network. Packets destined for stations that do not belong to the VLAN must be forwarded through a device that supports routing.

Multiple IP subnets can exist on a switched network, without the use of multiple VLANs. However, the devices will be in the same Layer 2 broadcast domain. This means that any Layer 2 broadcasts, such as an ARP request, will be received by all devices on the switched network, even by those not intended to receive the broadcast.

A VLAN creates a logical broadcast domain that can span multiple physical LAN segments. VLANs improve network performance by separating large broadcast domains into smaller ones. If a device in one VLAN sends a broadcast Ethernet frame, all devices in the VLAN receive the frame, but devices in other VLANs do not.

VLANs enable the implementation of access and security policies according to specific groupings of users. Each switch port can be assigned to only one VLAN (with the exception of a port connected to an IP phone or to another switch).

Refer to
Online Course
for Illustration

6.1.1.2   Benefits of VLANs

User productivity and network adaptability are important for business growth and success. VLANs make it easier to design a network to support the goals of an organization. The primary benefits of using VLANs are as follows:

- **Security** - Groups that have sensitive data are separated from the rest of the network, decreasing the chances of confidential information breaches. As shown in the figure, faculty computers are on VLAN 10 and completely separated from student and guest data traffic.

- **Cost reduction** - Cost savings result from reduced need for expensive network upgrades and more efficient use of existing bandwidth and uplinks.

- **Better performance** - Dividing flat Layer 2 networks into multiple logical workgroups (broadcast domains) reduces unnecessary traffic on the network and boosts performance.

- **Reduce the size of broadcast domains** - Dividing a network into VLANs reduces the number of devices in the broadcast domain. As shown in the figure, there are six computers on this network but there are three broadcast domains: Faculty, Student, and Guest.

- **Improved IT staff efficiency** - VLANs make it easier to manage the network because users with similar network requirements share the same VLAN. When a new switch is provisioned, all the policies and procedures already configured for the particular VLAN are implemented when the ports are assigned. It is also easy for the IT staff to identify the function of a VLAN by giving it an appropriate name. In the figure, for easy identification VLAN 10 has been named "Faculty", VLAN 20 is named "Student", and VLAN 30 "Guest".

- **Simpler project and application management** - VLANs aggregate users and network devices to support business or geographic requirements. Having separate functions makes managing a project or working with a specialized application easier; an example of such an application is an e-learning development platform for faculty.

Each VLAN in a switched network corresponds to an IP network. Therefore, VLAN design must take into consideration the implementation of a hierarchical network-addressing scheme. Hierarchical network addressing means that IP network numbers are applied to network segments or VLANs in an orderly fashion that takes the network as a whole into consideration. Blocks of contiguous network addresses are reserved for and configured on devices in a specific area of the network, as shown in the figure.

Refer to
Interactive Graphic
in online course

6.1.1.3 Types of VLANs

There are a number of distinct types of VLANs used in modern networks. Some VLAN types are defined by traffic classes. Other types of VLANs are defined by the specific function that they serve.

Data VLAN

A data VLAN is a VLAN that is configured to carry user-generated traffic. A VLAN carrying voice or management traffic would not be a data VLAN. It is common practice to separate voice and management traffic from data traffic. A data VLAN is sometimes referred to as a user VLAN. Data VLANs are used to separate the network into groups of users or devices.

Default VLAN

All switch ports become a part of the default VLAN after the initial boot up of a switch loading the default configuration. Switch ports that participate in the default VLAN are part of the same broadcast domain. This allows any device connected to any switch port to communicate with other devices on other switch ports. The default VLAN for Cisco switches is VLAN 1. In the figure, the **show vlan brief** command was issued on a switch running the default configuration. Notice that all ports are assigned to VLAN 1 by default.

VLAN 1 has all the features of any VLAN, except it cannot be renamed or deleted. By default, all Layer 2 control traffic is associated with VLAN 1.

Native VLAN

A native VLAN is assigned to an 802.1Q trunk port. Trunk ports are the links between switches that support the transmission of traffic associated with more than one VLAN. An

802.1Q trunk port supports traffic coming from many VLANs (tagged traffic), as well as traffic that does not come from a VLAN (untagged traffic). Tagged traffic refers to traffic that has a 4-byte tag inserted within the original Ethernet frame header, specifying the VLAN to which the frame belongs. The 802.1Q trunk port places untagged traffic on the native VLAN, which by default is VLAN 1.

Native VLANs are defined in the IEEE 802.1Q specification to maintain backward compatibility with untagged traffic common to legacy LAN scenarios. A native VLAN serves as a common identifier on opposite ends of a trunk link.

It is a best practice to configure the native VLAN as an unused VLAN, distinct VLAN 1 and other VLANs. In fact, it is not unusual to dedicate a fixed VLAN to serve the role of the native VLAN for all trunk ports in the switched domain.

Management VLAN

A management VLAN is any VLAN configured to access the management capabilities of a switch. VLAN 1 is the management VLAN by default. To create the management VLAN, the switch virtual interface (SVI) of that VLAN is assigned an IP address and a subnet mask, allowing the switch to be managed via HTTP, Telnet, SSH, or SNMP. Because the out-of-the-box configuration of a Cisco switch has VLAN 1 as the default VLAN, VLAN 1 would be a bad choice for the management VLAN.

In the past, the management VLAN for a 2960 switch was the only active SVI. On 15.x versions of the Cisco IOS for Catalyst 2960 Series switches, it is possible to have more than one active SVI. Cisco IOS 15.x requires that the particular active SVI assigned for remote management be documented. While theoretically a switch can have more than one management VLAN, having more than one increases exposure to network attacks.

In the figure, all ports are currently assigned to the default VLAN 1. No native VLAN is explicitly assigned and no other VLANs are active; therefore, the network is designed with the native VLAN the same as the management VLAN. This is considered a security risk.

Refer to
Online Course
for Illustration

6.1.1.4   Voice VLANs

A separate VLAN is needed to support Voice over IP (VoIP). VoIP traffic requires:

- Assured bandwidth to ensure voice quality

- Transmission priority over other types of network traffic

- Ability to be routed around congested areas on the network

- Delay of less than 150 ms across the network

To meet these requirements, the entire network has to be designed to support VoIP. The details of how to configure a network to support VoIP are beyond the scope of this course, but it is useful to summarize how a voice VLAN works between a switch, a Cisco IP phone, and a computer.

In the figure, VLAN 150 is designed to carry voice traffic. The student computer PC5 is attached to the Cisco IP phone, and the phone is attached to switch S3. PC5 is in VLAN 20, which is used for student data.

Refer to **Packet Tracer Activity** for this chapter

6.1.1.5   Packet Tracer – Who Hears the Broadcast?

Background/Scenario

In this activity, a 24-port Catalyst 2960 switch is fully populated. All ports are in use. You will observe broadcast traffic in a VLAN implementation and answer some reflection questions.

6.1.2   VLANs in a Multi-Switched Environment

Refer to **Online Course** for Illustration

6.1.2.1   VLAN Trunks

A trunk is a point-to-point link between two network devices that carries more than one VLAN. A VLAN trunk extends VLANs across an entire network. Cisco supports IEEE 802.1Q for coordinating trunks on Fast Ethernet, Gigabit Ethernet, and 10-Gigabit Ethernet interfaces.

VLANs would not be very useful without VLAN trunks. VLAN trunks allow all VLAN traffic to propagate between switches, so that devices which are in the same VLAN, but connected to different switches, can communicate without the intervention of a router.

A VLAN trunk does not belong to a specific VLAN; rather, it is a conduit for multiple VLANs between switches and routers. A trunk could also be used between a network device and server or other device that is equipped with an appropriate 802.1Q-capable NIC. By default, on a Cisco Catalyst switch, all VLANs are supported on a trunk port.

In the figure, the links between switches S1 and S2, and S1 and S3 are configured to transmit traffic coming from VLANs 10, 20, 30, and 99 across the network. This network could not function without VLAN trunks.

Refer to **Interactive Graphic** in online course

6.1.2.2   Controlling Broadcast Domains with VLANs

Network without VLANs

In normal operation, when a switch receives a broadcast frame on one of its ports, it forwards the frame out all other ports except the port where the broadcast was received. In the animation in Figure 1, the entire network is configured in the same subnet (172.17.40.0/24) and no VLANs are configured. As a result, when the faculty computer (PC1) sends out a broadcast frame, switch S2 sends that broadcast frame out all of its ports. Eventually the entire network receives the broadcast because the network is one broadcast domain.

In this example, all devices are on the same IPv4 subnet. If there were devices on other IPv4 subnets, they would also receive the same broadcast frame. Broadcasts such as an ARP request, are intended only for devices on the same subnet.

Network with VLANs

As shown in the animation in Figure 2, the network has been segmented using two VLANs. Faculty devices are assigned to VLAN 10 and student devices are assigned to VLAN 20. When a broadcast frame is sent from the faculty computer, PC1, to switch S2, the switch forwards that broadcast frame only to those switch ports configured to support VLAN 10.

The ports that comprise the connection between switches S2 and S1 (ports F0/1), and between S1 and S3 (ports F0/3) are trunks and have been configured to support all the VLANs in the network.

When S1 receives the broadcast frame on port F0/1, S1 forwards that broadcast frame out of the only other port configured to support VLAN 10, which is port F0/3. When S3 receives the broadcast frame on port F0/3, it forwards that broadcast frame out the only other port configured to support VLAN 10, which is port F0/11. The broadcast frame arrives at the only other computer in the network configured in VLAN 10, which is faculty computer PC4.

When VLANs are implemented on a switch, the transmission of unicast, multicast, and broadcast traffic from a host in a particular VLAN are restricted to the devices that are in that VLAN.

Refer to
Online Course
for Illustration

6.1.2.3   Tagging Ethernet Frames for VLAN Identification

Catalyst 2960 Series switches are Layer 2 devices. They use the Ethernet frame header information to forward packets. They do not have routing tables. The standard Ethernet frame header does not contain information about the VLAN to which the frame belongs; thus, when Ethernet frames are placed on a trunk, information about the VLANs to which they belong must be added. This process, called tagging, is accomplished by using the IEEE 802.1Q header, specified in the IEEE 802.1Q standard. The 802.1Q header includes a 4-byte tag inserted within the original Ethernet frame header, specifying the VLAN to which the frame belongs.

When the switch receives a frame on a port configured in access mode and assigned a VLAN, the switch inserts a VLAN tag in the frame header, recalculates the Frame Check Sequence (FCS), and sends the tagged frame out of a trunk port.

VLAN Tag Field Details

The VLAN tag field consists of a Type field, a Priority field, a Canonical Format Identifier field, and VLAN ID field:

- **Type** - A 2-byte value called the tag protocol ID (TPID) value. For Ethernet, it is set to hexadecimal 0x8100.

- **User priority** - A 3-bit value that supports level or service implementation.

- **Canonical Format Identifier (CFI)** - A 1-bit identifier that enables Token Ring frames to be carried across Ethernet links.

- **VLAN ID (VID)** - A 12-bit VLAN identification number that supports up to 4096 VLAN IDs.

After the switch inserts the Type and tag control information fields, it recalculates the FCS values and inserts the new FCS into the frame.

Refer to
Online Course
for Illustration

6.1.2.4   Native VLANs and 802.1Q Tagging

Tagged Frames on the Native VLAN

Some devices that support trunking add a VLAN tag to native VLAN traffic. Control traffic sent on the native VLAN should not be tagged. If an 802.1Q trunk port receives a tagged frame with the VLAN ID that is the same as the native VLAN, it drops the frame. Consequently, when configuring a switch port on a Cisco switch, configure devices so that they do not send tagged frames on the native VLAN. Devices from other vendors that support tagged frames on the native VLAN include IP phones, servers, routers, and non-Cisco switches.

Untagged Frames on the Native VLAN

When a Cisco switch trunk port receives untagged frames (which are unusual in a well-designed network), it forwards those frames to the native VLAN. If there are no devices associated with the native VLAN (which is not unusual) and there are no other trunk ports (which is not unusual), then the frame is dropped. The default native VLAN is VLAN 1. When configuring an 802.1Q trunk port, a default Port VLAN ID (PVID) is assigned the value of the native VLAN ID. All untagged traffic coming in or out of the 802.1Q port is forwarded based on the PVID value. For example, if VLAN 99 is configured as the native VLAN, the PVID is 99 and all untagged traffic is forwarded to VLAN 99. If the native VLAN has not been reconfigured, the PVID value is set to VLAN 1.

In the figure, PC1 is connected by a hub to an 802.1Q trunk link. PC1 sends untagged traffic, which the switches associate with the native VLAN configured on the trunk ports, and forward accordingly. Tagged traffic on the trunk received by PC1 is dropped. This scenario reflects poor network design for several reasons: it uses a hub, it has a host connected to a trunk link, and it implies that the switches have access ports assigned to the native VLAN. It also illustrates the motivation for the IEEE 802.1Q specification for native VLANs as a means of handling legacy scenarios.

Refer to
Interactive Graphic
in online course

6.1.2.5   Voice VLAN Tagging

Recall that to support VoIP, a separate voice VLAN is required.

An access port that is used to connect a Cisco IP phone can be configured to use two separate VLANs: one VLAN for voice traffic and another VLAN for data traffic from a device attached to the phone. The link between the switch and the IP phone acts as a trunk to carry both voice VLAN traffic and data VLAN traffic.

The Cisco IP Phone contains an integrated three-port 10/100 switch. The ports provide dedicated connections to these devices:

- Port 1 connects to the switch or other VoIP device.

- Port 2 is an internal 10/100 interface that carries the IP phone traffic.

- Port 3 (access port) connects to a PC or other device.

On the switch, the access is configured to send Cisco Discovery Protocol (CDP) packets that instruct an attached IP phone to send voice traffic to the switch in one of three ways, depending on the type of traffic:

■ In a voice VLAN tagged with a Layer 2 class of service (CoS) priority value

■ In an access VLAN tagged with a Layer 2 CoS priority value

■ In an access VLAN, untagged (no Layer 2 CoS priority value)

In Figure 1, the student computer PC5 is attached to a Cisco IP phone, and the phone is attached to switch S3. VLAN 150 is designed to carry voice traffic, while PC5 is in VLAN 20, which is used for student data.

Sample Configuration

Figure 2 shows a sample output. A discussion of voice Cisco IOS commands are beyond the scope of this course, but the highlighted areas in the sample output show the F0/18 interface configured with a VLAN configured for data (VLAN 20) and a VLAN configured for voice (VLAN 150).

Refer to
Interactive Graphic
in online course

6.1.2.6   Activity – Predict Switch Behavior

Refer to **Packet Tracer Activity** for this chapter

6.1.2.7   Packet Tracer – Investigating a VLAN Implementation

Background/Scenario

In this activity, you will observe how broadcast traffic is forwarded by the switches when VLANs are configured and when VLANs are not configured.

6.2   VLAN Implementations

6.2.1   VLAN Assignment

Refer to
Online Course
for Illustration

6.2.1.1   VLAN Ranges on Catalyst Switches

Different Cisco Catalyst switches support various numbers of VLANs. The number of supported VLANs is large enough to accommodate the needs of most organizations. For example, the Catalyst 2960 and 3560 Series switches support over 4,000 VLANs. Normal range VLANs on these switches are numbered 1 to 1,005 and extended range VLANs are numbered 1,006 to 4,094. The figure illustrates the available VLANs on a Catalyst 2960 switch running Cisco IOS Release 15.x.

Normal Range VLANs

■ Used in small- and medium-sized business and enterprise networks.

■ Identified by a VLAN ID between 1 and 1005.

■ IDs 1002 through 1005 are reserved for Token Ring and Fiber Distributed Data Interface (FDDI) VLANs.

- IDs 1 and 1002 to 1005 are automatically created and cannot be removed.

- Configurations are stored within a VLAN database file, called vlan.dat. The vlan.dat file is located in the flash memory of the switch.

- The VLAN Trunking Protocol (VTP), which helps manage VLAN configurations between switches, can only learn and store normal range VLANs.

Extended Range VLANs

- Enable service providers to extend their infrastructure to a greater number of customers. Some global enterprises could be large enough to need extended range VLAN IDs.

- Are identified by a VLAN ID between 1006 and 4094.

- Configurations are not written to the vlan.dat file.

- Support fewer VLAN features than normal range VLANs.

- Saved, by default, in the running configuration file.

- VTP does not learn extended range VLANs.

Note   4096 is the upper boundary for the number of VLANs available on Catalyst switches, because there are 12 bits in the VLAN ID field of the IEEE 802.1Q header.

Refer to
Interactive Graphic
in online course

6.2.1.2   Creating a VLAN

When configuring normal range VLANs, the configuration details are stored in flash memory on the switch, in a file called vlan.dat. Flash memory is persistent and does not require the **copy running-config startup-config** command. However, because other details are often configured on a Cisco switch at the same time that VLANs are created, it is good practice to save running configuration changes to the startup configuration.

Figure 1 displays the Cisco IOS command syntax used to add a VLAN to a switch and give it a name. Naming each VLAN is considered a best practice in switch configuration.

Figure 2 shows how the student VLAN (VLAN 20) is configured on switch S1. In the topology example, the student computer (PC2) has not been associated with a VLAN yet, but it does have an IP address of 172.17.20.22.

Use the Syntax Checker in Figure 3 to create a VLAN and use the **show vlan brief** command to display the contents of the vlan.dat file.

In addition to entering a single VLAN ID, a series of VLAN IDs can be entered separated by commas, or a range of VLAN IDs separated by hyphens using the **vlan** *vlan-id* command. For example, use the following command to create VLANs 100, 102, 105, 106, and 107:

```
S1(config)#  vlan 100,102,105-107
```

Refer to
Interactive Graphic
in online course

6.2.1.3   Assigning Ports to VLANs

After creating a VLAN, the next step is to assign ports to the VLAN. An access port can belong to only one VLAN at a time. One exception to this rule is that of a port connected to an IP phone, in which case, there are two VLANs associated with the port: one for voice and one for data.

Figure 1 displays the syntax for defining a port to be an access port and assigning it to a VLAN. The **switchport mode access** command is optional, but strongly recommended as a security best practice. With this command, the interface changes to permanent access mode.

Note   Use the **interface range** command to simultaneously configure multiple interfaces.

In the example in Figure 2, VLAN 20 is assigned to port F0/18 on switch S1; therefore, the student computer (PC2) is in VLAN 20. VLANs are configured on the switch port, not on the device. PC2 is configured with an IPv4 address and subnet mask associated with the VLAN which is configured on the switch port, VLAN 20 in this example. When VLAN 20 is configured on other switches, the network administrator knows to configure the other student computers to be in the same subnet as PC2 (172.17.20.0/24).

Use the Syntax Checker in Figure 3 to assign a VLAN and use the **show vlan brief** command to display the contents of the vlan.dat file.

The **switchport access vlan** command forces the creation of a VLAN if it does not already exist on the switch. For example, VLAN 30 is not present in the **show vlan brief** output of the switch. If the **switchport access vlan 30** command is entered on any interface with no previous configuration, then the switch displays the following:

```
% Access VLAN does not exist. Creating vlan 30
```

Refer to
Interactive Graphic
in online course

6.2.1.4   Changing VLAN Port Membership

There are a number of ways to change VLAN port membership. Figure 1 shows the syntax for changing a switch port to VLAN 1 membership with the **no switchport access vlan** interface configuration mode command.

Interface F0/18 was previously assigned to VLAN 20. The **no switchport access vlan** command is entered for interface F0/18. Examine the output in the **show vlan brief** command that immediately follows, as shown in Figure 2. The **show vlan brief** command displays the VLAN assignment and membership type for all switch ports. The **show vlan brief** command displays one line for each VLAN. The output for each VLAN includes the VLAN name, status, and switch ports.

VLAN 20 is still active, even though no ports are assigned to it. In Figure 3, the **show interfaces f0/18 switchport** output verifies that the access VLAN for interface F0/18 has been reset to VLAN 1.

A port can easily have its VLAN membership changed. It is not necessary to first remove a port from a VLAN to change its VLAN membership. When an access port has its VLAN membership reassigned to another existing VLAN, the new VLAN membership simply replaces the previous VLAN membership. In Figure 4, port F0/11 is assigned to VLAN 20.

Use the Syntax Checker in Figure 5 to change VLAN port membership.

Refer to
Online Course
for Illustration

6.2.1.5   Deleting VLANs

In the figure, the **no vlan** *vlan-id* global configuration mode command is used to remove VLAN 20 from the switch. Switch S1 had a minimal configuration with all ports in VLAN 1 and an unused VLAN 20 in the VLAN database. The **show vlan brief** command verifies that VLAN 20 is no longer present in the vlan.dat file after using the **no vlan 20** command.

Caution   Before deleting a VLAN, reassign all member ports to a different VLAN first. Any ports that are not moved to an active VLAN are unable to communicate with other hosts after the VLAN is deleted and until they are assigned to an active VLAN.

Alternatively, the entire vlan.dat file can be deleted using the **delete flash:vlan.dat** privileged EXEC mode command. The abbreviated command version (**delete vlan.dat**) can be used if the vlan.dat file has not been moved from its default location. After issuing this command and reloading the switch, the previously configured VLANs are no longer present. This effectively places the switch into its factory default condition with regard to VLAN configurations.

Note   For a Catalyst switch, the **erase startup-config** command must accompany the **delete vlan.dat** command prior to reload to restore the switch to its factory default condition.

Refer to
Interactive Graphic
in online course

6.2.1.6   Verifying VLAN Information

After a VLAN is configured, VLAN configurations can be validated using Cisco IOS show commands.

Figure 1 displays the **show vlan** and **show interfaces** command options.

In the example in Figure 2, the **show vlan name student** command produces output that is not easily interpreted. The **show vlan summary** command displays the count of all configured VLANs. The output in Figure 2 shows seven VLANs.

The **show interfaces vlan** *vlan-id* command displays details that are beyond the scope of this course. The important information appears on the second line in Figure 3, indicating that VLAN 20 is up.

Use the Syntax Checker in Figure 4 to display the VLAN and switch port information, and to verify VLAN assignments and mode.

Refer to **Packet Tracer Activity** for this chapter

6.2.1.7   Packet Tracer – Configuring VLANs

Background/Scenario

VLANs are helpful in the administration of logical groups, allowing members of a group to be easily moved, changed, or added. This activity focuses on creating and naming VLANs, and assigning access ports to specific VLANs.

6.2.2   VLAN Trunks

Refer to
Interactive Graphic
in online course

6.2.2.1   Configuring IEEE 802.1Q Trunk Links

A VLAN trunk is an OSI Layer 2 link between two switches that carries traffic for all VLANs (unless the allowed VLAN list is restricted manually or dynamically). To enable trunk links, configure the ports on either end of the physical link with parallel sets of commands.

To configure a switch port on one end of a trunk link, use the **switchport mode trunk** command. With this command, the interface changes to permanent trunking mode. The port enters into a Dynamic Trunking Protocol (DTP) negotiation to convert the link into a trunk link even if the interface connecting to it does not agree to the change. In this course, the **switchport mode trunk** command is the only method implemented for trunk configuration.

Note   DTP is beyond the scope of this course.

The Cisco IOS command syntax to specify a native VLAN (other than VLAN 1) is shown in Figure 1. In the example, VLAN 99 is configured as the native VLAN using the **switchport trunk native vlan 99** command.

Use the Cisco IOS **switchport trunk allowed vlan** *vlan-list* command to specify the list of VLANs to be allowed on the trunk link.

In Figure 2, VLANs 10, 20, and 30 support the Faculty, Student, and Guest computers (PC1, PC2, and PC3). The F0/1 port on switch S1 is configured as a trunk port and forwards traffic for VLANs 10, 20, and 30. VLAN 99 is configured as the native VLAN.

Figure 3 displays the configuration of port F0/1 on switch S1 as a trunk port. The native VLAN is changed to VLAN 99 and the allowed VLAN list is restricted to 10, 20, 30, and 99.

Note   This configuration assumes the use of Cisco Catalyst 2960 switches which automatically use 802.1Q encapsulation on trunk links. Other switches may require manual configuration of the encapsulation. Always configure both ends of a trunk link with the same native VLAN. If 802.1Q trunk configuration is not the same on both ends, Cisco IOS Software reports errors.

Refer to
Interactive Graphic
in online course

6.2.2.2   Resetting the Trunk to Default State

Figure 1 shows the commands to remove the allowed VLANs and reset the native VLAN of the trunk. When reset to the default state, the trunk allows all VLANs and uses VLAN 1 as the native VLAN.

Figure 2 shows the commands used to reset all trunking characteristics of a trunking interface to the default settings. The **show interfaces f0/1 switchport** command reveals that the trunk has been reconfigured to a default state.

In Figure 3, the sample output shows the commands used to remove the trunk feature from the F0/1 switch port on switch S1. The **show interfaces f0/1 switchport** command reveals that the F0/1 interface is now in static access mode.

Refer to
Interactive Graphic
in online course

6.2.2.3   Verifying Trunk Configuration

Figure 1 displays the configuration of switch port F0/1 on switch S1. The configuration is verified with the **show interfaces** *interface-ID* **switchport** command.

The top highlighted area shows that port F0/1 has its administrative mode set to **trunk**. The port is in trunking mode. The next highlighted area verifies that the native VLAN is VLAN 99. Further down in the output, the bottom highlighted area shows that all VLANs are enabled on the trunk.

Use the Syntax Checker in Figure 2 to configure a trunk supporting all VLANs on interface F0/1, with native VLAN 99. Verify the trunk configuration with the **show interfaces f0/1 switchport** command.

Refer to **Packet
Tracer Activity**
for this chapter

6.2.2.4   Packet Tracer – Configuring Trunks

Background/Scenario

Trunks are required to pass VLAN information between switches. A port on a switch is either an access port or a trunk port. Access ports carry traffic from a specific VLAN assigned to the port. A trunk port by default is a member of all VLANs; therefore, it carries traffic for all VLANs. This activity focuses on creating trunk ports, and assigning them to a native VLAN other than the default VLAN.

Refer to
Lab Activity
for this chapter

6.2.2.5   Lab – Configuring VLANs and Trunking

In this lab, you will complete the following objectives:

- Part 1: Build the Network and Configure Basic Device Settings

- Part 2: Create VLANs and Assign Switch Ports

- Part 3: Maintain VLAN Port Assignments and the VLAN Database

- Part 4: Configure an 802.1Q Trunk between the Switches

- Part 5: Delete the VLAN Database

6.2.3   Troubleshoot VLANs and Trunks

Refer to
Interactive Graphic
in online course

6.2.3.1   IP Addressing Issues with VLAN

Each VLAN must correspond to a unique IP subnet. If two devices in the same VLAN have different subnet addresses, they cannot communicate. This is a common problem, and it is easy to solve by identifying the incorrect configuration and changing the subnet address to the correct one.

In Figure 1, PC1 cannot connect to the Web/TFTP server shown.

A check of the IPv4 configuration settings of PC,1 shown in Figure 2, reveals the most common error in configuring VLANs: an incorrectly configured IPv4 address. PC1 is configured with an IPv4 address of 172.172.10.21, but it should have been configured with 172.17.10.21.

In Figure 3, the PC1 Fast Ethernet configuration dialog box shows the updated IPv4 address of 172.17.10.21. The output on the bottom reveals that PC1 has regained connectivity to the Web/TFTP server found at IPv4 address 172.17.10.30.

Refer to
Interactive Graphic
in online course

6.2.3.2   Missing VLANs

If there is still no connection between devices in a VLAN, but IP addressing issues have been ruled out, refer to the flowchart in Figure 1 to troubleshoot:

Step 1.   Use the **show vlan** command to check whether the port belongs to the expected VLAN. If the port is assigned to the wrong VLAN, use the **switchport access vlan** command to correct the VLAN membership. Use the **show mac address-table** command to check which addresses were learned on a particular port of the switch, and to which VLAN that port is assigned, as show in Figure 2.

Step 2.   If the VLAN to which the port is assigned is deleted, the port becomes inactive. The ports of a deleted VLAN will not be listed in the output of the **show vlan** command. Use the **show interfaces switchport** command to verify the inactive VLAN is assigned to the port, as shown in Figure 2.

The example in Figure 2 shows MAC addresses that were learned on the F0/1 interface. It can be seen that MAC address 000c.296a.a21c was learned on interface F0/1 in VLAN 10. If this number is not the expected VLAN number, change the port VLAN membership using the **switchport access vlan** command.

Each port in a switch belongs to a VLAN. If the VLAN to which the port belongs is deleted, the port becomes inactive. All ports belonging to the VLAN that was deleted are unable to communicate with the rest of the network. Use the **show interface f0/1 switchport** command to check whether the port is inactive. If the port is inactive, it is not functional until the missing VLAN is created using the **vlan** *vlan-id* global configuration command or the VLAN is removed from the port with the **no switchport access vlan** *vlan-id* command.

Refer to
Interactive Graphic
in online course

6.2.3.3   Introduction to Troubleshooting Trunks

A common task of a network administrator is to troubleshoot trunk formation, or ports incorrectly behaving as trunk ports. Sometimes a switch port may behave like a trunk port even if it is not configured as a trunk port. For example, an access port might accept frames from VLANs different from the VLAN to which it is assigned. This is called VLAN leaking.

Figure 1 displays a flowchart of general trunk troubleshooting guidelines.

To troubleshoot issues when a trunk is not forming or when VLAN leaking is occurring, proceed as follows:

Step 1.   Use the **show interfaces trunk** command to check whether the local and peer native VLANs match. If the native VLAN does not match on both sides, VLAN leaking occurs.

Step 2.   Use the **show interfaces trunk** command to check whether a trunk has been established between switches. Statically configure trunk links whenever possible. Cisco Catalyst switch ports use DTP by default and attempt to negotiate a trunk link.

To display the status of the trunk, the native VLAN used on that trunk link, and verify trunk establishment, use the **show interfaces trunk** command. The example in Figure 2 shows that the native VLAN on one side of the trunk link was changed to VLAN 2. If one end of the trunk is configured as native VLAN 99 and the other end is configured as native VLAN 2, a frame sent from VLAN 99 on one side is received on VLAN 2 on the other side. VLAN 99 leaks into the VLAN 2 segment.

CDP displays a notification of a native VLAN mismatch on a trunk link with this message:

```
*Mar 1 06:45:26.232: %CDP-4-NATIVE_VLAN_MISMATCH: Native VLAN mismatch
discovered on FastEthernet0/1 (2), with S2 FastEthernet0/1 (99).
```

Connectivity issues occur in the network if a native VLAN mismatch exists. Data traffic for VLANs, other than the two native VLANs configured, successfully propagates across the trunk link, but data associated with either of the native VLANs does not successfully propagate across the trunk link.

As shown in Figure 2, native VLAN mismatch issues do not keep the trunk from forming. To solve the native VLAN mismatch, configure the native VLAN to be the same VLAN on both sides of the link.

Refer to
Online Course
for Illustration

6.2.3.4   Common Problems with Trunks

Trunking issues are usually associated with incorrect configurations. When configuring VLANs and trunks on a switched infrastructure, the following types of configuration errors are the most common:

- **Native VLAN mismatches** - Trunk ports are configured with different native VLANs. This configuration error generates console notifications, and can cause inter-VLAN routing issues, among other problems. This poses a security risk.

- **Trunk mode mismatches** - One trunk port is configured in a mode that is not compatible for trunking on the corresponding peer port. This configuration error causes the trunk link to stop working. Be sure both sides of the trunk are configured with the **switchport mode trunk** command. Other trunk configuration commands are beyond the scope of this course.

- **Allowed VLANs on trunks** - The list of allowed VLANs on a trunk has not been updated with the current VLAN trunking requirements. In this situation, unexpected traffic (or no traffic) is being sent over the trunk.

If an issue with a trunk is discovered and if the cause is unknown, start troubleshooting by examining the trunks for a native VLAN mismatch. If that is not the cause, check for trunk mode mismatches, and finally check for the allowed VLAN list on the trunk. The next two pages examine how to fix the common problems with trunks.

Refer to
Interactive Graphic
in online course

6.2.3.5   Incorrect Port Mode

Trunk links are normally configured statically with the **switchport mode trunk** command. Cisco Catalyst switch trunk ports use DTP to negotiate the state of the link. When a port on a trunk link is configured with a trunk mode that is incompatible with the neighboring trunk port, a trunk link fails to form between the two switches.

In the scenario illustrated in Figure 1, PC4 cannot connect to the internal web server. The topology indicates a valid configuration. Why is there a problem?

Check the status of the trunk ports on switch S1 using the **show interfaces trunk** command. The output shown in Figure 2 reveals that interface Fa0/3 on switch S1 is not currently a trunk link. Examining the F0/3 interface reveals that the switch port is configured statically in trunk mode. An examination of the trunks on switch S3 reveals that there are no active trunk ports. Further checking reveals that the Fa0/3 interface is in static access mode. This is because the port was configured using the **switchport mode access** command. This explains why the trunk is down.

To resolve the issue, reconfigure the trunk mode of the F0/3 ports on switch S3, as shown in Figure 3. After the configuration change, the output of the **show interfaces** command indicates that the port on switch S3 is now in trunking. The output from PC4 indicates that it has regained connectivity to the Web/TFTP server found at IPv4 address 172.17.10.30.

Refer to **Interactive Graphic** in online course

6.2.3.6   Incorrect VLAN List

For traffic from a VLAN to be transmitted across a trunk, it must be allowed on the trunk. To do so, use the **switchport trunk allowed vlan** *vlan-id* command.

In Figure 1, VLAN 20 (Student) and PC5 have been added to the network. The documentation has been updated to show that the VLANs allowed on the trunk are 10, 20, and 99. In this scenario, PC5 cannot connect to the student email server.

Check the trunk ports on switch S1 using the **show interfaces trunk** command as shown in Figure 2. The **show interfaces trunk** command is an excellent tool for revealing common trunking problems. The command reveals that the interface F0/3 on switch S3 is correctly configured to allow VLANs 10, 20, and 99. An examination of the F0/3 interface on switch S1 reveals that interfaces F0/1 and F0/3 only allow VLANs 10 and 99. Someone updated the documentation but forgot to reconfigure the ports on the S1 switch.

Reconfigure F0/1 and F0/3 on switch S1 using the **switchport trunk allowed vlan 10,20,99** command as shown in Figure 3. The output shows that VLANs 10, 20, and 99 are now added to the F0/1 and F0/3 ports on switch S1. PC5 has regained connectivity to the student email server found at IPv4 address 172.17.20.10.

Refer to **Packet Tracer Activity** for this chapter

6.2.3.7 Packet Tracer – Troubleshooting a VLAN Implementation – Scenario 1

Background/Scenario

In this activity, you will troubleshoot connectivity problems between PCs on the same VLAN. The activity is complete when PCs on the same VLAN can ping each other. Any solution you implement must conform to the Addressing Table.

Refer to **Packet Tracer Activity** for this chapter

6.2.3.8   Packet Tracer – Troubleshooting a VLAN Implementation – Scenario 2

Background/Scenario

In this activity, you will troubleshoot a misconfigured VLAN environment. The initial network has errors. Your objective is to locate and correct the errors in the configurations and establish end-to-end connectivity. Your final configuration should match the Topology diagram and Addressing Table. The native VLAN for this topology is VLAN 56.

Refer to
Lab Activity
for this chapter

6.2.3.9 Lab – Troubleshooting VLAN Configurations

In this lab, you will complete the following objectives:

- Part 1: Build the Network and Configure Basic Device Settings

- Part 2: Troubleshoot VLAN 10

- Part 3: Troubleshoot VLAN 20

6.3 Inter-VLAN Routing Using Routers

6.3.1 Inter-VLAN Routing Operation

Refer to
Online Course
for Illustration

6.3.1.1 What is Inter-VLAN Routing?

VLANs are used to segment switched networks. Layer 2 switches, such as the Catalyst 2960 Series, can be configured with over 4,000 VLANs. A VLAN is a broadcast domain, so computers on separate VLANs are unable to communicate without the intervention of a routing device. Layer 2 switches have very limited IPv4 and IPv6 functionality and cannot perform the dynamic routing function of routers. While Layer 2 switches are gaining more IP functionality, such as the ability to perform static routing, this is insufficient to handle these large number of VLANs.

Any device that supports Layer 3 routing, such as a router or a multilayer switch, can be used to perform the necessary routing functionality. Regardless of the device used, the process of forwarding network traffic from one VLAN to another VLAN using routing is known as inter-VLAN routing.

There are three options for inter-VLAN routing :

- Legacy inter-VLAN routing

- Router-on-a-Stick

- Layer 3 switching using SVIs

Note   This chapter focuses on the first two options. Layer 3 switching using SVIs is beyond the scope of this course.

Refer to **Video**
in online course

6.3.1.2 Legacy Inter-VLAN Routing

Historically, the first solution for inter-VLAN routing relied on routers with multiple physical interfaces. Each interface had to be connected to a separate network and configured with a distinct subnet.

In this legacy approach, inter-VLAN routing is performed by connecting different physical router interfaces to different physical switch ports. The switch ports connected to the router are placed in access mode and each physical interface is assigned to a different VLAN. Each router interface can then accept traffic from the VLAN associated with the switch interface that it is connected to, and traffic can be routed to the other VLANs connected to the other interfaces.

Click Play in the figure to view an animation of legacy inter-VLAN routing.

As seen in the animation:

1. PC1 on VLAN 10 is communicating with PC3 on VLAN 30 through router R1.

2. PC1 and PC3 are on different VLANs and have IPv4 addresses on different subnets.

3. Router R1 has a separate interface configured for each of the VLANs.

4. PC1 sends unicast traffic destined for PC3 to switch S2 on VLAN 10, where it is then forwarded out the trunk interface to switch S1.

5. Switch S1 then forwards the unicast traffic through its interface F0/3 to interface G0/0 on router R1.

6. The router routes the unicast traffic through its interface G0/1, which is connected to VLAN 30.

7. The router forwards the unicast traffic to switch S1 on VLAN 30.

8. Switch S1 then forwards the unicast traffic to switch S2 through the active trunk link, after which switch S2 can then forward the unicast traffic to PC3 on VLAN 30.

In this example, the router was configured with two separate physical interfaces to interact with the different VLANs and perform the routing.

Note   This method of inter-VLAN routing is not efficient and is generally no longer implemented in switched networks. It is shown in this course for explanation purposes only.

6.3.1.3   Router-on-a-Stick Inter-VLAN Routing

Refer to **Video** in online course

While legacy inter-VLAN routing requires multiple physical interfaces on both the router and the switch, a more common, present-day implementation of inter-VLAN routing does not. Instead, some router software permits configuring a router interface as a trunk link, meaning only one physical interface is required on the router and the switch to route packets between multiple VLANs.

'Router-on-a-stick' is a type of router configuration in which a single physical interface routes traffic between multiple VLANs on a network. As seen in the figure, the router is connected to switch S1 using a single, physical network connection (a trunk).

The router interface is configured to operate as a trunk link and is connected to a switch port that is configured in trunk mode. The router performs inter-VLAN routing by accepting VLAN-tagged traffic on the trunk interface coming from the adjacent switch, and then, internally routing between the VLANs using subinterfaces. The router then forwards the routed traffic, VLAN-tagged for the destination VLAN, out the same physical interface as it used to receive the traffic.

Subinterfaces are software-based virtual interfaces, associated with a single physical interface. Subinterfaces are configured in software on a router and each subinterface is independently configured with an IP address and VLAN assignment. Subinterfaces are configured for different subnets corresponding to their VLAN assignment to facilitate logical routing. After a routing decision is made based on the destination VLAN, the data frames are VLAN-tagged and sent back out the physical interface.

Click Play in the figure to view an animation of how a router-on-a-stick performs its routing function.

As seen in the animation:

1. PC1 on VLAN 10 is communicating with PC3 on VLAN 30 through router R1 using a single, physical router interface.

2. PC1 sends its unicast traffic to switch S2.

3. Switch S2 then tags the unicast traffic as originating on VLAN 10 and forwards the unicast traffic out its trunk link to switch S1.

4. Switch S1 forwards the tagged traffic out the other trunk interface on port F0/3 to the interface on router R1.

5. Router R1 accepts the tagged unicast traffic on VLAN 10 and routes it to VLAN 30 using its configured subinterfaces.

6. The unicast traffic is tagged with VLAN 30 as it is sent out the router interface to switch S1.

7. Switch S1 forwards the tagged unicast traffic out the other trunk link to switch S2.

8. Switch S2 removes the VLAN tag of the unicast frame and forwards the frame out to PC3 on port F0/23.

Note   The router-on-a-stick method of inter-VLAN routing does not scale beyond 50 VLANs.

Refer to
Interactive Graphic
in online course

6.3.1.4   Activity – Identify the Types of Inter-VLAN Routing

6.3.2   Configure Legacy Inter-VLAN Routing

Refer to **Video**
in online course

6.3.2.1   Configure Legacy Inter-VLAN Routing: Preparation

Legacy inter-VLAN routing requires routers to have multiple physical interfaces. The router accomplishes the routing by having each of its physical interfaces connected to a unique VLAN. Each interface is also configured with an IPv4 address for the subnet associated with the particular VLAN to which it is connected. By configuring the IPv4 addresses on the physical interfaces, network devices connected to each of the VLANs can communicate with the router using the physical interface connected to the same VLAN. In this configuration, network devices can use the router as a gateway to access the devices connected to the other VLANs.

The routing process requires the source device to determine if the destination device is local or remote to the local subnet. The source device accomplishes this by comparing the source and destination IPv4 addresses against the subnet mask. When the destination IPv4 address has been determined to be on a remote network, the source device must identify where it needs to forward the packet to reach the destination device. The source device examines the local routing table to determine where it needs to send the data. Devices use their default gateway as the Layer 2 destination for all traffic that must leave the local subnet. The default gateway is the route that the device uses when it has no other explicitly defined route to the destination network. The IPv4 address of the router interface on the local subnet acts as the default gateway for the sending device.

When the source device has determined that the packet must travel through the local router interface on the connected VLAN, the source device sends out an ARP request to determine the MAC address of the local router interface. When the router sends its ARP reply back to the source device, the source device can use the MAC address to finish framing the packet before it sends it out on the network as unicast traffic.

Because the Ethernet frame has the destination MAC address of the router interface, the switch knows exactly which switch port to forward the unicast traffic out of to reach the router interface for that VLAN. When the frame arrives at the router, the router removes the source and destination MAC address information to examine the destination IPv4 address of the packet. The router compares the destination address to entries in its routing table to determine where it needs to forward the data to reach its final destination. If the router determines that the destination network is a locally connected network, as is the case with inter-VLAN routing, the router sends an ARP request out the interface that is physically connected to the destination VLAN. The destination device responds back to the router with its MAC address, which the router then uses to frame the packet. The router then sends the unicast traffic to the switch, which forwards it out the port where the destination device is connected.

Click Play in the figure to view how legacy inter-VLAN routing is accomplished.

Even though there are many steps in the process of inter-VLAN routing, when two devices on different VLANs communicate through a router, the entire process happens in a fraction of a second.

Refer to
Interactive Graphic
in online course

6.3.2.2   Configure Legacy Inter-VLAN Routing: Switch Configuration

To configure legacy inter-VLAN routing, start by configuring the switch.

As shown in the figure, router R1 is connected to switch ports F0/4 and F0/5, which have been configured for VLANs 10 and 30, respectively.

Use the **vlan** *vlan_id* global configuration mode command to create VLANs. In this example, VLANs 10 and 30 were created on switch S1.

After the VLANs have been created, the switch ports are assigned to the appropriate VLANs. The **switchport access vlan** *vlan_id* command is executed from interface configuration mode on the switch for each interface to which the router connects.

In this example, interfaces F0/4 and F0/11 have been assigned to VLAN 10 using the **switchport access vlan 10** command. The same process is used to assign interface F0/5 and F0/6 on switch S1 to VLAN 30.

Finally, to protect the configuration so that it is not lost after a reload of the switch, the **copy running-config startup-config** command is executed to back up the running configuration to the startup configuration.

Refer to
Interactive Graphic
in online course

6.3.2.3 Configure Legacy Inter-VLAN Routing: Router Interface Configuration

Now the router can be configured to perform inter-VLAN routing.

Router interfaces are configured in a manner similar to configuring VLAN interfaces on switches. To configure a specific interface, change to interface configuration mode from global configuration mode.

As shown in Figure 1, each interface is configured with an IPv4 address using the **ip address** *ip_address subnet_mask* command in interface configuration mode.

In the example, interface G0/0 is configured with IPv4 address 172.17.10.1 and subnet mask 255.255.255.0 using the **ip address 172.17.10.1 255.255.255.0** command.

Router interfaces are disabled by default and must be enabled using the **no shutdown** command before they are used. After the **no shutdown** interface configuration mode command has been issued, a notification displays, indicating that the interface state has changed to up. This indicates that the interface is now enabled.

The process is repeated for all router interfaces. Each router interface must be assigned to a unique subnet for routing to occur. In this example, the other router interface, G0/1, has been configured to use IPv4 address 172.17.30.1, which is on a different subnet than interface G0/0.

After the IPv4 addresses are assigned to the physical interfaces and the interfaces are enabled, the router is capable of performing inter-VLAN routing.

Examine the routing table using the **show ip route** command.

In Figure 2, there are two routes visible in the routing table. One route is to the 172.17.10.0 subnet, which is attached to the local interface G0/0. The other route is to the 172.17.30.0 subnet, which is attached to the local interface G0/1. The router uses this routing table to determine where to send the traffic it receives. For example, if the router receives a packet on interface G0/0 destined for the 172.17.30.0 subnet, the router would identify that it should send the packet out interface G0/1 to reach hosts on the 172.17.30.0 subnet.

Notice the letter C to the left of each of the route entries for the VLANs. This letter indicates that the route is local for a connected interface, which is also identified in the route entry.

Refer to
Lab Activity
for this chapter

6.3.2.4 Lab – Configuring Per-Interface Inter-VLAN Routing

In this lab, you will complete the following objectives:

- Part 1: Build the Network and Configure Basic Device Settings

- Part 2: Configure Switches with VLANs and Trunking

- Part 3: Verify Trunking, VLANs, Routing, and Connectivity

6.3.3 Configure Router-on-a-Stick Inter-VLAN Routing

Refer to **Video**
in online course

6.3.3.1 Configure Router-on-a-Stick: Preparation

Legacy inter-VLAN routing using physical interfaces has a significant limitation. Routers have a limited number of physical interfaces to connect to different VLANs. As the number of VLANs increases on a network, having one physical router interface per VLAN quickly exhausts the physical interface capacity of a router. An alternative in larger networks is to use VLAN trunking and subinterfaces. VLAN trunking allows a single physical router interface to route traffic for multiple VLANs. This technique is termed router-on-a-stick and uses virtual subinterfaces on the router to overcome the hardware limitations based on physical router interfaces.

Subinterfaces are software-based virtual interfaces that are assigned to physical interfaces. Each subinterface is configured independently with its own IP address and prefix length. This allows a single physical interface to simultaneously be part of multiple logical networks.

Note   The term prefix length can be used to refer to the IPv4 subnet mask when associated with an IPv4 address, and the IPv6 prefix length when associated with an IPv6 address.

When configuring inter-VLAN routing using the router-on-a-stick model, the physical interface of the router must be connected to a trunk link on the adjacent switch. On the router, subinterfaces are created for each unique VLAN on the network. Each subinterface is assigned an IP address specific to its subnet/VLAN and is also configured to tag frames for that VLAN. This way, the router can keep the traffic from each subinterface separate as it traverses the trunk link back to the switch.

Functionally, the router-on-a-stick model is the same as using the legacy inter-VLAN routing model, but instead of using the physical interfaces to perform the routing, subinterfaces of a single physical interface are used.

In the figure, PC1 wants to communicate with PC3. PC1 is on VLAN 10 and PC3 is on VLAN 30. For PC1 to communicate with PC3, PC1 must have its data routed through router R1 via subinterfaces.

Click Play in the figure to see how subinterfaces are used to route between VLANs. When the animation pauses, read the text to the left of the topology. Click Play again to continue the animation.

Using trunk links and subinterfaces decreases the number of router and switch ports used. Not only can this save money, it can also reduce configuration complexity. Consequently, the router subinterface approach can scale to a much larger number of VLANs than a configuration with one physical interface per VLAN design.

Refer to
Online Course
for Illustration

6.3.3.2   Configure Router-on-a-Stick: Switch Configuration

To enable inter-VLAN routing using router-on-a stick, start by enabling trunking on the switch port that is connected to the router.

In the figure, router R1 is connected to switch S1 on trunk port F0/5. VLANs 10 and 30 are added to switch S1.

Because switch port F0/5 is configured as a trunk port, the port does not need to be assigned to any VLAN. To configure switch port F0/5 as a trunk port, execute the **switchport mode trunk** command in interface configuration mode for port F0/5.

The router can now be configured to perform inter-VLAN routing.

Refer to
Interactive Graphic
in online course

6.3.3.3 Configure Router-on-a-Stick: Router Subinterface Configuration

The configuration of the router is different when a router-on-a-stick configuration is used, compared to legacy inter-VLAN routing. The figure shows that multiple subinterfaces are configured.

Each subinterface is created using the **interface** *interface_id subinterface_id* global configuration mode command. The syntax for the subinterface is the physical interface, in this case g0/0, followed by a period and a subinterface number. As shown in the figure subinterface GigabitEthernet0/0.10 is created using the **interface g0/0.10 global** configuration mode command. The subinterface number is typically configured to reflect the VLAN number.

Before assigning an IP address to a subinterface, the subinterface must be configured to operate on a specific VLAN using the **encapsulation dot1q** *vlan_id* command. In this example, subinterface G0/0.10 is assigned to VLAN 10.

Note   There is a **native** keyword option that can be appended to this command to set the IEEE 802.1Q native VLAN. In this example, the **native** keyword option was excluded to leave the native VLAN default as VLAN 1.

Next, assign the IPv4 address for the subinterface using the **ip address** *ip_address subnet_mask* subinterface configuration mode command. In this example, subinterface G0/0.10 is assigned the IPv4 address 172.17.10.1 using the **ip address 172.17.10.1 255.255.255.0** command.

This process is repeated for all router subinterfaces required to route between the VLANs configured on the network. Each router subinterface must be assigned an IP address on a unique subnet for routing to occur. For example, the other router subinterface, G0/0.30, is configured to use IPv4 address 172.17.30.1, which is on a different subnet from subinterface G0/0.10.

After a physical interface is enabled, subinterfaces will automatically be enabled upon configuration. Subinterfaces do not need to be enabled with the **no shutdown** command at the subinterface configuration mode level of the Cisco IOS software.

If the physical interface is disabled, all subinterfaces are disabled. In this example, the command **no shutdown** is entered in interface configuration mode for interface G0/0, which in turn, enables all of the configured subinterfaces.

Individual subinterfaces can be administratively shut down with the **shutdown** command. Also, individual subinterfaces can be enabled independently with the **no shutdown** command in the subinterface configuration mode.

Refer to
Interactive Graphic
in online course

6.3.3.4 Configure Router-on-a-Stick: Verifying Subinterfaces

By default, Cisco routers are configured to route traffic between local subinterfaces. As a result, routing does not specifically need to be enabled.

In Figure 1, the **show vlan** command displays information about the Cisco IOS VLAN subinterfaces. The output shows the two VLAN subinterfaces, GigabitEthernet0/0.10 and GigabitEthernet0/0.30.

Examine the routing table using the **show ip route** command (Figure 2). In the example, the routes defined in the routing table indicate that they are associated with specific subinterfaces, rather than separate physical interfaces. There are two routes in the routing table. One route is to the 172.17.10.0 subnet, which is attached to the local subinterface G0/0.10. The other route is to the 172.17.30.0 subnet, which is attached to the local subinterface G0/0.30. The router uses this routing table to determine where to send the traffic it receives. For example, if the router received a packet on subinterface G0/0.10 destined for the 172.17.30.0 subnet, the router would identify that it should send the packet out subinterface G0/0.30 to reach hosts on the 172.17.30.0 subnet.

Use the Syntax Checker, in Figure 3, to configure and verify router-on-a-stick on R1.

Refer to
Interactive Graphic
in online course

6.3.3.5   Configure Router-on-a-Stick: Verifying Routing

After the router and switch have been configured to perform inter-VLAN routing, the next step is to verify host-to-host connectivity. Access to devices on remote VLANs can be tested using the **ping** command.

For the example shown in the figure, a **ping** and a **tracert** are initiated from PC1 to the destination address of PC3.

Ping Test

The **ping** command sends an ICMP echo request to the destination address. When a host receives an ICMP echo request, it responds with an ICMP echo reply to confirm that it received the ICMP echo request. The **ping** command calculates the elapsed time using the difference between the time the echo request was sent and the time the echo reply was received. This elapsed time is used to determine the latency of the connection. Successfully receiving a reply confirms that there is a path between the sending device and the receiving device.

Tracert Test

Tracert is a useful utility for confirming the routed path taken between two devices. On UNIX systems, the utility is specified by **traceroute**. Tracert also uses ICMP to determine the path taken, but it uses ICMP echo requests with specific time-to-live values defined on the frame.

The time-to-live value determines exactly how many router hops away the ICMP echo is allowed to reach. The first ICMP echo request is sent with a time-to-live value set to expire at the first router on route to the destination device.

When the ICMP echo request times out on the first route, an ICMP message is sent back from the router to the originating device. The device records the response from the router and proceeds to send out another ICMP echo request, but this time with a greater time-to-live value. This allows the ICMP echo request to traverse the first router and reach the second device on route to the final destination. The process repeats recursively until finally the ICMP echo request is sent all the way to the final destination device. After the **tracert** utility finishes running, it displays a list of ingress router interfaces that the ICMP echo request reached on its way to the destination.

In the example, the **ping** utility was able to send an ICMP echo request to the IP address of PC3. Also, the **tracert** utility confirms that the path to PC3 is through the 172.17.10.1 subinterface IP address of router R1.

Refer to **Packet Tracer Activity** for this chapter

6.3.3.6   Packet Tracer – Configuring Router-on-a-Stick Inter-VLAN Routing

In this activity, you will check for connectivity prior to implementing inter-VLAN routing. You will then configure VLANs and inter-VLAN routing. Finally, you will enable trunking and verify connectivity between VLANs.

Refer to **Lab Activity** for this chapter

6.3.3.7   Lab – Configuring 801.2Q Trunk-Based Inter-VLAN Routing

In this lab, you will complete the following objectives:

- Part 1: Build the Network and Configure Basic Device Settings
- Part 2: Configure Switches with VLANs and Trunking
- Part 3: Configure Trunk-Based Inter-VLAN Routing

Refer to **Packet Tracer Activity** for this chapter

6.3.3.8   Packet Tracer – Inter-VLAN Routing Challenge

In this activity, you will troubleshoot a misconfigured VLAN environment. The initial network has errors. Your objective is to locate and correct the errors in the configurations and establish end-to-end connectivity. Your final configuration should match the Topology diagram and Addressing Table.

6.4   Summary

Refer to **Online Course** for Illustration

6.4.1.1   The Inside Track

Your company has just purchased a three-level building. You are the network administrator and must design the company inter-VLAN routing network scheme to serve a few employees on each floor.

Floor 1 is occupied by the HR Department, Floor 2 is occupied by the IT Department, and Floor 3 is occupied by the Sales Department. All Departments must be able to communicate with each other, but at the same time have their own separate, working networks.

You brought three Cisco 2960 switches and a Cisco 1941 series router from the old office location to serve network connectivity in the new building. There is no budget available for new equipment.

Refer to the PDF for this activity for further instructions.

Refer to **Packet Tracer Activity** for this chapter

6.4.1.2   Packet Tracer – Skills Integration Challenge

Background/Scenario

In this activity, two switches are completely configured. On a third switch, you are responsible for assigning IP addressing to the SVI, configuring VLANs, assigning VLANs to interfaces, configuring trunking, and performing basic switch security.

Refer to
Online Course
for Illustration

6.4.1.3 VLANs

This chapter introduced VLANS. VLANs are based on logical connections, instead of physical connections. VLANs are a mechanism to allow network administrators to create logical broadcast domains that can span across a single switch or multiple switches, regardless of physical proximity. This function is useful to reduce the size of broadcast domains or to allow groups or users to be logically grouped, without the need to be physically located in the same place.

There are several types of VLANs:

■ Default VLAN

■ Management VLAN

■ Native VLAN

■ User/Data VLANs

■ Voice VLAN

The **switchport access vlan** command is used to create a VLAN on a switch. After creating a VLAN, the next step is to assign ports to the VLAN. The **show vlan brief** command displays the VLAN assignment and membership type for all switch ports. Each VLAN must correspond to a unique IP subnet.

Use the **show vlan** command to check whether the port belongs to the expected VLAN. If the port is assigned to the wrong VLAN, use the **switchport access vlan** command to correct the VLAN membership. Use the **show mac address-table** command to check which addresses were learned on a particular port of the switch and to which VLAN that port is assigned.

A port on a switch is either an access port or a trunk port. Access ports carry traffic from a specific VLAN assigned to the port. A trunk port by default is a member of all VLANs; therefore, it carries traffic for all VLANs.

VLAN trunks facilitate inter-switch communication by carrying traffic associated with multiple VLANs. IEEE 802.1Q frame tagging differentiates between Ethernet frames associated with distinct VLANs as they traverse common trunk links. To enable trunk links, use the **switchport mode trunk** command. Use the **show interfaces trunk** command to check whether a trunk has been established between switches.

Trunk negotiation is managed by the Dynamic Trunking Protocol (DTP), which operates on a point-to-point basis only, between network devices. DTP is a Cisco proprietary protocol that is automatically enabled on Catalyst 2960 and Catalyst 3560 Series switches.

To place a switch into its factory default condition with 1 default VLAN, use the commands **delete flash:vlan.dat** and **erase startup-config.**

This chapter also examined the configuration, verification, and troubleshooting of VLANs and trunks using the Cisco IOS CLI.

Inter-VLAN routing is the process of routing traffic between different VLANs, using either a dedicated router or a multilayer switch. Inter-VLAN routing facilitates communication between devices isolated by VLAN boundaries.

Legacy inter-VLAN routing depended on a physical router port being available for each configured VLAN. This has been replaced by the router-on-a-stick topology that relies on an external router with subinterfaces trunked to a Layer 2 switch. With the router-on-a-stick option, appropriate IP addressing and VLAN information must be configured on each logical subinterface and a trunk encapsulation must be configured to match that of the trunking interface of the switch.

Go to the online course to take the quiz and exam.

Chapter 6   Quiz

This quiz is designed to provide an additional opportunity to practice the skills and knowledge presented in the chapter and to prepare for the chapter exam. You will be allowed multiple attempts and the grade does not appear in the gradebook.

Chapter 6   Exam

The chapter exam assesses your knowledge of the chapter content.

Your Chapter Notes

Access Control Lists

7.0   Introduction

Refer to
Online Course
for Illustration

7.0.1.1   Access Control Lists

One of the most important skills a network administrator needs is mastery of access control lists (ACLs). ACLs provide security for a network.

Network designers use firewalls to protect networks from unauthorized use. Firewalls are hardware or software solutions that enforce network security policies. Consider a lock on a door to a room inside a building. The lock allows only authorized users with a key or access card to pass through the door. Similarly, a firewall filters unauthorized or potentially dangerous packets from entering the network.

On a Cisco router, you can configure a simple firewall that provides basic traffic filtering capabilities using ACLs. Administrators use ACLs to stop traffic or permit only specified traffic on their networks.

This chapter explains how to configure and troubleshoot standard IPv4 ACLs on a Cisco router as part of a security solution. Included are tips, considerations, recommendations, and general guidelines on how to use ACLs. In addition, this chapter includes an opportunity to develop your mastery of ACLs with a series of lessons, activities, and lab exercises.

Refer to
Online Course
for Illustration

7.0.1.2   Permit Me to Assist You

Scenario

Each individual in the class will record five questions they would ask a candidate who is applying for a security clearance for a network assistant position within a small- to medium-sized business. The list of questions should be listed in order of importance to selecting a good candidate for the job. The preferred answers will also be recorded.

Two interviewers from the class will be selected. The interview process will begin. Candidates will be allowed or denied the opportunity to move to the next level of questions based upon their answers to the interviewer's questions.

Refer to the accompanying PDF for further instructions for this activity.

The entire class will then get together and discuss their observations regarding the process to permit or deny them the opportunity to continue on to the next level of interviews.

7.1   ACL Operation

7.1.1   Purpose of ACLs

Refer to
Online Course
for Illustration

7.1.1.1   What is an ACL?

An ACL is a series of IOS commands that control whether a router forwards or drops packets based on information found in the packet header. ACLs are among the most commonly used features of Cisco IOS software.

When configured, ACLs perform the following tasks:

- Limit network traffic to increase network performance. For example, if corporate policy does not allow video traffic on the network, ACLs that block video traffic could be configured and applied. This would greatly reduce the network load and increase network performance.

- Provide traffic flow control. ACLs can restrict the delivery of routing updates to ensure that the updates are from a known source.

- Provide a basic level of security for network access. ACLs can allow one host to access a part of the network and prevent another host from accessing the same area. For example, access to the Human Resources network can be restricted to authorized users.

- Filter traffic based on traffic type. For example, an ACL can permit email traffic, but block all Telnet traffic.

- Screen hosts to permit or deny access to network services. ACLs can permit or deny a user to access file types, such as FTP or HTTP.

By default, a router does not have ACLs configured; therefore, by default a router does not filter traffic. Traffic that enters the router is routed solely based on information within the routing table. However, when an ACL is applied to an interface, the router performs the additional task of evaluating all network packets as they pass through the interface to determine if the packet can be forwarded.

In addition to either permitting or denying traffic, ACLs can be used for selecting types of traffic to be analyzed, forwarded, or processed in other ways. For example, ACLs can be used to classify traffic to enable priority processing. This capability is similar to having a VIP pass at a concert or sporting event. The VIP pass gives selected guests privileges not offered to general admission ticket holders, such as priority entry or being able to enter a restricted area.

The figure shows a sample topology with ACLs applied.

Refer to
Online Course
for Illustration

7.1.1.2   Packet Filtering

An ACL is a sequential list of permit or deny statements, known as access control entries (ACEs). ACEs are also commonly called ACL statements. When network traffic passes through an interface configured with an ACL, the router compares the information within the packet against each ACE, in sequential order, to determine if the packet matches one of the ACEs. This process is called packet filtering.

Packet filtering controls access to a network by analyzing the incoming and outgoing packets and forwarding them or discarding them based on given criteria. Packet filtering can occur at Layer 3 or Layer 4, as shown in the figure. Standard ACLs only filter at Layer 3. Extended ACLs filter at Layer 3 and Layer 4.

Note   Extended ACLs are beyond the scope of this course.

The source IPv4 address is the filtering criteria set in each ACE of a standard IPv4 ACL. A router configured with a standard IPv4 ACL extracts the source IPv4 address from the packet header. The router starts at the top of the ACL and compares the address to each ACE sequentially. When a match is made, the router carries out the instruction, either permitting or denying the packet. After a match is made, the remaining ACEs in the ACL, if any, are not analyzed. If the source IPv4 address does not match any ACEs in the ACL, the packet is discarded.

The last statement of an ACL is always an implicit deny. This statement is automatically inserted at the end of each ACL even though it is not physically present. The implicit deny blocks all traffic. Because of this implicit deny, an ACL that does not have at least one permit statement will block all traffic.

Refer to
Online Course
for Illustration

7.1.1.3   ACL Operation

ACLs define the set of rules that give added control for packets that enter inbound interfaces, packets that relay through the router, and packets that exit outbound interfaces of the router. ACLs do not act on packets that originate from the router itself.

ACLs can be configured to apply to inbound traffic and outbound traffic as shown in the figure.

- **Inbound ACLs** - Incoming packets are processed before they are routed to the outbound interface. An inbound ACL is efficient because it saves the overhead of routing lookups if the packet is discarded. If the packet is permitted by the ACL, it is then processed for routing. Inbound ACLs are best used to filter packets when the network attached to an inbound interface is the only source of packets that need to be examined.

- **Outbound ACLs** - Incoming packets are routed to the outbound interface, and then they are processed through the outbound ACL. Outbound ACLs are best used when the same filter will be applied to packets coming from multiple inbound interfaces before exiting the same outbound interface.

Refer to **Packet
Tracer Activity**
for this chapter

7.1.1.4   Packet Tracer – ACL Demonstration

In this activity, you will observe how an access control list (ACL) can be used to prevent a ping from reaching hosts on remote networks. After removing the ACL from the configuration, the pings will be successful.

7.1.2   Wildcard Masks in ACLs

Refer to
Interactive Graphic
in online course

7.1.2.1   Introducing ACL Wildcard Masking

Wildcard Masking

IPv4 ACEs include the use of wildcard masks. A wildcard mask is a string of 32 binary digits used by the router to determine which bits of the address to examine for a match.

As with subnet masks, the numbers 1 and 0 in the wildcard mask identify how to treat the corresponding IPv4 address bits. However, in a wildcard mask, these bits are used for different purposes and follow different rules.

Subnet masks use binary 1s and 0s to identify the network, subnet, and host portion of an IPv4 address. Wildcard masks use binary 1s and 0s to filter individual IPv4 addresses or groups of IPv4 addresses to permit or deny access to resources.

Wildcard masks and subnet masks differ in the way they match binary 1s and 0s. Wildcard masks use the following rules to match binary 1s and 0s:

- Wildcard mask bit 0 - Match the corresponding bit value in the address.

- Wildcard mask bit 1 - Ignore the corresponding bit value in the address.

Figure 1 shows how different wildcard masks filter IPv4 addresses. In the example, remember that binary 0 signifies a bit that must match, and binary 1 signifies a bit that can be ignored.

Wildcard masks are often referred to as an inverse mask. The reason is that, unlike a subnet mask in which binary 1 is equal to a match and binary 0 is not a match, in a wildcard mask the reverse is true.

Using a Wildcard Mask

The table in Figure 2 shows the results of applying a 0.0.255.255 wildcard mask to a 32-bit IPv4 address. Remember that a binary 0 indicates a value that is matched.

Note   Unlike IPv4 ACLs, IPv6 ACLs do not use wildcard masks. Instead, the prefix-length is used to indicate how much of an IPv6 source or destination address should be matched. IPv6 ACLs are beyond the scope of this course.

Refer to
Interactive Graphic
in online course

7.1.2.2   Wildcard Mask Examples

Wildcard Masks to Match IPv4 Subnets

Calculating the wildcard mask can take some practice. Figure 1 provides three examples of wildcard masks.

In the first example the wildcard mask stipulates that every bit in the IPv4 192.168.1.1 must match exactly.

In the second example, the wildcard mask stipulates that anything will match.

In the third example, the wildcard mask stipulates that any host within the 192.168.1.0/24 network will match.

Wildcard Masks to Match Ranges

The two examples in Figure 2 are more complex. In example 1, the first two octets and first four bits of the third octet must match exactly. The last four bits in the third octet and the last octet can be any valid number. This results in a mask that checks for the range of networks 192.168.16.0 to 192.168.31.0.

Example 2 shows a wildcard mask that matches the first two octets, and the least significant bit in the third octet. The last octet and the first seven bits in the third octet can be any valid number. The result is a mask that would permit or deny all hosts from odd subnets from the 192.168.0.0 major network.

Refer to **Online Course** for Illustration

7.1.2.3 Calculating the Wildcard Mask

Calculating wildcard masks can be challenging. One shortcut method is to subtract the subnet mask from 255.255.255.255.

Wildcard Mask Calculation: Example 1

In the first example in the figure, assume you wanted to permit access to all users in the 192.168.3.0 network. Because the subnet mask is 255.255.255.0, you could take the 255.255.255.255 and subtract the subnet mask 255.255.255.0. The solution produces the wildcard mask 0.0.0.255.

Wildcard Mask Calculation: Example 2

In the second example in the figure, assume you wanted to permit network access for the 14 users in the subnet 192.168.3.32/28. The subnet mask for the IPv4 subnet is 255.255.255.240, therefore take 255.255.255.255 and subtract the subnet mask 255.255.255.240. The solution this time produces the wildcard mask 0.0.0.15.

Wildcard Mask Calculation: Example 3

In the third example in the figure, assume you wanted to match only networks 192.168.10.0 and 192.168.11.0. Again, you take the 255.255.255.255 and subtract the regular subnet mask which in this case would be 255.255.254.0. The result is 0.0.1.255.

You could accomplish the same result with statements like the two shown below:

```
R1(config)# access-list 10 permit 192.168.10.0
R1(config)# access-list 10 permit 192.168.11.0
```

It is far more efficient to configure the wildcard mask in the following way:

```
R1(config)# access-list 10 permit 192.168.10.0 0.0.1.255
```

Consider an example in which you need to match networks in the range between 192.168.16.0/24 to 192.168.31.0/24. These networks would summarize to 192.168.16.0/20. In this case, 0.0.15.255 is the correct wildcard mask to configure one efficient ACL statement, as shown below:

```
R1(config)# access-list 10 permit 192.168.16.0 0.0.15.255
```

Refer to
Online Course
for Illustration

7.1.2.4   Wildcard Mask Keywords

Working with decimal representations of binary wildcard mask bits can be tedious. To simplify this task, the keywords **host** and **any** help identify the most common uses of wildcard masking. These keywords eliminate entering wildcard masks when identifying a specific host or an entire network. These keywords also make it easier to read an ACL by providing visual clues as to the source or destination of the criteria.

The **host** keyword substitutes for the 0.0.0.0 mask. This mask states that all IPv4 address bits must match to filter just one host address.

The **any** option substitutes for the IPv4 address and 255.255.255.255 mask. This mask says to ignore the entire IPv4 address or to accept any addresses.

Example 1: Wildcard Masking Process with a Single IPv4 Address

In Example 1 in the figure, instead of entering **192.168.10.10 0.0.0.0**, you can use **host 192.168.10.10**.

Example 2: Wildcard Masking Process with a Match Any IPv4 Address

In Example 2 in the figure, instead of entering **0.0.0.0 255.255.255.255**, you can use the keyword **any** by itself.

Refer to
Online Course
for Illustration

7.1.2.5   Wildcard Mask Keyword Examples

Example 1 in the figure shows how to use the **any** keyword to substitute the IPv4 address 0.0.0.0 with a wildcard mask of 255.255.255.255.

Example 2 shows how to use the **host** keyword to substitute for the wildcard mask when identifying a single host.

Note   The syntax for configuring standard IPv4 ACLs is covered later in this chapter.

Refer to
Interactive Graphic
in online course

7.1.2.6   Activity – Determine the Correct Wildcard Mask

Refer to
Interactive Graphic
in online course

7.1.2.7   Activity – Determine the Permit or Deny

7.1.3   Guidelines for ACL Creation

Refer to
Online Course
for Illustration

7.1.3.1   General Guidelines for Creating ACLs

Writing ACLs can be a complex task. For every interface there may be multiple policies needed to manage the type of traffic allowed to enter or exit that interface. The router in the figure has two interfaces configured for IPv4 and IPv6. If we needed ACLs for both protocols, on both interfaces and in both directions, this would require eight separate ACLs. Each interface would have four ACLs; two ACLs for IPv4 and two ACLs for IPv6. For each protocol, one ACL is for inbound traffic and one for outbound traffic.

Note   ACLs do not have to be configured in both directions. The number of ACLs and their direction applied to the interface will depend on the requirements being implemented.

Here are some guidelines for using ACLs:

- Use ACLs in firewall routers positioned between your internal network and an external network such as the Internet.

- Use ACLs on a router positioned between two parts of your network to control traffic entering or exiting a specific part of your internal network.

- Configure ACLs on border routers, that is, routers situated at the edges of your networks. This provides a very basic buffer from the outside network, or between a less controlled area of your own network and a more sensitive area of your network.

- Configure ACLs for each network protocol configured on the border router interfaces.

Rules for Applying ACLs

You can configure one ACL per protocol, per direction, per interface:

- **One ACL per protocol** - To control traffic flow on an interface, an ACL must be defined for each protocol enabled on the interface.

- **One ACL per direction** - ACLs control traffic in one direction at a time on an interface. Two separate ACLs must be created to control inbound and outbound traffic.

- **One ACL per interface** - ACLs control traffic for an interface, for example, GigabitEthernet 0/0.

Refer to
Online Course
for Illustration

7.1.3.2   ACL Best Practices

Using ACLs requires attention to detail and great care. Mistakes can be costly in terms of downtime, troubleshooting efforts, and poor network service. Before configuring an ACL, basic planning is required. The figure presents guidelines that form the basis of an ACL best practices list.

Refer to
Interactive Graphic
in online course

7.1.3.3   Activity – ACL Operation

7.1.4   Guidelines for ACL Placement

Refer to
Online Course
for Illustration

7.1.4.1   Where to Place ACLs

The proper placement of an ACL can make the network operate more efficiently. An ACL can be placed to reduce unnecessary traffic. For example, traffic that will be denied at a remote destination should not be forwarded using network resources along the route to that destination.

Every ACL should be placed where it has the greatest impact on efficiency. As shown in the figure, the basic rules are:

- **Extended ACLs** - Locate extended ACLs as close as possible to the source of the traffic to be filtered. This way, undesirable traffic is denied close to the source network without crossing the network infrastructure.

- **Standard ACLs** - Because standard ACLs do not specify destination addresses, place them as close to the destination as possible. Placing a standard ACL at the source of the traffic will effectively prevent that traffic from reaching any other networks through the interface where the ACL is applied.

Placement of the ACL and therefore, the type of ACL used may also depend on:

- **The extent of the network administrator's control** - Placement of the ACL can depend on whether or not the network administrator has control of both the source and destination networks.

- **Bandwidth of the networks involved** - Filtering unwanted traffic at the source prevents transmission of the traffic before it consumes bandwidth on the path to a destination. This is especially important in low bandwidth networks.

- **Ease of configuration** - If a network administrator wants to deny traffic coming from several networks, one option is to use a single standard ACL on the router closest to the destination. The disadvantage is that traffic from these networks will use bandwidth unnecessarily. An extended ACL could be used on each router where the traffic originated. This will save bandwidth by filtering the traffic at the source but requires creating extended ACLs on multiple routers.

Note Although extended ACLs are beyond the scope of the ICND1/CCENT exam, you should know the general guideline for placing both standard and extended ACLs. For CCNA certification the general rule is that extended ACLs are placed as close as possible to the source and standard ACLs are placed as close as possible to the destination.

Refer to
Online Course
for Illustration

7.1.4.2 Standard ACL Placement

The topology in the figure is used to demonstration how a standard ACL can be placed. The administrator wants to prevent traffic originating in the 192.168.10.0/24 network from reaching the 192.168.30.0/24 network.

Following the basic placement guidelines of placing the standard ACL close to the destination, the figure shows two possible interfaces on R3 to apply the standard ACL:

- **R3 S0/0/1 interface** - Applying a standard ACL to prevent traffic from 192.168.10.0/24 from entering the S0/0/1 interface will prevent this traffic from reaching 192.168.30.0/24 and all other networks reachable by R3. This includes the 192.168.31.0/24 network. Because the intent of the ACL is to filter traffic destined only for 192.168.30.0/24, a standard ACL should not be applied to this interface.

- **R3 G0/0 interface** - Applying the standard ACL to traffic exiting the G0/0 interface will filter packets from 192.168.10.0/24 to 192.168.30.0/24. This will not affect other networks reachable by R3. Packets from 192.168.10.0/24 will still be able to reach 192.168.31.0/24.

7.2   Standard IPv4 ACLs

7.2.1   Configure Standard IPv4 ACLs

Refer to
Interactive Graphic
in online course

7.2.1.1   Numbered Standard IPv4 ACL Syntax

To use numbered standard ACLs on a Cisco router, you must first create the standard ACL and then activate the ACL on an interface.

The **access-list** global configuration command defines a standard ACL with a number in the range of 1 through 99. Cisco IOS Software Release 12.0.1 extended these numbers by allowing 1300 to 1999 to be used for standard ACLs. This allows for a maximum of 798 possible standard ACLs. These additional numbers are referred to as expanded IPv4 ACLs.

The full syntax of the standard ACL command is as follows:

```
Router(config)# access-list access-list-number { deny | permit |
remark } source [ source-wildcard ] [ log ]
```

Figure 1 provides a detailed explanation of the syntax for a standard ACL.

ACEs can permit or deny an individual host or a range of host addresses. To create a host statement in numbered ACL 10 that permits a specific host with the IPv4 address 192.168.10.10, you would enter:

```
R1(config)# access-list 10 permit host 192.168.10.10
```

As shown in Figure 2, to create a statement that will permit a range of IPv4 addresses in a numbered ACL 10 that permits all IPv4 addresses in the network 192.168.10.0/24, you would enter:

```
R1(config)# access-list 10 permit 192.168.10.0 0.0.0.255
```

To remove the ACL, the global configuration **no access-list** command is used. Issuing the **show access-list** command confirms that access list 10 has been removed.

Typically, when an administrator creates an ACL, the purpose of each statement is known and understood. However, to ensure that the administrator and others recall the purpose of a statement, remarks should be included. The **remark** keyword is used for documentation and makes access lists a great deal easier to understand. Each remark is limited to 100 characters. The ACL in Figure 3, although fairly simple, is used to provide an example. When reviewing the ACL in the configuration using the **show running-config** command, the remark is also displayed.

Refer to
Interactive Graphic
in online course

7.2.1.2   Applying Standard IPv4 ACLs to Interfaces

After a standard IPv4 ACL is configured, it is linked to an interface using the **ip access-group** command in interface configuration mode:

```
Router(config-if)# ip access-group { access-list-number |
access-list-name } { in | out }
```

To remove an ACL from an interface, first enter the **no ip access-group** command on the interface, and then enter the global **no access-list** command to remove the entire ACL.

Figure 1 lists the steps and syntax to configure and apply a numbered standard ACL on a router.

Figure 2 shows an example of an ACL designed to permit a single network.

This ACL allows only traffic from source network 192.168.10.0 to be forwarded out of interface S0/0/0. Traffic from networks other than 192.168.10.0 is blocked.

The first line identifies the ACL as access list 1. It permits traffic that matches the selected parameters. In this case, the IPv4 address and wildcard mask identifying the source network is 192.168.10.0 0.0.0.255. Recall that there is an implicit deny all statement that is equivalent to adding the line **access-list 1 deny 0.0.0.0 255.255.255.255** or **access-list deny any** to the end of the ACL.

The **ip access-group 1 out** interface configuration command links and ties ACL 1 to the Serial 0/0/0 interface as an outbound filter.

Therefore, ACL 1 only permits hosts from the 192.168.10.0/24 network to exit router R1. It denies any other network including the 192.168.11.0 network

Refer to
Interactive Graphic
in online course

7.2.1.3   Numbered Standard IPv4 ACL Examples

Figure 1 shows an example of an ACL that permits a specific subnet except for a specific host on that subnet.

The first command deletes the previous version of ACL 1. The next ACL statement, denies the PC1 host located at 192.168.10.10. Every other host on the 192.168.10.0/24 network is then permitted. Again the implicit deny statement matches every other network.

The ACL is reapplied to interface S0/0/0 in an outbound direction.

Figure 2 shows an example of an ACL that denies a specific host. This ACL replaces the previous example. This example still blocks traffic from host PC1 but permits all other traffic.

The first two commands are the same as the previous example. The first command deletes the previous version of ACL 1 and the next ACL statement denies the PC1 host that is located at 192.168.10.10.

The third line is new and permits all other hosts. This means that all hosts from the 192.168.10.0/24 network will be permitted except for PC1, which was denied in the previous statement.

This ACL is applied to interface G0/0 in the inbound direction. Because the filter only affects the 192.168.10.0/24 LAN on G0/0 it is more efficient to apply the ACL to the inbound interface. The ACL could be applied to S0/0/0 in the outbound direction but then R1 would have to examine packets from all networks including 192.168.11.0/24.

Refer to
Interactive Graphic
in online course

7.2.1.4   Named Standard IPv4 ACL Syntax

Naming an ACL makes it easier to understand its function. When you identify your ACL with a name instead of with a number, the configuration mode and command syntax are slightly different.

Figure 1 shows the steps required to create a standard named ACL.

Step 1. Starting from the global configuration mode, use the **ip access-list** command to create a named ACL. ACL names are alphanumeric, case sensitive, and must be unique. The **ip access-list standard** *name* command is used to create a standard named ACL. After entering the command, the router is in standard (std) named ACL (nacl) configuration mode as indicated by the second prompt in the Figure 1.

Note Numbered ACLs use the global configuration command **access-list**, whereas named IPv4 ACLs use the **ip access-list** command.

Step 2. From the named ACL configuration mode, use **permit** or **deny** statements to specify one or more conditions for determining whether a packet is forwarded or dropped. You can use **remark** to add a comment to the ACL.

Step 3. Apply the ACL to an interface using the **ip access-group** *name* command. Specify whether the ACL should be applied to packets as they enter the interface (**in**) or applied to packets as they exit the interface (**out**).

Figure 2 shows the commands used to configure a standard named ACL on router R1, interface G0/0, that denies host 192.168.11.10 access to the 192.168.10.0 network. The ACL is named NO_ACCESS.

Capitalizing ACL names is not required, but makes them stand out when viewing the running-config output. It also makes it less likely that you will accidentally create two different ACLs with the same name but with different uses of capitalization.

Refer to
Interactive Graphic
in online course

7.2.1.5   Activity – Configuring Standard IPv4 ACLs

Refer to **Packet Tracer Activity** *for this chapter*

7.2.1.6   Packet Tracer – Configuring Numbered Standard IPv4 ACLs

Standard access control lists (ACLs) are router configuration scripts that control whether a router permits or denies packets based on the source address. This activity focuses on defining filtering criteria, configuring standard ACLs, applying ACLs to router interfaces, and verifying and testing the ACL implementation. The routers are already configured, including IPv4 addresses and EIGRP routing.

Refer to **Packet Tracer Activity** *for this chapter*

7.2.1.7   Packet Tracer – Configuring Named Standard IPv4 ACLs

The senior network administrator has asked you to create a standard named ACL to prevent access to a file server. All clients from one network and one specific workstation from a different network should be denied access.

7.2.2   Modify IPv4 ACLs

Refer to **Online Course** *for Illustration*

7.2.2.1   Method 1 – Use a Text Editor

After someone is familiar with creating and editing ACLs, it may be easier to construct the ACL using a text editor such as Microsoft Notepad. This allows you to create or edit the ACL and then paste it into the router interface. For an existing ACL, you can use the **show running-config** command to display the ACL, copy and paste it into the text editor, make the necessary changes, and paste it back in to the router interface.

Configuration   For example, assume that the host IPv4 address in the figure was incorrectly entered. Instead of the 192.168.10.99 host, it should have been the 192.168.10.10 host. Here are the steps to edit and correct ACL 1:

Step 1.   Display the ACL using the **show running-config** command. The example in the figure uses the **include** keyword to display only the ACEs.

Step 2.   Highlight the ACL, copy it, and then paste it into Microsoft Notepad. Edit the list as required. After the ACL is correctly displayed in Microsoft Notepad, highlight it and copy it.

Step 3.   In global configuration mode, remove the access list using the **no access-list 1** command. Otherwise, the new statements would be appended to the existing ACL. Then paste the new ACL into the configuration of the router.

Step 4.   Using the **show running-config** command, verify the changes.

It should be mentioned that when using the **no access-list** command, different IOS software releases act differently. If the ACL that has been deleted is still applied to an interface, some IOS versions act as if no ACL is protecting your network while others deny all traffic. For this reason it is good practice to remove the reference to the access list from the interface before modifying the access list. If there is an error in the new list, disable it and troubleshoot the problem. In that instance, the network has no ACL during the correction process.

Refer to
Online Course
for Illustration

7.2.2.2   Method 2 – Use Sequence Numbers

As shown in the figure, the initial configuration of ACL 1 included a host statement for host 192.168.10.99. This was in error. The host should have been configured as 192.168.10.10. To edit the ACL using sequence numbers follow these steps:

Step 1.   Display the current ACL using the **show access-lists 1** command. The output from this command will be discussed in more detail later in this section. The sequence number is displayed at the beginning of each statement. The sequence number was automatically assigned when the access list statement was entered. Notice that the misconfigured statement has the sequence number 10.

Step 2.   Enter the **ip access-lists standard** command that is used to configure named ACLs. The ACL number 1, is used as the name. First, the misconfigured statement needs to be deleted using the **no 10** command with 10 referring to the sequence number. Next, a new sequence number 10 statement is added using the command, **10 deny host 192.168.10.10**.

Note   Statements cannot be overwritten using the same sequence number as an existing statement. The current statement must be deleted first, and then the new one can be added.

Step 3.   Verify the changes using the **show access-lists** command.

As discussed previously, Cisco IOS implements an internal logic to standard access lists. The order in which standard ACEs are entered may not be the order in which they are stored, displayed or processed by the router. The **show access-lists** command displays the ACEs with their sequence numbers.

Refer to
Online Course
for Illustration

7.2.2.3 Editing Standard Named ACLs

In a previous example, sequence numbers were used to edit a standard numbered IPv4 ACL. By referring to the statement sequence numbers, individual statements can easily be inserted or deleted. This method can also be used to edit standard named ACLs.

The figure shows an example of inserting a line to a named ACL.

- In the first **show** command output, you can see that the ACL named NO_ACCESS has two numbered lines indicating access rules for a workstation with the IPv4 address 192.168.11.10.

- From named access list configuration mode, statements can be inserted or removed.

- To add a statement to deny another workstation requires inserting a numbered line. In the example, the workstation with the IPv4 address 192.168.11.11 is being added using a new sequence number of 15.

- The final **show** command output verifies that the new workstation is now denied access.

Note   In named access list configuration mode, use the **no** *sequence-number* command to quickly delete individual statements.

Refer to
Interactive Graphic
in online course

7.2.2.4 Verifying ACLs

As shown in Figure 1, the **show ip interface** command is used to verify the ACL on the interface. The output from this command includes the number or name of the access list and the direction in which the ACL was applied. The output shows router R1 has the access list 1 applied to its S0/0/0 outbound interface and the access list NO_ACCESS applied to its g0/0 interface, also in the outbound direction.

The example in Figure 2 shows the result of issuing the **show access-lists** command on router R1. To view an individual access list use the **show access-lists** command followed by the access list number or name. The NO_ACCESS statements may look strange. Notice that sequence number 15 is displayed prior to sequence number 10. This is a result of the router's internal process and will be discussed later in this section.

Refer to
Interactive Graphic
in online course

7.2.2.5 ACL Statistics

After an ACL has been applied to an interface and some testing has occurred, the **show access-lists** command will show statistics for each statement that has been matched. In the output in Figure 1, note that some of the statements have been matched. When traffic is generated that should match an ACL statement, the matches shown in the **show access-lists** command output should increase. For instance, in this example, if a ping is issued from PC1 to PC3 or PC4, the output will show an increase in the matches for the deny statement of ACL 1.

Both permit and deny statements will track statistics for matches; however, recall that every ACL has an implied deny any as the last statement. This statement will not appear in the **show access-lists** command; therefore, statistics for that statement will not appear. To view statistics for the implied deny any statement, the statement can be configured manually and will appear in the output.

During testing of an ACL, the counters can be cleared using the **clear access-list counters** command. This command can be used alone or with the number or name of a specific ACL. As shown in Figure 2, this command clears the statistic counters for an ACL.

Refer to
Lab Activity
for this chapter

7.2.2.6   Lab – Configuring and Modifying Standard IPv4 ACLs

In this lab, you will complete the following objectives:

- Part 1: Set Up the Topology and Initialize Devices
- Part 2: Configure Devices and Verify Connectivity
- Part 3: Configure and Verify Standard Numbered and Named ACLs
- Part 4: Modify a Standard ACL

7.2.3   Securing VTY ports with a Standard IPv4 ACL

Refer to
Interactive Graphic
in online course

7.2.3.1   The access-class Command

You can improve the security of administrative lines by restricting VTY access. Restricting VTY access is a technique that allows you to define which IP addresses are allowed remote access to the router EXEC process. You can specify which IP addresses are allowed remote access to your router with an ACL and an **access-class** statement configured on your VTY lines. Use this technique with SSH to further improve administrative access security.

The **access-class** command configured in line configuration mode restricts incoming and outgoing connections between a particular VTY (into a Cisco device) and the addresses in an access list.

The command syntax of the **access-class** command is:

```
Router(config-line)# access-class access-list-number { in [ vrf-also ] |
out }
```

The parameter **in** restricts incoming connections between the addresses in the access list and the Cisco device, while the parameter **out** restricts outgoing connections between a particular Cisco device and the addresses in the access list.

An example allowing a range of addresses to access VTY lines 0 - 4 is shown in Figure 1. The ACL in the figure is configured to permit network 192.168.10.0 to access VTY lines 0 - 4 but deny all other networks.

The following should be considered when configuring access lists on VTYs:

- Both named and numbered access lists can be applied to VTYs.
- Identical restrictions should be set on all the VTYs, because a user can attempt to connect to any of them.

Use the Syntax Checker in Figure 2 to practice securing VTY access.

Note Access lists apply to packets that travel through a router. They are not designed to block packets that originate within the router. By default, an outbound ACL does not prevent remote access connections initiated from the router.

Refer to
Online Course
for Illustration

7.2.3.2   Verifying the VTY Port is Secured

After the ACL to restrict access to the VTY lines is configured, it is important to verify that it is working as expected. The figure shows two devices attempting to connect to R1 using SSH. Access list 21 has been configured on the VTY lines on R1. PC1 is successful while PC2 fails to establish a SSH connection. This is the expected behavior, as the configured access list permits VTY access from the 192.168.10.0/24 network while denying all other devices.

The output for R1 shows the result of issuing the **show access-lists** command after the SSH attempts by PC1 and PC2. The match in the permit line of the output is a result of a successful SSH connection by PC1. The match in the deny statement is due to the failed attempt to create an SSH connection by PC2, a device on the 192.168.11.0/24 network.

Refer to **Packet
Tracer Activity**
for this chapter

7.2.3.3   Packet Tracer – Configuring an IPv4 ACL on VTY Lines

As administrator of a network, you need to have remote access to your router. This access should not be available to other users of the network. Therefore, you will configure and apply an ACL that allows PC access to the Telnet lines, but denies all other source IPv4 addresses.

Refer to
Lab Activity
for this chapter

7.2.3.4   Lab – Configuring and Verifying VTY Restrictions

In this lab, you will complete the following objectives:

■ Part 1: Configure Basic Device Settings

■ Part 2: Configure and Apply the Access Control List on R1

■ Part 3: Verify the Access Control List Using Telnet

■ Part 4: Challenge – Configure and Apply the Access Control List on S1

7.3   Troubleshoot ACLs

7.3.1   Processing Packets with ACLs

Refer to
Online Course
for Illustration

7.3.1.1   The Implicit Deny Any

A single-entry ACL with only one deny entry has the effect of denying all traffic. At least one permit ACE must be configured in an ACL or all traffic is blocked.

For the network in the figure, applying either ACL 1 or ACL 2 to the S0/0/0 interface of R1 in the outbound direction will have the same effect. Network 192.168.10.0 will be permitted to access the networks reachable through S0/0/0, while 192.168.11.0 will not be allowed to access those networks. In ACL 1, if a packet does not match the permit statement, it is discarded.

Refer to
Interactive Graphic
in online course

7.3.1.2   The Order of ACEs in an ACL

Cisco IOS applies an internal logic when accepting and processing standard ACEs. As discussed previously, ACEs are processed sequentially; therefore, the order in which ACEs are entered is important.

For example, in Figure 1, ACL 3 contains two ACEs. The first ACE uses a wildcard mask to deny a range of addresses, which includes all hosts in the 192.168.10.0/24 network. The second ACE is a host statement that examines a specific host, 192.168.10.10, that belongs to the 192.168.10.0/24 network. The IOS internal logic for standard access lists rejects the second statement and returns an error message because it is a subset of the previous statement.

The configuration in Figure 2 of ACL 4 has the same two statements but in reverse order. This is a valid sequence of statements because the first statement refers a specific host, not a range of hosts.

In Figure 3, ACL 5 shows that a host statement can be configured after a statement that denotes a range of hosts. The host must not be within the range covered by a previous statement. The 192.168.11.10 host address is not a member of the 192.168.10.0/24 network so this is a valid statement.

Refer to
Interactive Graphic
in online course

7.3.1.3   Cisco IOS Reorders Standard ACLs

The order in which standard ACEs are entered may not be the order that they are stored, displayed, or processed by the router.

Figure 1 shows the configuration of a standard access list. Range statements that deny three networks are configured first followed by five host statements. The host statements are all valid statements because their host IPv4 addresses are not part of the previously entered range statements.

The **show running-config** command is used to verify the ACL configuration. Notice that the statements are listed in a different order than they were entered. We will use the **show access-lists** command to understand the logic behind this.

As shown in Figure 2, the **show access-lists** command displays ACEs along with their sequence numbers. We might expect the order of the statements in the output to reflect the order in which they were entered. However, the **show access-lists** output shows that this is not the case.

The order in which the standard ACEs are listed is the sequence used by the IOS to process the list. Notice that the statements are grouped into two sections, host statements followed by range statements. The sequence number indicates the order that the statement was entered, not the order the statement will be processed.

The host statements are listed first but not necessarily in the order that they were entered. The IOS puts host statements in an order using a special hashing function. The resulting order optimizes the search for a host ACL entry. The range statements are displayed after the host statements. These statements are listed in the order in which they were entered.

Note   The hashing function is only applied to host statements in an IPv4 standard access list. The details of the hashing function are beyond the scope of this course.

Recall that standard and numbered ACLs can be edited using sequence numbers. When inserting a new ACL statement, the sequence number will only affect the location of a range statement in the list. Host statements will always be put in order using the hashing function.

Continuing with the example, after saving the running-configuration, the router is reloaded. As shown in Figure 2, the **show access-lists** command displays the ACL in the same order, however the statements have been renumbered. The sequence numbers are now in numerical order.

Refer to **Interactive Graphic** in online course

7.3.1.4   Routing Processes and ACLs

The figure shows the logic of routing and ACL processes. When a packet arrives at a router interface, the router process is the same, whether ACLs are used or not. As a frame enters an interface, the router checks to see whether the destination Layer 2 address matches its interface Layer 2 address, or whether the frame is a broadcast frame.

If the frame address is accepted, the frame information is stripped off and the router checks for an ACL on the inbound interface. If an ACL exists, the packet is tested against the statements in the list.

If the packet matches a statement, the packet is either permitted or denied. If the packet is accepted, it is then checked against routing table entries to determine the destination interface. If a routing table entry exists for the destination, the packet is then switched to the outgoing interface, otherwise the packet is dropped.

Next, the router checks whether the outgoing interface has an ACL. If an ACL exists, the packet is tested against the statements in the list.

If the packet matches a statement, it is either permitted or denied.

If there is no ACL or the packet is permitted, the packet is encapsulated in the new Layer 2 protocol and forwarded out the interface to the next device.

7.3.2   Common IPv4 Standard ACL Errors

Refer to **Interactive Graphic** in online course

7.3.2.1   Troubleshooting Standard IPv4 ACLs – Example 1

Using the **show** commands described earlier reveals most of the more common ACL errors. The most common errors are entering ACEs in the wrong order and not specifying adequate ACL rules. Other common errors include applying the ACL using the wrong direction, the wrong interface, or the wrong source addresses.

Security Policy   PC2 should not be able to access the File Server.

In Figure 1, although PC2 cannot access the File Server, neither can PC1. When viewing the output of the **show access-list** command, only PC2 is explicitly denied. However, there is no permit statement allowing other access.

Solution   All access out the G0/0 interface to the 192.168.30.0/24 LAN is currently implicitly denied. Add a statement to ACL 10 to permit all other traffic, as shown in Figure 2. PC1 should now be able to access the file server. Output from the **show access-list** command verifies that a ping from PC1 to the File Server matches the permit any statement.

Refer to
Interactive Graphic
in online course

7.3.2.2   Troubleshooting Standard IPv4 ACLs – Example 2

Security Policy   The 192.168.11.0/24 network should not be able to access the 192.168.10.0/24 network.

In Figure 1, PC2 cannot access PC1. Nor can it access the Internet through R2. When viewing the output of the **show access-list** command, you can see that PC2 is matching the deny statement. ACL 20 seems to be configured correctly. You suspect that it must be incorrectly applied and view the interface configurations for R1

In Figure 2, the **show run** command filtered to view the interface configurations reveals that ACL 20 was applied to the wrong interface and in the wrong direction. All traffic from the 192.168.11.0/24 is denied inbound access through the G0/1 interface.

Solution   To correct this error, remove ACL 20 from the G0/1 interface and apply it outbound on the G0/0 interface, as shown in Figure 3. PC2 cannot access PC1, but can now access the Internet.

Refer to
Interactive Graphic
in online course

7.3.2.3   Troubleshooting Standard IPv4 ACLs – Example 3

Security Policy   Only PC1 is allowed SSH remote access to R1.

In Figure 1, PC1 is unable to remotely access R1 using an SSH connection. Viewing the running configuration section for the VTY lines reveals that an ACL named PC1-SSH is correctly applied for inbound connections. The VTY lines are correctly configured to only allow SSH connections. From the output of the show access-list command, you notice that the IPv4 address is the G0/0 interface for R1, not the IPv4 address of PC1. Also, notice that the administrator configured an explicit deny any statement in the ACL. This is helpful because, in this situation, you will see matches for failed attempts to remotely access R1.

Solution   Figure 2 shows the process for correcting the error. Because the statement that needs to be corrected is the first statement, we use the sequence number 10 to delete it by entering **no 10**. We then configure the correct IPv4 address for PC1. The **clear access-list counters** command resets the output to only show new matches. An attempt from PC2 to remotely access R1 is successful, as shown in the output for the **show access-list** command.

Refer to **Packet
Tracer Activity**
for this chapter

7.3.2.4   Packet Tracer – Troubleshooting Standard IPv4 ACLs

Scenario

Create a network that has the following three policies implemented:

- Hosts from the 192.168.0.0/24 network are unable to access any TCP service of Server3.

- Hosts from the 10.0.0.0/8 network are unable to access the HTTP service of Server1.

- Hosts from the 172.16.0.0/16 network are unable to access the FTP service of Server2.

**Refer to
Lab Activity
for this chapter**

7.3.2.5   Lab – Troubleshooting Standard IPv4 ACL Configuration and Placement

In this lab, you will complete the following objectives:

- Part 1: Build the Network and Configure Basic Device Settings
- Part 2: Troubleshoot Internal Access
- Part 3: Troubleshoot Remote Access

7.4   Summary

**Refer to
Online Course
for Illustration**

7.4.1.1   FTP Denied

Scenario

It was recently reported that viruses are on the rise within your small- to medium-sized business network. Your network administrator has been tracking network performance and has determined that one particular host is constantly downloading files from a remote FTP server. This host just may be the virus source perpetuating throughout the network!

Use Packet Tracer to complete this activity. Write a named ACL to deny the host access to the FTP server. Apply the ACL to the most effective interface on the router.

To complete the physical topology, you must use:

- One PC host station
- Two switches
- One Cisco 1941 series Integrated Services Router
- One server

Using the Packet Tracer text tool, record the ACL you prepared. Validate that the ACL works to deny access to the FTP server by trying to access the FTP server's address. Observe what happens while in simulation mode.

Save your file and be prepared to share it with another student, or with the entire class.

**Refer to Packet
Tracer Activity
for this chapter**

7.4.1.2   Packet Tracer – Skills Integration Challenge

In this challenge activity, you will finish the addressing scheme, configure routing, and implement named access control lists.

**Refer to
Online Course
for Illustration**

7.4.1.3   Access Control Lists

By default a router does not filter traffic. Traffic that enters the router is routed solely based on information within the routing table.

Packet filtering controls access to a network by analyzing the incoming and outgoing packets and passing or dropping them based on criteria such as the source IP address, destination IP addresses, and the protocol carried within the packet. A packet-filtering router uses rules to determine whether to permit or deny traffic. A router can also perform packet filtering at Layer 4, the transport layer.

An ACL is a sequential list of permit or deny statements. The last statement of an ACL is always an implicit deny which blocks all traffic. To prevent the implied deny any statement at the end of the ACL from blocking all traffic, the **permit any** statement can be added.

When network traffic passes through an interface configured with an ACL, the router compares the information within the packet against each entry, in sequential order, to determine whether the packet matches one of the statements. If a match is found, the packet is processed accordingly.

ACLs are configured to apply to inbound traffic or to apply to outbound traffic.

Standard ACLs can be used to permit or deny traffic only from source IPv4 addresses. The destination of the packet and the ports involved are not evaluated. The basic rule for placing a standard ACL is to place it close to the destination.

Extended ACLs filter packets based on several attributes: protocol type, source or destination IPv4 address, and source or destination ports. The basic rule for placing an extended ACL is to place it as close to the source as possible.

The **access-list** global configuration command defines a standard ACL with a number in the range of 1 through 99. The **ip access-list standard** *name* is used to create a standard named ACL.

After an ACL is configured, it is linked to an interface using the **ip access-group** command in interface configuration mode. Remember these rules: one ACL per protocol, one ACL per direction, one ACL per interface.

To remove an ACL from an interface, first enter the **no ip access-group** command on the interface, and then enter the global **no access-list** command to remove the entire ACL.

The **show running-config** and **show access-lists** commands are used to verify ACL configuration. The **show ip interface** command is used to verify the ACL on the interface and the direction in which it was applied.

The **access-class** command configured in line configuration mode restricts incoming and outgoing connections between a particular VTY and the addresses in an access list.

Go to the online course to take the quiz and exam.

Chapter 7 Quiz

This quiz is designed to provide an additional opportunity to practice the skills and knowledge presented in the chapter and to prepare for the chapter exam. You will be allowed multiple attempts and the grade does not appear in the gradebook.

Chapter 7 Exam

The chapter exam assesses your knowledge of the chapter content.

Your Chapter Notes

8.0 Introduction

Refer to
Online Course
for Illustration

8.0.1.1 DHCP

Every device that connects to a network needs a unique IP address. Network administrators assign static IP addresses to routers, servers, printers, and other network devices whose locations (physical and logical) are not likely to change. These are usually devices that provide services to users and devices on the network; therefore, the addresses assigned to them should remain constant. Additionally, static addresses enable administrators to manage these devices remotely. It is easier for network administrators to access a device when they can easily determine its IP address.

However, computers and users in an organization often change locations, physically and logically. It can be difficult and time consuming for administrators to assign new IP addresses every time an employee moves. Additionally, for mobile employees working from remote locations, manually setting the correct network parameters can be challenging. Even for desktop clients, the manual assignment of IP addresses and other addressing information presents an administrative burden, especially as the network grows.

Introducing a Dynamic Host Configuration Protocol (DHCP) server to the local network simplifies IP address assignment to both desktop and mobile devices. Using a centralized DHCP server enables organizations to administer all dynamic IP address assignments from a single server. This practice makes IP address management more effective and ensures consistency across the organization, including branch offices.

DHCP is available for both IPv4 (DHCPv4) and for IPv6 (DHCPv6). This chapter explores the functionality, configuration, and troubleshooting of both DHCPv4 and DHCPv6.

8.1 DHCPv4

8.1.1 DHCPv4 Operation

Refer to
Online Course
for Illustration

8.1.1.1 Introducing DHCPv4

DHCPv4 assigns IPv4 addresses and other network configuration information dynamically. Because desktop clients typically make up the bulk of network nodes, DHCPv4 is an extremely useful and timesaving tool for network administrators.

A dedicated DHCPv4 server is scalable and relatively easy to manage. However, in a small branch or SOHO location, a Cisco router can be configured to provide DHCPv4 services without the need for a dedicated server. Cisco IOS software supports an optional, full-featured DHCPv4 server.

The DHCPv4 server dynamically assigns, or leases, an IPv4 address from a pool of addresses for a limited period of time chosen by the server, or until the client no longer needs the address.

Clients lease the information from the server for an administratively defined period. Administrators configure DHCPv4 servers to set the leases to time out at different intervals. The lease is typically anywhere from 24 hours to a week or more. When the lease expires, the client must ask for another address, although the client is typically reassigned the same address.

Refer to **Interactive Graphic** in online course

8.1.1.2 DHCPv4 Operation

As shown in Figure 1, DHCPv4 works in a client/server mode. When a client communicates with a DHCPv4 server, the server assigns or leases an IPv4 address to that client. The client connects to the network with that leased IP address until the lease expires. The client must contact the DHCP server periodically to extend the lease. This lease mechanism ensures that clients that move or power off do not keep addresses that they no longer need. When a lease expires, the DHCP server returns the address to the pool where it can be reallocated as necessary.

Lease Origination

When the client boots (or otherwise wants to join a network), it begins a four step process to obtain a lease. As shown in Figure 2, a client starts the process with a broadcast DHCPDISCOVER message with its own MAC address to discover available DHCPv4 servers.

DHCP Discover (DHCPDISCOVER)

The DHCPDISCOVER message finds DHCPv4 servers on the network. Because the client has no valid IPv4 information at bootup, it uses Layer 2 and Layer 3 broadcast addresses to communicate with the server.

DHCP Offer (DHCPOFFER)

When the DHCPv4 server receives a DHCPDISCOVER message, it reserves an available IPv4 address to lease to the client. The server also creates an ARP entry consisting of the MAC address of the requesting client and the leased IPv4 address of the client. As shown in Figure 3, the DHCPv4 server sends the binding DHCPOFFER message to the requesting client. The DHCPOFFER message is sent as a unicast, using the Layer 2 MAC address of the server as the source address and the Layer 2 MAC address of the client as the destination.

DHCP Request (DHCPREQUEST)

When the client receives the DHCPOFFER from the server, it sends back a DHCPRE-QUEST message as shown in Figure 4. This message is used for both lease origination and lease renewal. When used for lease origination, the DHCPREQUEST serves as a binding acceptance notice to the selected server for the parameters it has offered and an implicit decline to any other servers that may have provided the client a binding offer.

Many enterprise networks use multiple DHCPv4 servers. The DHCPREQUEST message is sent in the form of a broadcast to inform this DHCPv4 server and any other DHCPv4 servers about the accepted offer.

DHCP Acknowledgment (DHCPACK)

On receiving the DHCPREQUEST message, the server verifies the lease information with an ICMP ping to that address to ensure it is not being used already, creates a new ARP entry for the client lease, and replies with a unicast DHCPACK message as shown in Figure 5. The DHCPACK message is a duplicate of the DHCPOFFER, except for a change in the message type field. When the client receives the DHCPACK message, it logs the configuration information and performs an ARP lookup for the assigned address. If there is no reply to the ARP, the client knows that the IPv4 address is valid and starts using it as its own.

Lease Renewal

DHCP Request (DHCPREQUEST)

As shown in Figure 6, before the lease expires, the client sends a DHCPREQUEST message directly to the DHCPv4 server that originally offered the IPv4 address. If a DHCPACK is not received within a specified amount of time, the client broadcasts another DHCPREQUEST so that one of the other DHCPv4 servers can extend the lease.

DHCP Acknowledgment (DHCPACK)

On receiving the DHCPREQUEST message, the server verifies the lease information by returning a DHCPACK, as shown in Figure 7.

Refer to **Interactive Graphic** in online course

8.1.1.3   DHCPv4 Message Format

The DHCPv4 message format is used for all DHCPv4 transactions. DHCPv4 messages are encapsulated within the UDP transport protocol. DHCPv4 messages sent from the client use UDP source port 68 and destination port 67. DHCPv4 messages sent from the server to the client use UDP source port 67 and destination port 68.

The figure shows the format of a DHCPv4 message. The fields are as follows:

- **Operation (OP) Code** - Specifies the general type of message. A value of 1 indicates a request message; a value of 2 is a reply message.

- **Hardware Type** - Identifies the type of hardware used in the network. For example, 1 is Ethernet, 15 is Frame Relay, and 20 is a serial line. These are the same codes used in ARP messages.

- **Hardware Address Length** - Specifies the length of the address.

- **Hops** - Controls the forwarding of messages. Set to 0 by a client before transmitting a request.

- **Transaction Identifier** - Used by the client to match the request with replies received from DHCPv4 servers.

- **Seconds** - Identifies the number of seconds elapsed since a client began attempting to acquire or renew a lease. Used by DHCPv4 servers to prioritize replies when multiple client requests are outstanding.

- **Flags** - Used by a client that does not know its IPv4 address when it sends a request. Only one of the 16 bits is used, which is the broadcast flag. A value of 1 in this field tells the DHCPv4 server or relay agent receiving the request that the reply should be sent as a broadcast.

- **Client IP Address** - Used by a client during lease renewal when the address of the client is valid and usable, not during the process of acquiring an address. The client puts its own IPv4 address in this field if and only if it has a valid IPv4 address while in the bound state; otherwise, it sets the field to 0.

- **Your IP Address** - Used by the server to assign an IPv4 address to the client.

- **Server IP Address** - Used by the server to identify the address of the server that the client should use for the next step in the bootstrap process, which may or may not be the server sending this reply. The sending server always includes its own IPv4 address in a special field called the Server Identifier DHCPv4 option.

- **Gateway IP Address** - Routes DHCPv4 messages when DHCPv4 relay agents are involved. The gateway address facilitates communications of DHCPv4 requests and replies between the client and a server that are on different subnets or networks.

- **Client Hardware Address** - Specifies the physical layer of the client.

- **Server Name** - Used by the server sending a DHCPOFFER or DHCPACK message. The server may optionally put its name in this field. This can be a simple text nickname or a DNS domain name, such as dhcpserver.netacad.net.

- **Boot Filename** - Optionally used by a client to request a particular type of boot file in a DHCPDISCOVER message. Used by a server in a DHCPOFFER to fully specify a boot file directory and filename.

- **DHCP Options** - Holds DHCP options, including several parameters required for basic DHCP operation. This field is variable in length. Both client and server may use this field.

Refer to
Interactive Graphic
in online course

8.1.1.4 DHCPv4 Discover and Offer Messages

If a client is configured to receive its IPv4 settings dynamically and wants to join the network, it requests addressing values from the DHCPv4 server. The client transmits a DHCPDISCOVER message on its local network when it boots or senses an active network connection. Because the client has no way of knowing the subnet to which it belongs, the DHCPDISCOVER message is an IPv4 broadcast (destination IPv4 address of 255.255.255.255). The client does not have a configured IPv4 address yet, so the source IPv4 address of 0.0.0.0 is used.

As shown in Figure 1, the client IPv4 address (CIADDR), default gateway address (GIADDR), and subnet mask are all marked to indicate that the address 0.0.0.0 is used.

Note   Unknown information is sent as 0.0.0.0.

When the DHCPv4 server receives the DHCPDISCOVER message, it responds with a DHCPOFFER message. This message contains initial configuration information for the client, including the IPv4 address that the server offers, the subnet mask, the lease duration, and the IPv4 address of the DHCPv4 server making the offer.

The DHCPOFFER message can be configured to include other information, such as the lease renewal time and DNS address.

As shown in Figure 2, the DHCP server responds to the DHCPDISCOVER by assigning values to the CIADDR and subnet mask. The frame is constructed using the client hardware address (CHADDR) and sent to the requesting client.

The client and server send acknowledgment messages, and the process is complete.

Refer to
Interactive Graphic
in online course

8.1.1.5   Activity – Identify the Steps in DHCPv4 Operation

8.1.2   Configuring a Basic DHCPv4 Server

Refer to
Interactive Graphic
in online course

8.1.2.1   Configuring a Basic DHCPv4 Server

A Cisco router running Cisco IOS software can be configured to act as a DHCPv4 server. The Cisco IOS DHCPv4 server assigns and manages IPv4 addresses from specified address pools within the router to DHCPv4 clients. The topology shown in Figure 1 is used to illustrate this functionality.

Step 1.   **Excluding IPv4 Addresses**
The router functioning as the DHCPv4 server assigns all IPv4 addresses in a DHCPv4 address pool unless configured to exclude specific addresses. Typically, some IPv4 addresses in a pool are assigned to network devices that require static address assignments. Therefore, these IPv4 addresses should not be assigned to other devices. To exclude specific addresses, use the **ip dhcp excluded-address** command as shown in Figure 2.

A single address or a range of addresses can be excluded by specifying the low-address and high-address of the range. Excluded addresses should include the addresses assigned to routers, servers, printers, and other devices that have been or will be manually configured.

Step 2.   **Configuring a DHCPv4 Pool**
Configuring a DHCPv4 server involves defining a pool of addresses to assign. As shown in Figure 3, the **ip dhcp pool** *pool-name* command creates a pool with the specified name and puts the router in DHCPv4 configuration mode, which is identified by this prompt Router(dhcp-config)#.

Step 3.   **Configuring Specific Tasks**
Figure 4 lists the tasks to complete the DHCPv4 pool configuration. Some of these are optional, while others must be configured.

The address pool and default gateway router must be configured. Use the **network** statement to define the range of available addresses.

Use the **default-router** command to define the default gateway router. Typically, the gateway is the LAN interface of the router closest to the client devices. One gateway is required, but you can list up to eight addresses if there are multiple gateways.

Other DHCPv4 pool commands are optional. For example, the IPv4 address of the DNS server that is available to a DHCPv4 client is configured using the **dns-server** command. The **domain-name** *domain* command is used to define the domain name. The duration of the DHCPv4 lease can be changed using the **lease** command. The default lease value is one day. The **netbios-name-server** command is used to define the NetBIOS WINS server.

DHCPv4 Example

A sample configuration with basic DHCPv4 parameters configured on router R1 is shown in Figure 5. R1 is configured as a DHCPv4 server for the 192.168.10.0/24 LAN using the example topology from Figure 1.

Disabling DHCPv4

The DHCPv4 service is enabled, by default. To disable the service, use the **no service dhcp** global configuration mode command. Use the **service dhcp** global configuration mode command to re-enable the DHCPv4 server process. Enabling the service has no effect if the parameters are not configured.

Use the Syntax Checker activity in Figure 6 to configure similar DHCPv4 parameters on R1 for the 192.168.11.0/24 LAN.

> Refer to
> **Interactive Graphic**
> in online course

8.1.2.2   Verifying DHCPv4

The topology shown in Figure 1 is used in the example output. In this example, R1 has been configured to provide DHCPv4 services. PC1 has not been powered up and, therefore, does not have an IP address.

As shown in Figure 2, the **show running-config | section dhcp** command output displays the DHCPv4 commands configured on R1. The **| section** parameter displays only the commands associated with DHCPv4 configuration.

As shown in Figure 3, the operation of DHCPv4 can be verified using the **show ip dhcp binding** command. This command displays a list of all IPv4 address to MAC address bindings that have been provided by the DHCPv4 service. The second command in Figure 3, **show ip dhcp server statistics**, is used to verify that messages are being received or sent by the router. This command displays count information regarding the number of DHCPv4 messages that have been sent and received.

As seen in the output for these commands, currently there are no bindings and the statistics indicate no messages sent or received. At this point no devices have requested DHCPv4 services from router R1.

In Figure 4, the commands are issued after PC1 and PC2 have been powered on and have completed the booting process.

Notice that the binding information now displays that the IPv4 addresses of 192.168.10.10 and 192.168.11.10 have been bound to MAC addresses. The statistics are also displaying DHCPDISCOVER, DHCPREQUEST, DHCPOFFER, and DHCPACK activity.

As shown in Figure 5, the **ipconfig /all** command, when issued on PC1, displays the TCP/IP parameters. Because PC1 was connected to the network segment 192.168.10.0/24, it automatically received a DNS suffix, IPv4 address, subnet mask, default gateway, and DNS server address from that pool. No DHCP-specific router interface configuration is required. If a PC is connected to a network segment that has a DHCPv4 pool available, the PC can obtain an IPv4 address from the appropriate pool automatically.

Refer to
Interactive Graphic
in online course

8.1.2.3   DHCPv4 Relay

What is DHCP Relay?

In a complex hierarchical network, enterprise servers are usually located in a server farm. These servers may provide DHCP, DNS, TFTP, and FTP services for the network. Network clients are not typically on the same subnet as those servers. In order to locate the servers and receive services, clients often use broadcast messages.

In Figure 1, PC1 is attempting to acquire an IPv4 address from a DHCP server using a broadcast message. In this scenario, router R1 is not configured as a DHCPv4 server and does not forward the broadcast. Because the DHCPv4 server is located on a different network, PC1 cannot receive an IP address using DHCP.

In Figure 2, PC1 is attempting to renew its IPv4 address. To do so, the **ipconfig /release** command is issued. Notice that the IPv4 address is released and the address is shown to be 0.0.0.0. Next, the **ipconfig /renew** command is issued. This command causes PC1 to broadcast a DHCPDISCOVER message. The output shows that PC1 is unable to locate the DHCPv4 server. Because routers do not forward broadcasts, the request is not successful.

As a solution to this problem, an administrator can add DHCPv4 servers on all the subnets. However, running these services on several computers creates additional cost and administrative overhead.

A better solution is to configure a Cisco IOS helper address. This solution enables a router to forward DHCPv4 broadcasts to the DHCPv4 server. When a router forwards address assignment/parameter requests, it is acting as a DHCPv4 relay agent. In the example topology, PC1 would broadcast a request to locate a DHCPv4 server. If R1 was configured as a DHCPv4 relay agent, it would forward the request to the DHCPv4 server located on subnet 192.168.11.0.

As shown in Figure 3, the interface on R1 receiving the broadcast is configured with the **ip helper-address** interface configuration mode command. The address of the DHCPv4 server is configured as the only parameter.

When R1 has been configured as a DHCPv4 relay agent, it accepts broadcast requests for the DHCPv4 service and then forwards those requests as a unicast to the IPv4 address 192.168.11.6. The **show ip interface** command is used to verify the configuration.

As shown in Figure 4, PC1 is now able to acquire an IPv4 address from the DHCPv4 server.

DHCPv4 is not the only service that the router can be configured to relay. By default, the **ip helper-address** command forwards the following eight UDP services:

- Port 37: Time
- Port 49: TACACS
- Port 53: DNS
- Port 67: DHCP/BOOTP client
- Port 68: DHCP/BOOTP server

- Port 69: TFTP
- Port 137: NetBIOS name service
- Port 138: NetBIOS datagram service

Using the Syntax Checker in Figure 5, configure the DHCPv4 relay commands on the correct router so that PC3 can receive IPv4 addressing information from the DHCPv4 server. Refer back to Figure 1 to view the network topology.

Refer to
Lab Activity
for this chapter

8.1.2.4   Lab – Configuring Basic DHCPv4 on a Router
In this lab, you will complete the following objectives:

- Part 1: Build the Network and Configure Basic Device Settings
- Part 2: Configure a DHCPv4 Server and a DHCP Relay Agent

Refer to
Lab Activity
for this chapter

8.1.2.5   Lab – Configuring Basic DHCPv4 on a Switch
In this lab, you will complete the following objectives:

- Part 1: Build the Network and Configure Basic Device Settings
- Part 2: Change the SDM Preference
- Part 3: Configure DHCPv4
- Part 4: Configure DHCP for Multiple VLANs
- Part 5: Enable IP Routing

8.1.3   Configure DHCPv4 Client

Refer to
Interactive Graphic
in online course

8.1.3.1   Configuring a Router as DHCPv4 Client

Sometimes, Cisco routers in small office/home office (SOHO) and branch sites have to be configured as DHCPv4 clients in a similar manner to client computers. The method used depends on the ISP. However, in its simplest configuration, the Ethernet interface is used to connect to a cable or DSL modem. To configure an Ethernet interface as a DHCP client, use the **ip address dhcp** interface configuration mode command.

In Figure 1, assume that an ISP has been configured to provide select customers with IP addresses from the 209.165.201.0/27 network range. After the G0/1 interface is configured with the **ip address dhcp** command, the **show ip interface g0/1** command confirms that the interface is up and that the address was allocated by a DHCPv4 server.

Use the Syntax Checker in Figure 2 to configure the interface that is connected to the ISP to acquire an address from the DHCP server.

Refer to
Online Course
for Illustration

8.1.3.2   Configuring a Wireless Router as a DHCPv4 Client

Typically, wireless routers for home or small office use connect to an ISP using a DSL or cable modem. In most cases, wireless routers are set to receive IPv4 addressing information automatically from the ISP.

For example, the figure shows the default WAN setup page for a Packet Tracer wireless router. Notice that the Internet connection type is set to **Automatic Configuration - DHCP**. This selection is used when the router is connected to a DSL or cable modem and acts as a DHCPv4 client, requesting an IPv4 address from the ISP.

Refer to **Packet Tracer Activity** for this chapter

8.1.3.3   Packet Tracer – Configuring DHCPv4 Using Cisco IOS

A dedicated DHCP server is scalable and relatively easy to manage, but there are situations where it is not cost effective. For example, in a small branch or SOHO location, a Cisco router can be configured to provide DHCPv4 services without the need for a dedicated server. Cisco IOS software supports an optional, full-featured DHCPv4 server. The DHCPv4 server leases configurations for 24 hours by default. As the network technician for your company, you are tasked with configuring a Cisco router as a DHCP server to provide dynamic allocation of addresses to clients on the network. You are also required to configure the edge router as a DHCP client so that it receives an IP address from the ISP network.

8.1.4   Troubleshoot DHCPv4

Refer to **Interactive Graphic** in online course

8.1.4.1   Troubleshooting Tasks

DHCPv4 problems can arise for a multitude of reasons, such as software defects in operating systems, NIC drivers, or DHCP relay agents, but the most common are configuration issues. Because of the number of potentially problematic areas, a systematic approach to troubleshooting is required, as shown in Figure 1.

Troubleshooting Task 1: Resolve IPv4 Address Conflicts

An IPv4 address lease can expire on a client still connected to a network. If the client does not renew the lease, the DHCPv4 server can reassign that IPv4 address to another client. When the client reboots, it requests an IPv4 address. If the DHCPv4 server does not respond quickly, the client uses the last IPv4 address. The situation then arises where two clients are using the same IPv4 address, creating a conflict.

The **show ip dhcp conflict** command displays all address conflicts recorded by the DHCPv4 server, as shown in Figure 2. The server uses the **ping** command to detect clients. The client uses Address Resolution Protocol (ARP) to detect conflicts. If an address conflict is detected, the address is removed from the pool and not assigned until an administrator resolves the conflict.

This output displays IP addresses that have conflicts with the DHCP server. It shows the detection method and detection time for conflicting IP addresses that the DHCP server has offered.

Troubleshooting Task 2: Verify Physical Connectivity

First, use the **show interfaces** *interface* command to confirm that the router interface acting as the default gateway for the client is operational. If the state of the interface is anything other than up, the port does not pass traffic, including DHCP client requests.

Troubleshooting Task 3: Test Connectivity using a Static IP Address

When troubleshooting any DHCPv4 issue, verify network connectivity by configuring static IPv4 address information on a client workstation. If the workstation is unable to reach network resources with a statically configured IPv4 address, the root cause of the problem is not DHCPv4. At this point, network connectivity troubleshooting is required.

Troubleshooting Task 4: Verify Switch Port Configuration

If the DHCPv4 client is unable to obtain an IPv4 address from the DHCPv4 server on startup, attempt to obtain an IPv4 address from the DHCPv4 server by manually forcing the client to send a DHCPv4 request.

Note   If there is a switch between the client and the DHCPv4 server, and the client is unable to obtain the DHCP configuration, switch port configuration issues may be the cause. These causes may include issues from trunking and channeling, STP, and RSTP. PortFast and edge port configurations resolve the most common DHCPv4 client issues that occur with an initial installation of a Cisco switch.

Troubleshooting Task 5: Test DHCPv4 Operation on the Same Subnet or VLAN

It is important to distinguish whether DHCPv4 is functioning correctly when the client is on the same subnet or VLAN as the DHCPv4 server. If DHCPv4 is working correctly when the client is on the same subnet or VLAN, the problem may be the DHCP relay agent. If the problem persists even with testing DHCPv4 on the same subnet or VLAN as the DHCPv4 server, the problem may actually be with the DHCPv4 server.

Refer to
Online Course
for Illustration

8.1.4.2   Verify Router DHCPv4 Configuration

When the DHCPv4 server is located on a separate LAN from the client, the router interface facing the client must be configured to relay DHCPv4 requests by configuring the IPv4 helper address. If the IPv4 helper address is not configured properly, client DHCPv4 requests are not forwarded to the DHCPv4 server.

Follow these steps to verify the router configuration:

Step 1.   Verify that the **ip helper-address** command is configured on the correct interface. It must be present on the inbound interface of the LAN containing the DHCPv4 client workstations and must be directed to the correct DHCPv4 server. In the figure, the output of the **show running-config** command verifies that the DHCPv4 relay IPv4 address is referencing the DHCPv4 server address at 192.168.11.6.

The **show ip interface** command can also be used to verify the DHCPv4 relay on an interface.

Step 2.   Verify that the global configuration command **no service dhcp** has not been configured. This command disables all DHCP server and relay functionality on the router. The command **service dhcp** does not appear in the running-config, because it is the default configuration.

In the figure, the **show running-config | include no service dhcp** command verifies that the DHCPv4 service is enabled since there is no match for the **show running-config | include no service dhcp** command. If the service had been disabled, the **no service dhcp** command would be displayed in the output.

Refer to
Online Course
for Illustration

8.1.4.3   Debugging DHCPv4

On routers configured as DHCPv4 servers, the DHCPv4 process fails if the router is not receiving requests from the client. As a troubleshooting task, verify that the router is receiving the DHCPv4 request from the client. This troubleshooting step involves configuring an ACL for debugging output.

Note   Although you can copy the extended ACL shown in the figure and use it to filter DHCP messages, the configuration of extended ACLs are beyond the scope of this course.

The figure shows an extended ACL permitting only packets with UDP destination ports of 67 or 68. These are the typical ports used by DHCPv4 clients and servers when sending DHCPv4 messages. The extended ACL is used with the **debug ip packet** command to display only DHCPv4 messages.

The output in the figure shows that the router is receiving DHCP requests from the client. The source IP address is 0.0.0.0 because the client does not yet have an IP address. The destination is 255.255.255.255 because the DHCP discovery message from the client is sent as a broadcast. This output only shows a summary of the packet and not the DHCPv4 message itself. Nevertheless, the router did receive a broadcast packet with the source and destination IP and UDP ports that are correct for DHCPv4. The complete debug output shows all the packets in the DHCPv4 communications between the DHCPv4 server and client.

Another useful command for troubleshooting DHCPv4 operation is the **debug ip dhcp server events** command. This command reports server events, like address assignments and database updates.

Refer to
Lab Activity
for this chapter

8.1.4.4   Lab – Troubleshooting DHCPv4

In this lab, you will complete the following objectives:

- Part 1: Build the Network and Configure Basic Device Settings
- Part 2: Troubleshoot DHCPv4 Issues

8.2   DHCPv6

8.2.1   SLAAC and DHCPv6

Refer to
Online Course
for Illustration

8.2.1.1   Stateless Address Autoconfiguration (SLAAC)

Similar to IPv4, IPv6 global unicast addresses can be configured manually or dynamically. However, there are two methods in which IPv6 global unicast addresses can be assigned dynamically:

- Stateless Address Autoconfiguration (SLAAC), as shown in the figure
- Dynamic Host Configuration Protocol for IPv6 (Stateful DHCPv6)

Introducing SLAAC

SLAAC is a method in which a device can obtain an IPv6 global unicast address without the services of a DHCPv6 server. At the core of SLAAC is ICMPv6. ICMPv6 is similar to ICMPv4 but includes additional functionality and is a much more robust protocol. SLAAC uses ICMPv6 Router Solicitation and Router Advertisement messages to provide addressing and other configuration information that would normally be provided by a DHCP server:

- **Router Solicitation (RS) message** - When a client is configured to obtain its addressing information automatically using SLAAC, the client sends an RS message to the router. The RS message is sent to the IPv6 all-routers multicast address FF02::2.

- **Router Advertisement (RA) message** - RA messages are sent by routers to provide addressing information to clients configured to obtain their IPv6 addresses automatically. The RA message includes the prefix and prefix length of the local segment. A client uses this information to create its own IPv6 global unicast address. A router sends an RA message periodically, or in response to an RS message. By default, Cisco routers send RA messages every 200 seconds. RA messages are always sent to the IPv6 all-nodes multicast address FF02::1.

As the name indicates, SLAAC is stateless. A stateless service means there is no server that maintains network address information. Unlike DHCP, there is no SLAAC server that knows which IPv6 addresses are being used and which ones are available.

Refer to
Interactive Graphic
in online course

8.2.1.2   SLAAC Operation

A router must have IPv6 routing enabled before it can send RA messages:

```
Router(config)# ipv6 unicast-routing
```

1. In the example topology shown in Figure 1, PC1 is configured to obtain IPv6 address information automatically. Since booting, PC1 has not received an RA message, so it sends an RS message to the all-routers multicast address to inform the local IPv6 router that it needs an RA.

2. As shown in Figure 2, R1 receives the RS message and responds with an RA message. Included in the RA message are the prefix and prefix length of the network. The RA message is sent to the IPv6 all-nodes multicast address FF02::1, with the link-local address of the router as the IPv6 source address.

3. PC1 receives the RA message containing the prefix and prefix length for the local network. PC1 will use this information to create its own IPv6 global unicast address. PC1 now has a 64-bit network prefix, but needs a 64-bit Interface ID (IID) to create a global unicast address.

   There are two ways PC1 can create its own unique IID:

   - **EUI-64** - Using the EUI-64 process, PC1 will create an IID using its 48-bit MAC address.

   - **Randomly generated** - The 64-bit IID can be a random number generated by the client operating system.

As shown in Figure 3, PC1 can create a 128-bit IPv6 global unicast address by combining the 64-bit prefix with the 64-bit IID. PC1 will use the link-local address of the router as its IPv6 default gateway address.

4. Because SLAAC is a stateless process, PC1 must verify that this newly created IPv6 address is unique before it can be used. As shown in Figure 4, PC1 sends an ICMPv6 Neighbor Solicitation message with a specially constructed multicast address, called a solicited-node multicast address, which duplicates the last 24 bits of PC1's IPv6 address. If no other devices respond with a Neighbor Advertisement message, then the address is virtually guaranteed to be unique and can be used by PC1. If a Neighbor Advertisement is received by PC1 then the address is not unique and the operating system has to determine a new Interface ID to use.

This process is part of ICMPv6 Neighbor Discovery and is known as Duplicate Address Detection (DAD).

Refer to **Online Course** for Illustration

8.2.1.3   SLAAC and DHCPv6

The decision of whether a client is configured to obtain its IPv6 address information automatically using SLAAC, DHCPv6, or a combination of both depends on the settings within the RA message.

The two flags are the Managed Address Configuration flag (M flag) and the Other Configuration flag (O flag).

Using different combinations of the M and O flags, RA messages have one of three addressing options for the IPv6 device, as shown in the figure:

- SLAAC (Router Advertisement only)

- Stateless DHCPv6 (Router Advertisement and DHCPv6)

- Stateful DHCPv6 (DHCPv6 only)

Regardless of the option used, it is recommended by RFC 4861 that all IPv6 devices perform Duplicate Address Detection (DAD) on any unicast address, including addresses configured using SLAAC or DHCPv6. DAD is implemented using ICMPv6, which is specified by RFC 4443.

Note   Although the RA message specifies the process the client should use in obtaining an IPv6 address dynamically, the client operating system may choose to ignore the RA message and use the services of a DHCPv6 server exclusively.

Refer to **Online Course** for Illustration

8.2.1.4   SLAAC Option

SLAAC Option (Router Advertisement only)

SLAAC is the default option on Cisco routers. Both the M flag and the O flag are set to 0 in the RA, as shown in the figure.

This option instructs the client to use the information in the RA message exclusively. This includes prefix, prefix-length, DNS server, MTU, and default gateway information. There is no further information available from a DHCPv6 server. The IPv6 global unicast address is created by combining the prefix from RA and an Interface ID using either EUI-64 or a randomly generated value.

RA messages are configured on an individual interface of a router. To re-enable an interface for SLAAC that might have been set to another option, the M and O flags need to be reset to their initial values of 0. This is done using the following interface configuration mode commands:

```
Router(config-if)# no ipv6 nd managed-config-flag
```

```
Router(config-if)# no ipv6 nd other-config-flag
```

Refer to
Online Course
for Illustration

8.2.1.5   Stateless DHCPv6 Option

Although DHCPv6 is similar to DHCPv4 in what it provides, the two protocols are independent of each other. DHCPv6 is defined in RFC 3315. There has been a lot of work done on this specification over the years as indicated by the fact that DHCPv6 RFC has the highest revision number of any Internet draft.

Stateless DHCPv6 Option (Router Advertisement and DHCPv6)

The stateless DHCPv6 option informs the client to use the information in the RA message for addressing, but additional configuration parameters are available from a DHCPv6 server.

Using the prefix and prefix length in the RA message, along with EUI-64 or a randomly generated IID, the client creates its IPv6 global unicast address.

The client will then communicate with a stateless DHCPv6 server to obtain additional information not provided in the RA message. This may be a list of DNS server IPv6 addresses, for example. This process is known as stateless DHCPv6 because the server is not maintaining any client state information (i.e., a list of available and allocated IPv6 addresses). The stateless DHCPv6 server is only providing configuration parameters for clients, not IPv6 addresses.

For stateless DHCPv6, the O flag is set to 1 and the M flag is left at the default setting of 0. The O flag value of 1 is used to inform the client that additional configuration information is available from a stateless DHCPv6 server.

To modify the RA message sent on the interface of a router to indicate stateless DHCPv6, use the following command:

```
Router(config-if)# ipv6 nd other-config-flag
```

Refer to
Online Course
for Illustration

8.2.1.6   Stateful DHCPv6 Option

Stateful DHCPv6 (DHCPv6 only)

This option is the most similar to DHCPv4. In this case, the RA message informs the client not to use the information in the RA message. All addressing information and configuration information must be obtained from a stateful DHCPv6 server. This is known as stateful DHCPv6 because the DHCPv6 server maintains IPv6 state information. This is similar to a DHCPv4 server allocating addresses for IPv4.

The M flag indicates whether or not to use stateful DHCPv6. The O flag is not involved. The following command is used to change the M flag from 0 to 1 to signify stateful DHCPv6:

```
Router(config-if)# ipv6 nd managed-config-flag
```

Refer to
Interactive Graphic
in online course

8.2.1.7   DHCPv6 Operations

As shown in Figure 1, stateless or stateful DHCPv6, or both begin with an ICMPv6 RA message from the router. The RA message might have been a periodic message or solicited by the device using an RS message.

If stateless or stateful DHCPv6 is indicated in the RA message, then the device begins DHCPv6 client/server communications.

DHCPv6 Communications

When stateless DHCPv6 or stateful DHCPv6 is indicated by the RA, DHCPv6 operation is invoked. DHCPv6 messages are sent over UDP. DHCPv6 messages from the server to the client use UDP destination port 546. The client sends DHCPv6 messages to the server using UDP destination port 547.

The client, now a DHCPv6 client, needs to locate a DHCPv6 server. In Figure 2, the client sends a DHCPv6 SOLICIT message to the reserved IPv6 multicast all-DHCPv6-servers address FF02::1:2. This multicast address has link-local scope, which means routers do not forward the messages to other networks.

One or more DHCPv6 servers respond with a DHCPv6 ADVERTISE unicast message as shown in Figure 3. The ADVERTISE message informs the DHCPv6 client that the server is available for DHCPv6 service.

In Figure 4, the client responds with a DHCPv6 REQUEST or INFORMATION-REQUEST unicast message to the server, depending on whether it is using stateful or stateless DHCPv6.

- **Stateless DHCPv6 client** - The client sends a DHCPv6 INFORMATION-REQUEST message to the DHCPv6 server requesting only configuration parameters, such as DNS server address. The client generated its own IPv6 address using the prefix from the RA message and a self-generated Interface ID.

- **Stateful DHCPv6 client** - The client sends a DHCPv6 REQUEST message to the server to obtain an IPv6 address and all other configuration parameters from the server.

The server sends a DHCPv6 REPLY unicast message to the client containing the information requested in the REQUEST or INFORMATION-REQUEST message as shown in Figure 5.

Refer to
Interactive Graphic
in online course

8.2.1.8   Activity – Identify the Steps in DHCPv6 Operation

8.2.2   Stateless DHCPv6

Refer to
Interactive Graphic
in online course

8.2.2.1   Configuring a Router as a Stateless DHCPv6 Server

As shown in Figure 1, there are four steps to configure a router as a DHCPv6 server:

Step 1.   Enable IPv6 Routing

The **ipv6 unicast-routing** command is required to enable IPv6 routing. This command is not necessary for the router to be a stateless DHCPv6 server, but it is required for the router to source ICMPv6 RA messages.

Step 2.   Configure a DHCPv6 Pool

The **ipv6 dhcp pool** *pool-name* command creates a pool and enters the router in DHCPv6 configuration mode, which is identified by the Router(config-dhcpv6)# prompt.

Step 3.   Configure Pool Parameters

During the SLAAC process, the client received the information it needed to create an IPv6 global unicast address. The client also received the default gateway information using the source IPv6 address from the RA message, which is the link-local address of the router. However, the stateless DHCPv6 server can be configured to provide other information that might not have been included in the RA message such as DNS server address and the domain name.

Step 4.   Configure the DHCPv6 Interface

The **ipv6 dhcp server** *pool-name* interface configuration mode command binds the DHCPv6 pool to the interface. The router responds to stateless DHCPv6 requests on this interface with the information contained in the pool. The O flag needs to be changed from 0 to 1 using the interface command **ipv6 nd other-config-flag**. RA messages sent on this interface indicate that additional information is available from a stateless DHCPv6 server.

DHCPv6 Stateless Server Example

Figure 2 shows a sample configuration for a router to be configured as a stateless DHCPv6 server. Notice that router R3 is shown as a DHCPv6 client. R3 is configured as a client to help verify the stateless DHCPv6 operations.

Refer to
Online Course
for Illustration

8.2.2.2   Configuring a Router as a Stateless DHCPv6 Client

In the example shown in the figure, a Cisco router is used as the stateless DHCPv6 client. This is not a typical scenario and is used for demonstration purposes only. Typically, a stateless DHCPv6 client is a device, such as a computer, tablet, mobile device, or webcam.

The client router needs an IPv6 link-local address on the interface to send and receive IPv6 messages, such as RS messages and DHCPv6 messages. The link-local address of a router is created automatically when IPv6 is enabled on the interface. This can happen when a global unicast address is configured on the interface or by using the **ipv6 enable** command. After the router receives a link-local address, it can participate in IPv6 neighbor discovery.

In this example, the **ipv6 enable** command is used because the router does not yet have a global unicast address.

The **ipv6 address autoconfig** command enables automatic configuration of IPv6 addressing using SLAAC. By assumption, the server router is configured for stateless DHCPv6 so it sends an RA message to inform the client router to use stateless DHCPv6 to obtain DNS information.

Refer to
Interactive Graphic
in online course

8.2.2.3 Verifying Stateless DHCPv6

Verifying the Stateless DHCPv6 Server

In Figure 1, the **show ipv6 dhcp pool** command verifies the name of the DHCPv6 pool and its parameters. The number of active clients is 0, because there is no state being maintained by the server.

The **show running-config** command can also be used to verify all the commands that were previously configured.

Verifying the Stateless DHCPv6 Client

In this example, a router is used as a stateless DHCPv6 client. In Figure 2, the output from the **show ipv6 interface** command shows that the router has "Stateless address autoconfig enabled" and has an IPv6 global unicast address. The IPv6 global unicast address was created using SLAAC, which includes the prefix contained in the RA message. The IID was generated using EUI-64. DHCPv6 was not used to assign the IPv6 address.

The default router information is also from the RA message. This was the source IPv6 address of the packet that contained the RA message and the link-local address of the router.

The Figure 3 output from the **debug ipv6 dhcp detail** command shows the DHCPv6 messages exchanged between the client and the server. In this example, the command has been entered on the client. The INFORMATION-REQUEST message is shown because it is sent from a stateless DHCPv6 client. Notice that the client, router R3, is sending the DHCPv6 messages from its link-local address to the All_DHCPv6_Relay_Agents_and_Servers address FF02::1:2.

The debug output displays all the DHCPv6 messages sent between the client and the server including the DNS server and domain name options that were configured on the server.

Use the Syntax Checker in Figure 4 to configure and verify stateless DHCPv6 on the router.

8.2.3 Stateful DHCPv6 Server

Refer to
Interactive Graphic
in online course

8.2.3.1 Configuring a Router as a Stateful DHCPv6 Server

Configuring a stateful DHCPv6 server is similar to configuring a stateless server. The most significant difference is that a stateful server also includes IPv6 addressing information similar to a DHCPv4 server.

Step 1. Enable IPv6 Routing

As shown in Figure 1, the **ipv6 unicast-routing** command is required to enable IPv6 routing. This command is not necessary for the router to be a stateful DHCPv6 server, but it is required for the router to source ICMPv6 RA messages.

Step 2.   Configure a DHCPv6 Pool

The **ipv6 dhcp pool** *pool-name* command creates a pool and enters the router in DHCPv6 configuration mode, which is identified by the Router(config-dhcpv6)# prompt.

Step 3.   Configure Pool Parameters

With stateful DHCPv6 all addressing and other configuration parameters must be assigned by the DHCPv6 server. The **address prefix** command is used to indicate the pool of addresses to be allocated by the server. The **lifetime** option indicates the valid and preferred lease times in seconds. As with stateless DHCPv6, the client uses the source IPv6 address from the packet that contained the RA message.

Other information provided by the stateful DHCPv6 server typically includes DNS server address and the domain name.

Step 4.   Interface Commands

The **ipv6 dhcp server** *pool-name* interface command binds the DHCPv6 pool to the interface. The router responds to stateless DHCPv6 requests on this interface with the information contained in the pool. The M flag needs to be changed from 0 to 1 using the interface command **ipv6 nd managed-config-flag**. This informs the device not to use SLAAC but to obtain IPv6 addressing and all configuration parameters from a stateful DHCPv6 server.

DHCPv6 Stateful Server Example

Figure 2 shows an example of stateful DHCPv6 server commands for a router configured on R1. Notice that a default gateway is not specified because the router will automatically send its own link-local address as the default gateway. Router R3 is configured as a client to help verify the stateful DHCPv6 operations.

Refer to
Online Course
for Illustration

8.2.3.2   Configuring a Router as a Stateful DHCPv6 Client

As shown in the figure, use the **ipv6 enable** interface configuration mode command to allow the router to receive a link-local address to send RS messages and participate in DHCPv6.

The **ipv6 address dhcp** interface configuration mode command enables the router to behave as a DHCPv6 client on this interface.

Refer to
Interactive Graphic
in online course

8.2.3.3   Verifying Stateful DHCPv6

Verifying the Stateful DHCPv6 Server

In Figure 1, the **show ipv6 dhcp pool** command verifies the name of the DHCPv6 pool and its parameters. The number of active clients is 1, which reflects client R3 receiving its IPv6 global unicast address from this server.

The **show ipv6 dhcp binding** command, as shown in Figure 2, displays the automatic binding between the link-local address of the client and the address assigned by the server. FE80::32F7:DFF:FE25:2DE1 is the link-local address of the client. In this example, this is the G0/1 interface of R3. This address is bound to the IPv6 global unicast address, 2001:DB8:CAFE:1:5844:47B2:2603:C171, which was assigned by R1, the DHCPv6 server. This information is maintained by a stateful DHCPv6 server and not by a stateless DHCPv6 server.

Verifying the Stateful DHCPv6 Client

The output from the **show ipv6 interface** command shown in Figure 3 verifies the IPv6 global unicast address on DHCPv6 client R3 that was assigned by the DHCPv6 server. The default router information is not from the DHCPv6 server, but was determined by using the source IPv6 address from the RA message. Although the client does not use the information contained in the RA message, it is able to use the source IPv6 address for its default gateway information.

Use the Syntax Checker in Figure 4 to configure and verify stateless DHCPv6.

Refer to
Interactive Graphic
in online course

8.2.3.4 Configuring a Router as a DHCPv6 Relay Agent

If the DHCPv6 server is located on a different network than the client, then the IPv6 router can be configured as a DHCPv6 relay agent. The configuration of a DHCPv6 relay agent is similar to the configuration of an IPv4 router as a DHCPv4 relay.

Note   Although the configuration of a DHCPv6 relay agent is similar to DHCPv4, IPv6 router or relay agents forward DHCPv6 messages slightly differently than DHCPv4 relays. The messages and the process are beyond the scope of this curriculum.

Figure 1 shows an example topology where a DHCPv6 server is located on the 2001:DB8:CAFE:1::/64 network. The network administrator wants to use this DHCPv6 server as a central, stateful DHCPv6 server to allocate IPv6 addresses to all clients. Therefore, clients on other networks such as PC1 on the 2001:DB8:CAFE:A::/64 network, must communicate with the DHCPv6 server.

DHCPv6 messages from clients are sent to the IPv6 multicast address FF02::1:2. All_ DHCPv6_Relay_Agents_and_Servers address. This address has link-local scope which means routers do not forward these messages. The router must be configured as a DHCPv6 relay agent to enable the DHCPv6 client and server to communicate.

Configuring the DHCPv6 Relay Agent

As shown in Figure 2, a DHCPv6 relay agent is configured using the **ipv6 dhcp relay destination** command. This command is configured on the interface facing the DHCPv6 client using the address of the DHCPv6 server as the destination.

The **show ipv6 dhcp interface** command verifies the G0/0 interface is in relay mode with 2001:DB8:CAFE:1::6 configured as the DHCPv6 server.

Using the Syntax Checker in Figure 3, configure the DHCPv6 relay commands on the correct router so that PC3 can receive IPv6 addressing information from the DHCPv6 server. Refer to Figure 1 to view the network topology.

Refer to
Lab Activity
for this chapter

8.2.3.5 Lab – Configuring Stateless and Stateful DHCPv6

In this lab, you will complete the following objectives:

- Part 1: Build the Network and Configure Basic Device Settings

- Part 2: Configure the Network for SLAAC

- Part 3: Configure the Network for Stateless DHCPv6

- Part 4: Configure the Network for Stateful DHCPv6

8.2.4   Troubleshoot DHCPv6

Refer to
Online Course
for Illustration

8.2.4.1   Troubleshooting Tasks

Troubleshooting DHCPv6 is similar to troubleshooting DHCPv4.

Troubleshooting Task 1: Resolve Conflicts

Similar to IPv4 addresses, an IPv6 address lease can expire on a client that still needs to connect to the network. The **show ipv6 dhcp conflict** command displays any address conflicts logged by the stateful DHCPv6 server. If an IPv6 address conflict is detected, the client typically removes the address and generates a new address using either SLAAC or stateful DHCPv6.

Troubleshooting Task 2: Verify Allocation Method

The **show ipv6 interface** *interface* command can be used to verify the method of address allocation indicated in the RA message as indicated by the settings of the M and O flags. This information is displayed in the last lines of the output. If a client is not receiving its IPv6 address information from a stateful DHCPv6 server, it could be due to incorrect M and O flags in the RA message.

Troubleshooting Task 3: Test with a Static IPv6 Address

When troubleshooting any DHCP issue, whether it is DHCPv4 or DHCPv6, network connectivity can be verified by configuring a static IP address on a client workstation. In the case of IPv6, if the workstation is unable to reach network resources with a statically configured IPv6 address, the root cause of the problem is not SLAAC or DHCPv6. At this point, network connectivity troubleshooting is required.

Troubleshooting Task 4: Verify Switch Port Configuration

If the DHCPv6 client is unable to obtain information from a DHCPv6 server, verify that the switch port is enabled and is operating correctly.

Note   If there is a switch between the client and the DHCPv6 server, and the client is unable to obtain the DHCP configuration, switch port configuration issues may be the cause. These causes may include issues related to trunking, channeling, or spanning tree. PortFast and edge port configurations resolve the most common DHCPv6 client issues that occur with an initial installation of a Cisco switch.

Troubleshooting Task 5: Test DHCPv6 Operation on the Same Subnet or VLAN

If the stateless or stateful DHCPv6 server is functioning correctly, but is on a different IPv6 network or VLAN than the client, the problem may be with the DHCPv6 relay agent. The client facing interface on the router must be configured with the **ipv6 dhcp relay destination** command.

Refer to
Interactive Graphic
in online course

8.2.4.2   Verify Router DHCPv6 Configuration

The router configurations for stateless and stateful DHCPv6 services have many similarities but also include significant differences. Figure 1 shows the configuration commands for both types of DHCPv6 services.

Stateful DHCPv6

A router configured for stateful DHCPv6 services has the **address prefix** command to provide addressing information.

For stateful DHCPv6 services the **ipv6 nd managed-config-flag** interface configuration mode command is used. In this instance, the client ignores the addressing information in the RA message and communicates with a DHCPv6 server for both addressing and other information.

Stateless DHCPv6

For stateless DHCPv6 services the **ipv6 nd other-config-flag** interface configuration mode command is used. This informs the device to use SLAAC for addressing information and a stateless DHCPv6 server for other configuration parameters.

The **show ipv6 interface** command can be used to view the current configuration to determine the allocation method. As shown in Figure 2, the last line of the output indicates how clients obtain addresses and other parameters.

Refer to
Online Course
for Illustration

8.2.4.3   Debugging DHCPv6

When the router is configured as a stateless or stateful DHCPv6 server, the **debug ipv6 dhcp detail** command is useful to verify the receipt and transmission of DHCPv6 messages. As shown in the figure, a stateful DHCPv6 router has received a SOLICIT message from a client. The router is using the addressing information in its IPV6-STATEFUL pool for binding information.

Refer to
Lab Activity
for this chapter

8.2.4.4   Lab – Troubleshooting DHCPv6

In this lab, you will complete the following objectives:

- Part 1: Build the Network and Configure Basic Device Settings
- Part 2: Troubleshoot IPv6 Connectivity
- Part 3: Troubleshoot Stateless DHCPv6

8.3 Summary

Refer to **Online Course** for Illustration

8.3.1.1 Class Activity – IoE and DHCP

This chapter presents the concept of using the DHCP process in a small- to medium-sized business network; however, DHCP also has other uses!

With the advent of the Internet of Everything (IoE), any device in your home capable of wired or wireless connectivity to a network will be able to be accessed from just about anywhere.

Using Packet Tracer for this modeling activity, perform the following tasks:

- Configure a Cisco 1941 router (or DHCP-server-capable ISR device) for IPv4 or IPv6 DHCP addressing.

- Think of five devices in your home you would like to receive IP addresses from the router's DHCP service. Set the end devices to claim DHCP addresses from the DHCP server.

- Show output validating that each end device secures an IP address from the server. Save your output information via a screen capture program or use the **PrtScrn** key command.

- Present your findings to a fellow classmate or to the class.

Refer to **Packet Tracer Activity** for this chapter

8.3.1.2 Packet Tracer – Skills Integration Challenge

Scenario

In this culminating activity, you will configure VLANs, trunks, DHCPv4 servers, DHCPv4 relay agents, and configure a router as a DHCP client.

Refer to **Online Course** for Illustration

8.3.1.3 DHCP

All nodes on a network require a unique IP address to communicate with other devices. The static assignment of IP addressing information on a large network results in an administrative burden that can be eliminated by using DHCPv4 and DHCPv6 to dynamically assign IPv4 and IPv6 addressing information, respectively.

- DHCPv4 dynamically assigns, or leases, an IPv4 address from a pool of addresses for a limited period of time, as configured on the server, or until the client no longer needs the address.

DHCPv4 involves the exchange of several different packets between the DHCPv4 server and the DHCPv4 client resulting in the lease of valid addressing information for a predefined period of time.

Messages originating from the client (DHCPDISCOVER, DHCPREQUEST) are broadcast to allow all DHCPv4 servers on the network to hear the client request for, and receipt of, addressing information. Messages originating from the DHCPv4 server (DHCPOFFER, DHCPACK) are sent as unicasts directly to the client.

There are two methods available for the dynamic configuration of IPv6 global unicast addresses.

- Stateless Address Autoconfiguration (SLAAC)
- Dynamic Host Configuration Protocol for IPv6 (Stateful DHCPv6)

With stateless autoconfiguration, the client uses information provided by the IPv6 RA message to automatically select and configure a unique IPv6 address. The stateless DHCPv6 option informs the client to use the information in the RA message for addressing, but additional configuration parameters are available from a DHCPv6 server.

Stateful DHCPv6 is similar to DHCPv4. In this case, the RA message informs the client not to use the information in the RA message. All addressing information and DNS configuration information is obtained from a stateful DHCPv6 server. The DHCPv6 server maintains IPv6 state information similar to a DHCPv4 server allocating addresses for IPv4.

If the DHCP server is located on a different network segment than the DHCP client then it is necessary to configure a relay agent. The relay agent forwards specific broadcast or multicast messages, including DHCP messages, originating from a host on a LAN segment and destined for a specific server located on a different LAN segment.

Troubleshooting issues with DHCPv4 and DHCPv6 involve the same tasks:

- Resolve Address Conflicts
- Verify Physical Connectivity
- Test Connectivity using a Static IP Address
- Verify Switch Port Configuration
- Test Operation on the Same Subnet or VLAN

Go to the online course to take the quiz and exam.

Chapter 8 Quiz

This quiz is designed to provide an additional opportunity to practice the skills and knowledge presented in the chapter and to prepare for the chapter exam. You will be allowed multiple attempts and the grade does not appear in the gradebook.

Chapter 8 Exam

The chapter exam assesses your knowledge of the chapter content.

Your Chapter Notes

NAT for IPv4

9.0 Introduction

Refer to
Online Course
for Illustration

9.0.1.1 NAT for IPv4

All public IPv4 addresses that transverse the Internet must be registered with a Regional Internet Registry (RIR). Organizations can lease public addresses from a service provider. The registered holder of a public IP address can assign that address to a network device.

With a theoretical maximum of 4.3 billion addresses, IPv4 address space is severely limited. When Bob Kahn and Vint Cerf first developed the suite of TCP/IP protocols including IPv4 in 1981, they never envisioned what the Internet would become. At the time, the personal computer was mostly a curiosity for hobbyists and the World Wide Web was still more than a decade away.

With the proliferation of personal computing and the advent of the World Wide Web, it soon became obvious that 4.3 billion IPv4 addresses would not be enough. The long term solution was IPv6, but more immediate solutions to address exhaustion were required. For the short term, several solutions were implemented by the IETF including Network Address Translation (NAT) and RFC 1918 private IPv4 addresses. The chapter discusses how NAT, combined with the use of private address space, is used to both conserve and more efficiently use IPv4 addresses to provide networks of all sizes access to the Internet. This chapter covers:

- NAT characteristics, terminology, and general operations
- The different types of NAT, including static NAT, dynamic NAT, and NAT with overloading
- The benefits and disadvantages of NAT
- The configuration, verification, and analysis of static NAT, dynamic NAT, and NAT with overloading
- How port forwarding can be used to access internal devices from the Internet
- Troubleshooting NAT using **show** and **debug** commands
- How NAT for IPv6 is used to translate between IPv6 addresses and IPv4 addresses

Refer to
Online Course
for Illustration

9.0.1.2 Conceptual NAT

Scenario

You work for a large university or school system.

Because you are the network administrator, many professors, administrative workers, and other network administrators need your assistance with their networks on a daily basis. They call you at all working hours of the day and, because of the number of telephone calls, you cannot complete your regular network administration tasks.

You need to find a way to limit when you take calls and from whom. You also need to mask your telephone number so that when you call someone, another number is displayed to the recipient.

This scenario describes a very common problem for most small- to medium-sized businesses. Visit, "How Network Address Translation Works", located here, to view more information about how the digital world handles these types of workday interruptions.

Use the PDF provided accompanying this activity to reflect further on how a process, known as NAT, could be the answer to this scenario's challenge.

9.1   NAT Operation

9.1.1   NAT Characteristics

Refer to
Interactive Graphic
in online course

9.1.1.1   IPv4 Private Address Space

There are not enough public IPv4 addresses to assign a unique address to each device connected to the Internet. Networks are commonly implemented using private IPv4 addresses, as defined in RFC 1918. Figure 1 shows the range of addresses included in RFC 1918. It is very likely that the computer that you use to view this course is assigned a private address.

These private addresses are used within an organization or site to allow devices to communicate locally. However, because these addresses do not identify any single company or organization, private IPv4 addresses cannot be routed over the Internet. To allow a device with a private IPv4 address to access devices and resources outside of the local network, the private address must first be translated to a public address.

As shown in Figure 2, NAT provides the translation of private addresses to public addresses. This allows a device with a private IPv4 address to access resources outside of their private network, such as those found on the Internet. NAT combined with private IPv4 addresses, has proven to be a useful method of preserving public IPv4 addresses. A single, public IPv4 address can be shared by hundreds, even thousands of devices, each configured with a unique private IPv4 address.

Without NAT, the exhaustion of the IPv4 address space would have occurred well before the year 2000. However, NAT has certain limitations, which will be explored later in this chapter. The solution to the exhaustion of IPv4 address space and the limitations of NAT is the eventual transition to IPv6.

Refer to
Online Course
for Illustration

9.1.1.2   What is NAT?

NAT has many uses, but its primary use is to conserve public IPv4 addresses. It does this by allowing networks to use private IPv4 addresses internally and providing translation to a public address only when needed. NAT has an added benefit of adding a degree of privacy and security to a network, because it hides internal IPv4 addresses from outside networks.

NAT-enabled routers can be configured with one or more valid public IPv4 addresses. These public addresses are known as the NAT pool. When an internal device sends traffic out of the network, the NAT-enabled router translates the internal IPv4 address of the device to a public address from the NAT pool. To outside devices, all traffic entering and exiting the network appears to have a public IPv4 address from the provided pool of addresses.

A NAT router typically operates at the border of a stub network. A stub network is a network that has a single connection to its neighboring network, one way in and one way out of the network. In the example in the figure, R2 is a border router. As seen from the ISP, R2 forms a stub network.

When a device inside the stub network wants to communicate with a device outside of its network, the packet is forwarded to the border router. The border router performs the NAT process, translating the internal private address of the device to a public, outside, routable address.

Note The connection to the ISP may use a private address or a public address that is shared among customers. For the purposes of this chapter, a public address is shown.

Refer to **Online Course** for Illustration

9.1.1.3 NAT Terminology

In NAT terminology, the inside network is the set of networks that is subject to translation. The outside network refers to all other networks.

When using NAT, IPv4 addresses have different designations based on whether they are on the private network, or on the public network (Internet), and whether the traffic is incoming or outgoing.

NAT includes four types of addresses:

- Inside local address
- Inside global address
- Outside local address
- Outside global address

When determining which type of address is used, it is important to remember that NAT terminology is always applied from the perspective of the device with the translated address:

- **Inside address** - The address of the device which is being translated by NAT.
- **Outside address** - The address of the destination device.

NAT also uses the concept of local or global with respect to addresses:

- **Local address** - A local address is any address that appears on the inside portion of the network.
- **Global address** - A global address is any address that appears on the outside portion of the network.

In the figure, PC1 has an inside local address of 192.168.10.10. From the perspective of PC1, the web server has an outside address of 209.165.201.1. When packets are sent from PC1 to the global address of the web server, the inside local address of PC1 is translated to 209.165.200.226 (inside global address). The address of the outside device is not typically translated, because that address is usually a public IPv4 address.

Notice that PC1 has different local and global addresses, whereas the web server has the same public IPv4 address for both. From the perspective of the web server, traffic originating from PC1 appears to have come from 209.165.200.226, the inside global address.

The NAT router, R2 in the figure, is the demarcation point between the inside and outside networks and as between local and global addresses.

Refer to
Online Course
for Illustration

9.1.1.4   NAT Terminology (Cont.)

The terms, inside and outside, are combined with the terms local and global to refer to specific addresses. In the figure, router R2 has been configured to provide NAT. It has a pool of public addresses to assign to inside hosts.

- **Inside local address** - The address of the source as seen from inside the network. In the figure, the IPv4 address 192.168.10.10 is assigned to PC1. This is the inside local address of PC1.

- **Inside global address** - The address of source as seen from the outside network. In the figure, when traffic from PC1 is sent to the web server at 209.165.201.1, R2 translates the inside local address to an inside global address. In this case, R2 changes the IPv4 source address from 192.168.10.10 to 209.165.200.226. In NAT terminology, the inside local address of 192.168.10.10 is translated to the inside global address of 209.165.200.226.

- **Outside global address** - The address of the destination as seen from the outside network. It is a globally routable IPv4 address assigned to a host on the Internet. For example, the web server is reachable at IPv4 address 209.165.201.1. Most often the outside local and outside global addresses are the same.

- **Outside local address** - The address of the destination as seen from the inside network. In this example, PC1 sends traffic to the web server at the IPv4 address 209.165.201.1. While uncommon, this address could be different than the globally routable address of the destination.

The figure shows how traffic is addressed that is sent from an internal PC to an external web server, across the NAT-enabled router. It also shows how return traffic is initially addressed and translated.

Note   The use of the outside local address is outside the scope of this course.

Refer to **Video**
in online course

9.1.1.5   How NAT Works

In this example, PC1 with private address 192.168.10.10 wants to communicate with an outside web server with public address 209.165.201.1.

Click the Play button in the figure to start the animation.

PC1 sends a packet addressed to the web server. The packet is forwarded by R1 to R2.

When the packet arrives at R2, the NAT-enabled router for the network, R2 reads the source IPv4 address of the packet to determine if the packet matches the criteria specified for translation.

In this case, the source IPv4 address does match the criteria and is translated from 192.168.10.10 (inside local address) to 209.165.200.226 (inside global address). R2 adds this mapping of the local to global address to the NAT table.

R2 sends the packet with the translated source address toward the destination.

The web server responds with a packet addressed to the inside global address of PC1 (209.165.200.226).

R2 receives the packet with destination address 209.165.200.226. R2 checks the NAT table and finds an entry for this mapping. R2 uses this information and translates the inside global address (209.165.200.226) to the inside local address (192.168.10.10), and the packet is forwarded toward PC1.

Refer to
Interactive Graphic
in online course

9.1.1.6   Activity – Identify the NAT Terminology

9.1.2   Types of NAT

Refer to
Online Course
for Illustration

9.1.2.1   Static NAT

There are three types of NAT translation:

- **Static address translation (static NAT)** - One-to-one address mapping between local and global addresses.

- **Dynamic address translation (dynamic NAT)** - Many-to-many address mapping between local and global addresses. Translations are made on an as-available basis; for example, if there are 100 inside local addresses and 10 inside global addresses, then at any given time only 10 of the 100 inside local addresses can be translated. This limitation of dynamic NAT makes it much less useful for production networks than port address translation.

- **Port Address Translation (PAT)** - Many-to-one address mapping between local and global addresses. This method is also known as overloading (NAT overloading). For example, if there are 100 inside local addresses and 10 inside global addresses, PAT uses ports as an additional parameter to provide a multiplier effect, making it possible to reuse any one of the 10 inside global addresses up to 65,536 times (depending on whether the flow is based on UDP, TCP, or ICMP).

Static NAT

Static NAT uses a one-to-one mapping of local and global addresses. These mappings are configured by the network administrator and remain constant.

In the figure, R2 is configured with static mappings for the inside local addresses of Svr1, PC2, and PC3. When these devices send traffic to the Internet, their inside local addresses are translated to the configured inside global addresses. To outside networks, these devices have public IPv4 addresses.

Static NAT is particularly useful for web servers or devices that must have a consistent address that is accessible from the Internet, such as a company web server. It is also useful for devices that must be accessible by authorized personnel when offsite, but not by the general public on the Internet. For example, a network administrator from PC4 can SSH to Svr1's inside global address (209.165.200.226). R2 translates this inside global address to the inside local address and connects the administrator's session to Svr1.

Static NAT requires that enough public addresses are available to satisfy the total number of simultaneous user sessions.

Refer to **Interactive Graphic** in online course

9.1.2.2   Dynamic NAT

Dynamic NAT uses a pool of public addresses and assigns them on a first-come, first-served basis. When an inside device requests access to an outside network, dynamic NAT assigns an available public IPv4 address from the pool.

In the figure, PC3 has accessed the Internet using the first available address in the dynamic NAT pool. The other addresses are still available for use. Similar to static NAT, dynamic NAT requires that enough public addresses are available to satisfy the total number of simultaneous user sessions.

Refer to **Video** in online course

9.1.2.3   Port Address Translation (PAT)

Port Address Translation (PAT), also known as NAT overload, maps multiple private IPv4 addresses to a single public IPv4 address or a few addresses. This is what most home routers do. The ISP assigns one address to the router, yet several members of the household can simultaneously access the Internet. This is the most common form of NAT.

With PAT, multiple addresses can be mapped to one or to a few addresses, because each private address is also tracked by a port number. When a device initiates a TCP/IP session, it generates a TCP or UDP source port value or a specially assigned query ID for ICMP, to uniquely identify the session. When the NAT router receives a packet from the client, it uses its source port number to uniquely identify the specific NAT translation.

PAT ensures that devices use a different TCP port number for each session with a server on the Internet. When a response comes back from the server, the source port number, which becomes the destination port number on the return trip, determines to which device the router forwards the packets. The PAT process also validates that the incoming packets were requested, thus adding a degree of security to the session.

Click the Play and Pause buttons in the figure to control the animation.

The animation illustrates the PAT process. PAT adds unique source port numbers to the inside global address to distinguish between translations.

As R2 processes each packet, it uses a port number (1331 and 1555, in this example) to identify the device from which the packet originated. The source address (SA) is the inside local address with the TCP/IP assigned port number added. The destination address (DA) is the outside local address with the service port number added. In this example, the service port is 80, which is HTTP.

For the source address, R2 translates the inside local address to an inside global address with the port number added. The destination address is not changed, but is now referred to as the outside global IPv4 address. When the web server replies, the path is reversed.

Refer to **Video** in online course

9.1.2.4   Next Available Port

In the previous example, the client port numbers, 1331 and 1555, did not change at the NAT-enabled router. This is not a very likely scenario, because there is a good chance that these port numbers may have already been attached to other active sessions.

PAT attempts to preserve the original source port. However, if the original source port is already used, PAT assigns the first available port number starting from the beginning of the appropriate port group 0–511, 512–1,023, or 1,024–65,535. When there are no more ports available and there is more than one external address in the address pool, PAT moves to the next address to try to allocate the original source port. This process continues until there are no more available ports or external IPv4 addresses.

Click the Play button in the figure to view PAT operation. In this example, PAT has assigned the next available port (1445) to the second host address.

In the animation, the hosts have chosen the same port number 1444. This is acceptable for the inside address, because the hosts have unique private IPv4 addresses. However, at the NAT router, the port numbers must be changed; otherwise, packets from two different hosts would exit R2 with the same source address. This example assumes that the first 420 ports in the range 1,024-65,535 are already in use, so the next available port number, 1445, is used.

Refer to **Online Course** for Illustration

9.1.2.5   Comparing NAT and PAT

Summarizing the differences between NAT and PAT helps your understanding of each.

As the figure shows, NAT translates IPv4 addresses on a 1:1 basis between private IPv4 addresses and public IPv4 addresses. However, PAT modifies both the address and the port number.

NAT forwards incoming packets to their inside destination by referring to the incoming source IPv4 address given by the host on the public network. With PAT, there is generally only one or a very few publicly exposed IPv4 addresses. Incoming packets from the public network are routed to their destinations on the private network by referring to a table in the NAT router. This table tracks public and private port pairs. This is called connection tracking.

Packets without a Layer 4 Segment

What about IPv4 packets carrying data other than a TCP or UDP segment? These packets do not contain a Layer 4 port number. PAT translates most common protocols carried by IPv4 that do not use TCP or UDP as a transport layer protocol. The most common of these is ICMPv4. Each of these types of protocols is handled differently by PAT. For example, ICMPv4 query messages, echo requests, and echo replies include a Query ID. ICMPv4 uses the Query ID to identify an echo request with its corresponding echo reply. The Query ID is incremented with each echo request sent. PAT uses the Query ID instead of a Layer 4 port number.

Note   Other ICMPv4 messages do not use the Query ID. These messages and other protocols that do not use TCP or UDP port numbers vary and are beyond the scope of this curriculum.

Refer to **Packet Tracer Activity** for this chapter

9.1.2.6   Packet Tracer - Investigating NAT Operation

You know that as a frame travels across a network, the MAC addresses change. But IPv4 addresses can also change when a packet is forwarded by a device configure with NAT. In this activity we will see what happens to IPv4 addresses during the NAT process.

9.1.3   NAT Advantages

Refer to **Online Course** for Illustration

9.1.3.1   Advantages of NAT

NAT provides many benefits, including:

- NAT conserves the legally registered addressing scheme by allowing the privatization of intranets. NAT conserves addresses through application port-level multiplexing. With NAT overload, internal hosts can share a single public IPv4 address for all external communications. In this type of configuration, very few external addresses are required to support many internal hosts.

- NAT increases the flexibility of connections to the public network. Multiple pools, backup pools, and load-balancing pools can be implemented to ensure reliable public network connections.

- NAT provides consistency for internal network addressing schemes. On a network not using private IPv4 addresses and NAT, changing the public IPv4 address scheme requires the readdressing of all hosts on the existing network. The costs of readdressing hosts can be significant. NAT allows the existing private IPv4 address scheme to remain while allowing for easy change to a new public addressing scheme. This means an organization could change ISPs and not need to change any of its inside clients.

- NAT hides user IPv4 addresses. Using RFC 1918 IPv4 addresses, NAT provides the side effect of hiding users and other devices' IPv4 addresses. Some people consider this a security feature, however most experts agree that NAT does not provide security. A stateful firewall is what provides security on the edge of the network.

Refer to **Online Course** for Illustration

9.1.3.2   Disadvantages of NAT

NAT does have some drawbacks. The fact that hosts on the Internet appear to communicate directly with the NAT-enabled device, rather than with the actual host inside the private network, creates a number of issues.

One disadvantage of using NAT is related to network performance, particularly for real time protocols such as VoIP. NAT increases forwarding delays because the translation of each IPv4 address within the packet headers takes time. The first packet is always process-switched going through the slower path. The router must look at every packet to decide whether it needs translation. The router must alter the IPv4 header, and possibly alter the TCP or UDP header. The IPv4 header checksum, along with the TCP or UDP checksum must be recalculated each time a translation is made. Remaining packets go through the fast-switched path if a cache entry exists; otherwise, they too are delayed.

Another disadvantage of using NAT is that end-to-end addressing is lost. Many Internet protocols and applications depend on end-to-end addressing from the source to the destination. Some applications do not work with NAT. For example, some security applications, such as digital signatures, fail because the source IPv4 address changes before reaching the destination. Applications that use physical addresses, instead of a qualified domain name, do not reach destinations that are translated across the NAT router. Sometimes, this problem can be avoided by implementing static NAT mappings.

End-to-end IPv4 traceability is also lost. It becomes much more difficult to trace packets that undergo numerous packet address changes over multiple NAT hops, making troubleshooting challenging.

Using NAT also complicates the use of tunneling protocols, such as IPsec, because NAT modifies values in the headers, causing integrity checks to fail.

Services that require the initiation of TCP connections from the outside network, or stateless protocols, such as those using UDP, can be disrupted. Unless the NAT router has been configured to support such protocols, incoming packets cannot reach their destination. Some protocols can accommodate one instance of NAT between participating hosts (passive mode FTP, for example), but fail when both systems are separated from the Internet by NAT.

9.2   Configure NAT

9.2.1   Configuring Static NAT

Refer to
Interactive Graphic
in online course

9.2.1.1   Configure Static NAT

Static NAT is a one-to-one mapping between an inside address and an outside address. Static NAT allows external devices to initiate connections to internal devices using the statically assigned public address. For instance, an internal web server may be mapped to a specific inside global address so that it is accessible from outside networks.

Figure 1 shows an inside network containing a web server with a private IPv4 address. Router R2 is configured with static NAT to allow devices on the outside network (Internet) to access the web server. The client on the outside network accesses the web server using a public IPv4 address. Static NAT translates the public IPv4 address to the private IPv4 address.

There are two basic tasks when configuring static NAT translations.

Step 1.   The first task is to create a mapping between the inside local address and the inside global addresses. For example, the 192.168.10.254 inside local address and the 209.165.201.5 inside global address in Figure 1 are configured as a static NAT translation.

Step 2.   After the mapping is configured, the interfaces participating in the translation are configured as inside or outside relative to NAT. In the example, the Serial 0/0/0 interface of R2 is an inside interface and Serial 0/1/0 is an outside interface.

Packets arriving on the inside interface of R2 (Serial 0/0/0) from the configured inside local IPv4 address (192.168.10.254) are translated and then forwarded towards the outside network. Packets arriving on the outside interface of R2 (Serial 0/1/0), that are addressed to the configured inside global IPv4 address (209.165.201.5), are translated to the inside local address (192.168.10.254) and then forwarded to the inside network.

Figure 2 outlines the commands needed to configure static NAT.

Figure 3 shows the commands needed on R2 to create a static NAT mapping to the web server in the example topology. With the configuration shown, R2 translates packets from the web server with address 192.168.10.254 to public IPv4 address 209.165.201.5. The Internet client directs web requests to the public IPv4 address 209.165.201.5. R2 forwards that traffic to the web server at 192.168.10.254.

Use the Syntax Checker in Figure 4 to configure an additional static NAT entry on R2.

Refer to
Interactive Graphic
in online course

9.2.1.2   Analyzing Static NAT

Using the previous configuration, the figure illustrates the static NAT translation process between the client and the web server. Usually static translations are used when clients on the outside network (Internet) need to reach servers on the inside (internal) network.

1. The client wants to open a connection to the web server. The client sends a packet to the web server using the public IPv4 destination address of 209.165.201.5. This is the inside global address of the web server.

2. The first packet that R2 receives from the client on its NAT outside interface causes R2 to check its NAT table. The destination IPv4 address is located in the NAT table and is translated.

3. R2 replaces the inside global address of 209.165.201.5 with the inside local address of 192.168.10.254. R2 then forwards the packet towards the web server.

4. The web server receives the packet and responds to the client using the inside local address, 192.168.10.254.

5a. R2 receives the packet from the web server on its NAT inside interface with source address of the inside local address of the web server, 192.168.10.254.

5b. R2 checks the NAT table for a translation for the inside local address. The address is found in the NAT table. R2 translates the source address to the inside global address of 209.165.201.5 and forwards the packet toward the client.

6. The client receives the packet and continues the conversation. The NAT router performs Steps 2 to 5b for each packet. (Step 6 is not shown in the figure.)

Refer to
Interactive Graphic
in online course

9.2.1.3   Verifying Static NAT

A useful command to verify NAT operation is **show ip nat translations**. This command shows active NAT translations. Static translations, unlike dynamic translations, are always in the NAT table. Figure 1 shows the output from this command using the previous configuration example. Because the example is a static NAT configuration, the translation is always present in the NAT table regardless of any active communications. If the command is issued during an active session, the output also indicates the address of the outside device as shown in Figure 1.

Another useful command is **show ip nat statistics**. As shown in Figure 2, the **show ip nat statistics** command displays information about the total number of active translations, NAT configuration parameters, the number of addresses in the pool, and the number of addresses that have been allocated.

To verify that the NAT translation is working, it is best to clear statistics from any past translations using the **clear ip nat statistics** command before testing.

Prior to any communications with the web server, the **show ip nat statistics** command shows no current hits. After the client establishes a session with the web server, the **show ip nat statistics** displays an increase to five hits on the Inside (Serial0/0/0) interface. This verifies that the static NAT translation is taking place on R2.

Refer to **Packet Tracer Activity** for this chapter

9.2.1.4 Packet Tracer – Configuring Static NAT

In IPv4 configured networks, clients and servers use private addressing. Before packets with private addressing can cross then Internet, they need to be translated to public addressing. Servers that are accessed from outside the organization are usually assigned both a public and a private static IPv4 address. In this activity, you will configure static NAT so that outside devices can access and inside server at its public address.

9.2.2 Configure Dynamic NAT

Refer to **Online Course** for Illustration

9.2.2.1 Dynamic NAT Operation

While static NAT provides a permanent mapping between an inside local address and an inside global address, dynamic NAT allows the automatic mapping of inside local addresses to inside global addresses. These inside global addresses are typically public IPv4 addresses. Dynamic NAT uses a group, or pool of public IPv4 addresses for translation.

Dynamic NAT, like static NAT, requires the configuration of the inside and outside interfaces participating in NAT. However, where static NAT creates a permanent mapping to a single address, dynamic NAT uses a pool of addresses.

Note Translating between public and private IPv4 addresses is by far the most common use of NAT. However, NAT translations can occur between any pair of addresses.

The example topology shown in the figure has an inside network using addresses from the RFC 1918 private address space. Attached to router R1 are two LANs, 192.168.10.0/24 and 192.168.11.0/24. Router R2, the border router, is configured for dynamic NAT using a pool of public IPv4 addresses 209.165.200.226 through 209.165.200.240.

The pool of public IPv4 addresses (inside global address pool) is available to any device on the inside network on a first-come first-served basis. With dynamic NAT, a single inside address is translated to a single outside address. With this type of translation there must be enough addresses in the pool to accommodate all the inside devices needing access to the outside network at the same time. If all of the addresses in the pool have been used, a device must wait for an available address before it can access the outside network.

Refer to **Interactive Graphic** in online course

9.2.2.2 Configuring Dynamic NAT

Figure 1 shows the steps and the commands used to configure dynamic NAT.

Step 1. Define the pool of addresses that will be used for translation using the **ip nat pool** command. This pool of addresses is typically a group of public addresses. The addresses are defined by indicating the starting IPv4 address and the ending IPv4 address of the pool. The **netmask** or **prefix-length** keyword indicates which address bits belong to the network and which bits belong to the host for the range of addresses.

Step 2. Configure a standard ACL to identify (permit) only those addresses that are to be translated. An ACL that is too permissive can lead to unpredictable results. Remember there is an implicit **deny all** statement at the end of each ACL.

Step 3. Bind the ACL to the pool. The **ip nat inside source list** *access-list-number* **pool** *pool name* command is used to bind the ACL to the pool. This configuration is used by the router to identify which devices (**list**) receive which addresses (**pool**).

Step 4. Identify which interfaces are inside, in relation to NAT; that is, any interface that connects to the inside network.

Step 5. Identify which interfaces are outside, in relation to NAT; that is, any interface that connects to the outside network.

Figure 2 shows an example topology and configuration. This configuration allows translation for all hosts on the 192.168.0.0/16 network, which includes the 192.168.10.0 and 192.168.11.0 LANs, when they generate traffic that enters S0/0/0 and exits S0/1/0. These hosts are translated to an available address in the pool in the range 209.165.200.226 - 209.165.200.240.

Figure 3 shows the topology used for the Syntax Checker configuration. Use the Syntax Checker in Figure 4 to configure dynamic NAT on R2.

> Refer to
> **Interactive Graphic**
> in online course

9.2.2.3   Analyzing Dynamic NAT

Using the previous configuration, the figures illustrate the dynamic NAT translation process between two clients and the web server:

In Figure 1, the traffic flow from inside to outside is shown:

1. The hosts with the source IPv4 addresses (192.168.10.10 (PC1) and 192.168.11.10 (PC2)) send packets requesting a connection to the server at the public IPv4 address (209.165.200.254).

2. R2 receives the first packet from host 192.168.10.10. Because this packet was received on an interface configured as an inside NAT interface, R2 checks the NAT configuration to determine if this packet should be translated. The ACL permits this packet, so R2 will translate the packet. R2 checks its NAT table. Because there is no translation entry for this IPv4 address, R2 determines that the source address 192.168.10.10 must be translated dynamically. R2 selects an available global address from the dynamic address pool and creates a translation entry, 209.165.200.226. The original source IPv4 address (192.168.10.10) is the inside local address and the translated address is the inside global address (209.165.200.226) in the NAT table.

   For the second host, 192.168.11.10, R2 repeats the procedure, selects the next available global address from the dynamic address pool, and creates a second translation entry, 209.165.200.227.

3. R2 replaces the inside local source address of PC1, 192.168.10.10, with the translated inside global address of 209.165.200.226 and forwards the packet. The same process occurs for the packet from PC2 using the translated address for PC2 (209.165.200.227).

In Figure 2, the traffic flow from outside to inside is shown:

4. The server receives the packet from PC1 and responds using the IPv4 destination address of 209.165.200.226. When the server receives the second packet, it responds to PC2 using the IPv4 destination address of 209.165.200.227.

5a. When R2 receives the packet with the destination IPv4 address of 209.165.200.226; it performs a NAT table lookup. Using the mapping from the table, R2 translates the address back to the inside local address (192.168.10.10) and forwards the packet toward PC1.

5b. When R2 receives the packet with the destination IPv4 address of 209.165.200.227; it performs a NAT table lookup. Using the mapping from the table, R2 translates the address back to the inside local address (192.168.11.10) and forwards the packet toward PC2.

6. PC1 at 192.168.10.10 and PC2 at 192.168.11.10 receive the packets and continue the conversation. The router performs Steps 2 to 5 for each packet. (Step 6 is not shown in the figures.)

Refer to
Interactive Graphic
in online course

9.2.2.4 Verifying Dynamic NAT

The output of the **show ip nat translations** command shown in Figure 1 displays the details of the two previous NAT assignments. The command displays all static translations that have been configured and any dynamic translations that have been created by traffic.

Adding the **verbose** keyword displays additional information about each translation, including how long ago the entry was created and used.

By default, translation entries time out after 24 hours, unless the timers have been reconfigured with the **ip nat translation timeout** *timeout-seconds* command in global configuration mode.

To clear dynamic entries before the timeout has expired, use the **clear ip nat translation** privileged EXEC mode command (Figure 2). It is useful to clear the dynamic entries when testing the NAT configuration. As shown in the table, this command can be used with keywords and variables to control which entries are cleared. Specific entries can be cleared to avoid disrupting active sessions. Use the **clear ip nat translation *** privileged EXEC command to clear all translations from the table.

Note Only the dynamic translations are cleared from the table. Static translations cannot be cleared from the translation table.

In Figure 3, the **show ip nat statistics** command displays information about the total number of active translations, NAT configuration parameters, the number of addresses in the pool, and how many of the addresses have been allocated.

Alternatively, use the **show running-config** command and look for NAT, ACL, interface, or pool commands with the required values. Examine these carefully and correct any errors discovered.

Refer to **Packet Tracer Activity** for this chapter

9.2.2.5   Packet Tracer – Configuring Dynamic NAT

In this Packet Tracer, you will complete the following objectives:

- Part 1: Configure Dynamic NAT
- Part 2: Verify NAT Implementation

Refer to **Lab Activity** for this chapter

9.2.2.6   Lab – Configuring Dynamic and Static NAT

In this lab, you will complete the following objectives:

- Part 1: Build the Network and Verify Connectivity
- Part 2: Configure and Verify Static NAT
- Part 3: Configure and Verify Dynamic NAT

9.2.3   Configure PAT

Refer to **Interactive Graphic** in online course

9.2.3.1   Configuring PAT: Address Pool

PAT (also called NAT overload) conserves addresses in the inside global address pool by allowing the router to use one inside global address for many inside local addresses. In other words, a single public IPv4 address can be used for hundreds, even thousands of internal private IPv4 addresses. When this type of translation is configured, the router maintains enough information from higher-level protocols, TCP or UDP port numbers, for example, to translate the inside global address back into the correct inside local address. When multiple inside local addresses map to one inside global address, the TCP or UDP port numbers of each inside host distinguish between the local addresses.

Note   The total number of internal addresses that can be translated to one external address could theoretically be as high as 65,536 per IPv4 address. However, the number of internal addresses that can be assigned a single IPv4 address is around 4,000.

There are two ways to configure PAT, depending on how the ISP allocates public IPv4 addresses. In the first instance, the ISP allocates more than one public IPv4 address to the organization, and in the other, it allocates a single public IPv4 address that is required for the organization to connect to the ISP.

Configuring PAT for a Pool of Public IPv4 Addresses

If a site has been issued more than one public IPv4 address, these addresses can be part of a pool that is used by PAT. This is similar to dynamic NAT, except that there are not enough public addresses for a one-to-one mapping of inside to outside addresses. The small pool of addresses is shared among a larger number of devices.

Figure 1 shows the steps to configure PAT to use a pool of addresses. The primary difference between this configuration and the configuration for dynamic, one-to-one NAT is that the **overload** keyword is used. The **overload** keyword enables PAT.

The example configuration shown in Figure 2 establishes overload translation for the NAT pool named NAT-POOL2. NAT-POOL2 contains addresses 209.165.200.226 to

209.165.200.240. Hosts in the 192.168.0.0/16 network are subject to translation. The S0/0/0 interface is identified as an inside interface and the S0/1/0 interface is identified as an outside interface.

Use the Syntax Checker in Figure 3 to configure PAT using an address pool on R2.

Refer to
Interactive Graphic
in online course

9.2.3.2   Configuring PAT: Single Address

Configuring PAT for a Single Public IPv4 Address

Figure 1 shows the topology of a PAT implementation for a single public IPv4 address translation. In the example, all hosts from network 192.168.0.0/16 (matching ACL 1) that send traffic through router R2 to the Internet will be translated to IPv4 address 209.165.200.225 (IPv4 address of interface S0/1/0). The traffic flows will be identified by port numbers in the NAT table because the **overload** keyword was used.

Figure 2 shows the steps to follow to configure PAT with a single IPv4 address. If only a single public IPv4 address is available, the overload configuration typically assigns the public address to the outside interface that connects to the ISP. All inside addresses are translated to the single IPv4 address when leaving the outside interface.

Step 1.   Define an ACL to permit the traffic to be translated.

Step 2.   Configure source translation using the **interface** and **overload** keywords. The **interface** keyword identifies which interface IPv4 address to use when translating inside addresses. The **overload** keyword directs the router to track port numbers with each NAT entry.

Step 3.   Identify which interfaces are inside in relation to NAT. That is any interface that connects to the inside network.

Step 4.   Identify which interface is outside in relation to NAT. This should be the same interface identified in the source translation statement from Step 2.

The configuration is similar to dynamic NAT, except that instead of a pool of addresses, the **interface** keyword is used to identify the outside IPv4 address. Therefore, no NAT pool is defined.

Use the Syntax Checker in Figure 3 to configure PAT using a single address on R2.

Refer to
Interactive Graphic
in online course

9.2.3.3 Analyzing PAT

The process of NAT overload is the same whether a pool of addresses is used or a single address is used. Continuing with the previous PAT example, using a single public IPv4 address, PC1 wants to communicate with the web server, Svr1. At the same time another client, PC2, wants to establish a similar session with the web server Svr2. Both PC1 and PC2 are configured with private IPv4 addresses, with R2 enabled for PAT.

PC to Server Process

1. Figure 1 shows both PC1 and PC2 sending packets to Svr1 and Svr2, respectively. PC1 has the source IPv4 address 192.168.10.10 and is using TCP source port 1444. PC2 has the source IPv4 address 192.168.10.11 and is coincidentally assigned the same source port of 1444.

2. The packet from PC1 reaches R2 first. Using PAT, R2 modifies the source IPv4 address to 209.165.200.225 (inside global address). There are no other devices in the NAT table using port 1444, so PAT maintains the same port number. The packet is then forwarded towards Svr1 at 209.165.201.1.

3. Next, the packet from PC2 arrives at R2. PAT is configured to use a single inside global IPv4 address for all translations, 209.165.200.225. Similar to the translation process for PC1, PAT changes PC2's source IPv4 address to the inside global address 209.165.200.225. However, PC2 has the same source port number as a current PAT entry, the translation for PC1. PAT increments the source port number until it is a unique value in its table. In this instance, the source port entry in the NAT table and the packet for PC2 receives 1445.

   Although PC1 and PC2 are using the same translated address, the inside global address of 209.165.200.225, and the same source port number of 1444; the modified port number for PC2 (1445) makes each entry in the NAT table unique. This will become evident with the packets sent from the servers back to the clients.

Server to PC Process

4. As shown in Figure 2, in a typical client-server exchange, Svr1 and Svr2 respond to the requests received from PC1 and PC2, respectively. The servers use the source port from the received packet as the destination port, and the source address as the destination address for the return traffic. The servers seem as if they are communicating with the same host at 209.165.200.225; however, this is not the case.

5. As the packets arrive, R2 locates the unique entry in its NAT table using the destination address and the destination port of each packet. In the case of the packet from Svr1, the destination IPv4 address of 209.165.200.225 has multiple entries but only one with the destination port 1444. Using the entry in its table, R2 changes the destination IPv4 address of the packet to 192.168.10.10, with no change required for the destination port. The packet is then forwarded toward PC1.

6. When the packet from Svr2 arrives R2 performs a similar translation. The destination IPv4 address of 209.165.200.225 is located, again with multiple entries. However, using the destination port of 1445, R2 is able to uniquely identify the translation entry. The destination IPv4 address is changed to 192.168.10.11. In this case, the destination port must also be modified back to its original value of 1444, which is stored in the NAT table. The packet is then forwarded toward PC2.

Refer to
Interactive Graphic
in online course

9.2.3.4   Verifying PAT

Router R2 has been configured to provide PAT to the 192.168.0.0/16 clients. When the internal hosts exit router R2 to the Internet, they are translated to an IPv4 address from the PAT pool with a unique source port number.

The same commands used to verify static and dynamic NAT are used to verify PAT, as shown in Figure 1. The **show ip nat translations** command displays the translations from two different hosts to different web servers. Notice that two different inside hosts are allocated the same IPv4 address of 209.165.200.226 (inside global address). The source port numbers in the NAT table differentiate the two transactions.

As shown in Figure 2, the **show ip nat statistics** command verifies that NAT-POOL2 has allocated a single address for both translations. Included in the output is information about the number and type of active translations, NAT configuration parameters, the number of addresses in the pool, and how many have been allocated.

Refer to **Interactive Graphic** in online course

9.2.3.5   Activity – Identify the Address Information at Each Hop

Refer to **Packet Tracer Activity** for this chapter

9.2.3.6   Packet Tracer – Implementing Static and Dynamic NAT

In this Packet Tracer, you will complete the following objectives:

- Part 1: Configure Dynamic NAT with PAT

- Part 2: Configure Static NAT

- Part 3: Verify NAT Implementation

Refer to **Lab Activity** for this chapter

9.2.3.7   Lab – Configuring Port Address Translation (PAT)

In this lab, you will complete the following objectives:

- Part 1: Build the Network and Verify Connectivity

- Part 2: Configure and Verify NAT Pool Overload

- Part 3: Configure and Verify PAT

9.2.4   Configure Port Forwarding

Refer to **Interactive Graphic** in online course

9.2.4.1   Port Forwarding

Port forwarding is the act of forwarding traffic addressed to a specific network port from one network node to another. This technique allows an external user to reach a port on a private IPv4 address (inside a LAN) from the outside, through a NAT-enabled router.

Typically, peer-to-peer file-sharing programs and operations, such as web serving and outgoing FTP, require that router ports be forwarded or opened to allow these applications to work, as shown in Figure 1. Because NAT hides internal addresses, peer-to-peer only works from the inside out where NAT can map outgoing requests against incoming replies.

The problem is that NAT does not allow requests initiated from the outside. This situation can be resolved with manual intervention. Port forwarding can be configured to identify specific ports that can be forwarded to inside hosts.

Recall that Internet software applications interact with user ports that need to be open or available to those applications. Different applications use different ports. This makes it predictable for applications and routers to identify network services. For example, HTTP operates through the well-known port 80. When someone enters the **http://cisco.com** address, the browser displays the Cisco Systems, Inc. website. Notice that they do not have to specify the HTTP port number for the page request, because the application assumes port 80.

If a different port number is required, it can be appended to the URL separated by a colon (:). For example, if the web server is listening on port 8080, the user would type **http:// www.example.com:8080**.

Port forwarding allows users on the Internet to access internal servers by using the WAN port address of the router and the matched external port number. The internal servers are typically configured with RFC 1918 private IPv4 addresses. When a request is sent to the IPv4 address of the WAN port via the Internet, the router forwards the request to the appropriate server on the LAN. For security reasons, broadband routers do not by default permit any external network request to be forwarded to an inside host.

Figure 2 shows a small business owner using a point of sale (PoS) server to track sales and inventories at the store. The server can be accessed within the store, but because it has a private IPv4 address, it is not publically accessible from the Internet. Enabling the local router for port forwarding allows the owner to access the point of sale server from anywhere on the Internet. Port forwarding on the router is configured using the destination port number and the private IPv4 address of the point of sale server. To access the server, the client software would use the public IPv4 address of the router and the destination port of the server.

Refer to
Online Course
for Illustration

9.2.4.2 Wireless Router Example

The figure shows the Single Port Forwarding configuration window for a Packet Tracer wireless router. By default, port forwarding is not enabled on the router.

Port forwarding can be enabled for applications by specifying the inside local address that requests should be forwarded to. In the figure, HTTP service requests, coming into wireless router, are forwarded to the web server with the inside local address of 192.168.1.254. If the external WAN IPv4 address of the wireless router is 209.165.200.225, the external user can enter **http://www.example.com** and the wireless router redirects the HTTP request to the internal web server at IPv4 address 192.168.1.254, using the default port number 80.

A port other than the default port 80 can be specified. However, the external user would have to know the specific port number to use. To specify a different port, the value of the External Port in the Single Port Forwarding window would be modified.

The approach taken to configure port forwarding depends on the brand and model of the broadband router in the network. However, there are some generic steps to follow. If the instructions supplied by the ISP, or those that came with the router, do not provide adequate guidance, the website http://www.portforward.com provides guides for several broadband routers. You can follow the instructions to add or delete ports as required to meet the needs of any applications you want to allow or deny.

Refer to
Interactive Graphic
in online course

9.2.4.3 Configuring Port Forwarding with IOS

Implementing port forwarding with IOS commands is similar to the commands used to configure static NAT. Port forwarding is essentially a static NAT translation with a specified TCP or UDP port number.

Figure 1 shows the static NAT command used to configure port forwarding using IOS.

Figure 2 shows an example of configuring port forwarding using IOS commands on router R2. 192.168.10.254 is the inside local IPv4 address of the web server listening on port 80. Users will access this internal web server using the global IPv4 address 209.165.200.225, a globally unique public IPv4 address. In this case, it is the address of the Serial 0/1/0 interface of R2. The global port is configured as 8080. This will be the destination port used, along with the global IPv4 address of 209.165.200.225 to access the internal web server. Notice within the NAT configuration, the following command parameters:

- `local-ip` = 192.168.10.254
- `local-port` = 80
- `global-ip` = 209.165.200.225
- `global-port` = 8080

When a well-known port number is not being used, the client must specify the port number in the application.

Like other types of NAT, port forwarding requires the configuration of both the inside and outside NAT interfaces.

Similar to static NAT, the **show ip nat translations** command can be used to verify the port forwarding, as shown in Figure 3.

In the example, when the router receives the packet with the inside global IPv4 address of 209.165.200.225 and a TCP destination port 8080, the router performs a NAT table lookup using the destination IPv4 address and destination port as the key. The router then translates the address to the inside local address of host 192.168.10.254 and destination port 80. R2 then forwards the packet to the web server. For return packets from the web server back to the client, this process is reversed.

Refer to **Packet Tracer Activity** for this chapter

9.2.4.4   Packet Tracer – Configuring Port Forwarding on a Wireless Router

Scenario

Your friend wants to play a game with you on your server. Both of you are at your respective homes, connected to the Internet. You need to configure your wireless router to port forward HTTP requests to your server so that your friend can access the game lobby web page.

9.2.5   NAT and IPv6

Refer to **Online Course** for Illustration

9.2.5.1   NAT for IPv6?

Since the early 1990s, the concern about the depletion of IPv4 address space has been a priority of the IETF. The combination of RFC 1918 private IPv4 addresses and NAT has been instrumental in slowing this depletion. NAT has significant disadvantages, and in January of 2011, IANA allocated the last of its IPv4 addresses to RIRs.

One of the unintentional benefits of NAT for IPv4 is that it hides the private network from the public Internet. NAT has the advantage of providing a perceived level of security by denying computers in the public Internet from accessing internal hosts. However, it should not be considered a substitute for proper network security, such as that provided by a firewall.

In RFC 5902, the Internet Architecture Board (IAB) included the following quote concerning IPv6 network address translation:

"It is commonly perceived that a NAT box provides one level of protection because external hosts cannot directly initiate communication with hosts behind a NAT. However, one should not confuse NAT boxes with firewalls. As discussed Section 2.2 in RFC4864, the act of translation does not provide security in itself. The stateful filtering function can provide the same level of protection without requiring a translation function".

IPv6, with a 128-bit address, provides 340 undecillion addresses. Therefore, address space is not an issue. IPv6 was developed with the intention of making NAT for IPv4 with its translation between public and private IPv4 addresses unnecessary. However, IPv6 does implement a form of NAT. IPv6 includes both its own IPv6 private address space and NAT, which are implemented differently than they are for IPv4.

Refer to
Online Course
for Illustration

9.2.5.2 IPv6 Unique Local Addresses

IPv6 unique local addresses (ULA) are similar to RFC 1918 private addresses in IPv4, but there are significant differences as well. The intent of ULA is to provide IPv6 address space for communications within a local site; it is not meant to provide additional IPv6 address space, nor is it meant to provide a level of security.

As shown in the figure, ULA have the prefix FC00::/7, which results in a first hextet range of FC00 to FDFF. The next 1 bit is set to 1 if the prefix is locally assigned. Set to 0 may be defined in the future. The next 40 bits is a global ID followed by a 16-bit Subnet ID. These first 64 bits combine to make the ULA prefix. This leaves the remaining 64 bits for the interface ID, or in IPv4 terms, the host portion of the address.

Unique local addresses are defined in RFC 4193. ULAs are also known as local IPv6 addresses (not to be confused with IPv6 link-local addresses) and have several characteristics including:

■ Allows sites to be combined or privately interconnected, without creating any address conflicts or requiring renumbering of interfaces that use these prefixes.

■ Independent of any ISP and can be used for communications within a site without having any Internet connectivity.

■ Not routable across the Internet, however, if accidentally leaked by routing or DNS, there is not conflict with other addresses.

ULA is not quite as straight-forward as RFC 1918 addresses. Unlike private IPv4 addresses, it has not been the intention of the IETF to use a form of NAT to translate between unique local addresses and IPv6 global unicast addresses.

The implementation and potential uses for IPv6 unique local addresses are still being examined by the Internet community. For example, the IETF is considering allowing the option of having the 40-bit global ID centrally assigned when using the FC00::/8 ULA prefix, and the 40-bit global ID randomly generated, or perhaps manually assigned, when using the ULA prefix FD00::/8. The rest of the address remains the same. We still use 16 bits for the subnet ID and 64 bits for the interface ID.

Note The original IPv6 specification allocated address space for site-local addresses, defined in RFC 3513. Site-local addresses have been deprecated by the IETF in RFC 3879 because the term "site" was somewhat ambiguous. Site-local addresses had the prefix range of FEC0::/10 and may still be found in some older IPv6 documentation.

Refer to
Online Course
for Illustration

9.2.5.3   NAT for IPv6

NAT for IPv6 is used in a much different context than NAT for IPv4. The varieties of NAT for IPv6 are used to transparently provide access between IPv6-only and IPv4-only networks. It is not used as a form of private IPv6 to global IPv6 translation.

Ideally, IPv6 should be run natively wherever possible. This means IPv6 devices communicating with each other over IPv6 networks. However, to aid in the move from IPv4 to IPv6, the IETF has developed several transition techniques to accommodate a variety of IPv4-to-IPv6 scenarios, including dual-stack, tunneling, and translation.

Dual-stack is when the devices are running protocols associated with both the IPv4 and IPv6. Tunneling for IPV6 is the process of encapsulating an IPv6 packet inside an IPv4 packet. This allows the IPv6 packet to be transmitted over an IPv4-only network.

NAT for IPv6 should not be used as a long term strategy, but as a temporary mechanism to assist in the migration from IPv4 to IPv6. Over the years, there have been several types of NAT for IPv6 including Network Address Translation-Protocol Translation (NAT-PT). NAT-PT has been deprecated by IETF in favor of its replacement, NAT64. NAT64 is beyond the scope of this curriculum.

9.3   Troubleshoot NAT

9.3.1   NAT Troubleshooting Commands

Refer to
Interactive Graphic
in online course

9.3.1.1   The show ip nat Commands

Figure 1 shows R2 enabled for PAT, using the range of addresses 209.165.200.226 to 209.165.200.240.

When there are IPv4 connectivity problems in a NAT environment, it is often difficult to determine the cause of the problem. The first step in solving the problem is to rule out NAT as the cause. Follow these steps to verify that NAT is operating as expected:

Step 1.   Based on the configuration, clearly define what NAT is supposed to achieve. This may reveal a problem with the configuration.

Step 2.   Verify that correct translations exist in the translation table using the **show ip nat translations** command.

Step 3.   Use the **clear** and **debug** commands to verify that NAT is operating as expected. Check to see if dynamic entries are recreated after they are cleared.

Step 4.   Review in detail what is happening to the packet, and verify that routers have the correct routing information to move the packet.

Figure 2 shows the output of the **show ip nat statistics** and **show ip nat translations** commands. Prior to using the **show** commands, the NAT statistics and entries in the NAT table are cleared with the **clear ip nat statistics** and **clear ip nat translation *** commands. After the host at 192.168.10.10 telnets to the server at 209.165.201.1, the NAT statistics and NAT table are displayed to verify NAT is working as expected.

In a simple network environment, it is useful to monitor NAT statistics with the **show ip nat statistics** command. The **show ip nat statistics** command displays information about the total number of active translations, NAT configuration parameters, the number of addresses in the pool, and the number that have been allocated. However, in a more complex NAT environment, with several translations taking place, this command may not clearly identify the issue. It may be necessary to run **debug** commands on the router.

Refer to
Interactive Graphic
in online course

9.3.1.2   The debug ip nat Command

Use the **debug ip nat** command to verify the operation of the NAT feature by displaying information about every packet that is translated by the router. The **debug ip nat detailed** command generates a description of each packet considered for translation. This command also provides information about certain errors or exception conditions, such as the failure to allocate a global address. The **debug ip nat detailed** command generates more overhead than the **debug ip nat** command, but it can provide the detail that may be needed to troubleshoot the NAT problem. Always turn off debugging when finished.

Figure 1 shows a sample **debug ip nat** output. The output shows that the inside host (192.168.10.10) initiated traffic to the outside host (209.165.201.1) and the source address was translated to address 209.165.200.226.

When decoding the debug output, note what the following symbols and values indicate:

- *** (asterisk)** - The asterisk next to NAT indicates that the translation is occurring in the fast-switched path. The first packet in a conversation is always process-switched, which is slower. The remaining packets go through the fast-switched path if a cache entry exists.

- **s=** - This symbol refers to the source IPv4 address.

- **a.b.c.d--->w.x.y.z** - This value indicates that source address a.b.c.d is translated to w.x.y.z.

- **d=** - This symbol refers to the destination IPv4 address.

- **[xxxx]** - The value in brackets is the IPv4 identification number. This information may be useful for debugging in that it enables correlation with other packet traces from protocol analyzers.

Note   Verify that the ACL referenced in the NAT command is permitting all of the necessary networks. In Figure 2, only 192.168.0.0/16 addresses are eligible to be translated. Packets from the inside network destined for the Internet with source addresses that are not explicitly permitted by ACL 1 are not translated by R2.

Refer to
Interactive Graphic
in online course

9.3.1.3   NAT Troubleshooting Scenario

Case Study

Figure 1 shows that hosts from the 192.168.0.0/16 LANs, PC1, and PC2 cannot ping servers on the outside network, Svr1, and Svr2.

To begin troubleshooting the problem, use the **show ip nat translations** command to see if any translations are currently in the NAT table. The output in Figure 1 shows that no translations are in the table.

The **show ip nat statistics** command is used to determine whether any translations have taken place. It also identifies the interfaces that translation should be occurring between.

As shown in the output of Figure 2, the NAT counters are at 0, verifying that no translation has occurred. By comparing the output with the topology shown in Figure 1, notice that the router interfaces are incorrectly defined as NAT inside or NAT outside. The incorrect configuration can also be verified using the **show running-config** command.

The current NAT interface configuration must be deleted from the interfaces before applying the correct configuration.

After correctly defining the NAT inside and outside interfaces, another ping from PC1 to Svr1 fails. Using the **show ip nat translations** and **show ip nat statistics** commands again verifies that translations are still not occurring.

As shown in Figure 3, the **show access-lists** command is used to determine whether the ACL that the NAT command references is permitting all of the necessary networks. Examining the output indicates that an incorrect wildcard bit mask has been used in the ACL that defines the addresses which need to be translated. The wildcard mask is only permitting the 192.168.0.0/24 subnet. The access list is first removed and then reconfigured using the correct wildcard mask.

After configurations are corrected, another ping is generated from PC1 to Svr1, and this time the ping succeeds. As shown in Figure 4, the **show ip nat translations** and **show ip nat statistics** commands are used to verify that the NAT translation is occurring.

Refer to **Packet Tracer Activity** for this chapter

9.3.1.4   Packet Tracer - Verifying and Troubleshooting NAT Configurations

A contractor restored an old configuration to a new router running NAT. But the network has changed, and a new subnet was added after the old configuration was backed up. It is your job to get the network working again.

Refer to **Lab Activity** for this chapter

9.3.1.5   Lab – Troubleshooting NAT Configurations

In this lab, you will complete the following objectives:

- Part 1: Build the Network and Configure Basic Device Settings
- Part 2: Troubleshoot Static NAT
- Part 3: Troubleshoot Dynamic NAT

9.4   Summary

Refer to **Online Course** for Illustration

9.4.1.1   NAT Check

Scenario

Network address translation is not currently included in your company's network design. It has been decided to configure some devices to use NAT services for connecting to the mail server.

Before deploying NAT live on the network, you prototype it using a network simulation program.

For further instructions, refer to the PDF which accompanies this activity.

Refer to **Packet Tracer Activity** for this chapter

9.4.1.2   Packet Tracer – Skills Integration Challenge

Scenario

This culminating activity includes many of the skills that you have acquired during this course. First, you will complete the documentation for the network. So make sure you have a printed version of the instructions. During implementation, you will configure VLANs, trunking, port security, and SSH remote access on a switch. Then, you will implement inter-VLAN routing and NAT on a router. Finally, you will use your documentation to verify your implementation by testing end-to-end connectivity.

Refer to **Online Course** for Illustration

9.4.1.3   NAT for IPv4

This chapter has outlined how NAT is used to help alleviate the depletion of IPv4 address space. NAT for IPv4 allows network administrators to use RFC 1918 private address space while providing connectivity to the Internet, using a single or limited number of public addresses.

NAT conserves public address space and saves considerable administrative overhead in managing adds, moves, and changes. NAT and PAT can be implemented to conserve public address space without affecting the ISP connection. However, NAT has drawbacks in terms of its negative effects on device performance, mobility, and end-to-end connectivity and should be considered a short term implementation for address exhaustion with the long term solution being IPv6.

This chapter discussed NAT for IPv4, including:

- NAT characteristics, terminology, and general operations

- The different types of NAT including static NAT, dynamic NAT, and PAT

- The benefits and disadvantages of NAT

- The configuration, verification, and analysis of static NAT, dynamic NAT, and PAT

- How port forwarding can be used to access an internal device from the Internet

- Why NAT is available but not integral to IPv6 networking

- Troubleshooting NAT using **show** and **debug** commands

Go to the online course to take the quiz and exam.

Chapter 9 Quiz

This quiz is designed to provide an additional opportunity to practice the skills and knowledge presented in the chapter and to prepare for the chapter exam. You will be allowed multiple attempts and the grade does not appear in the gradebook.

Chapter 9 Exam

The chapter exam assesses your knowledge of the chapter content.

Your Chapter Notes

Device Discovery, Management, and Maintenance

10.0 Introduction

Refer to
Online Course
for Illustration

10.0.1.1 Device Discovery, Management, and Maintenance

In this chapter, you will explore the tools network administrators can use for device discovery, device management, and device maintenance. Cisco Discovery Protocol (CDP) and Link Layer Discover Protocol (LLDP) are both capable of discovering information about directly connected devices.

Network Time Protocol (NTP) can be effectively used to synchronize the time across all your networking devices, which is especially important when trying to compare log files from different devices. Those log files are generated by the syslog protocol. Syslog messages can be captured and sent to a syslog server to aid in device management tasks.

Device maintenance includes ensuring that Cisco IOS images and configuration files are backed up in a safe location in the event that the device memory is corrupted or erased, either maliciously or inadvertently. Maintenance also includes keeping the IOS image up to date. The device maintenance section of the chapter includes topics for file maintenance, image management, and software licensing.

10.1 Device Discovery

10.1.1 Device Discovery with CDP

Refer to
Online Course
for Illustration

10.1.1.1 CDP Overview

Cisco Discovery Protocol (CDP) is a Cisco proprietary Layer 2 protocol that is used to gather information about Cisco devices which share the same data link. CDP is media and protocol independent and runs on all Cisco devices, such as routers, switches, and access servers.

The device sends periodic CDP advertisements to connected devices, as shown in the figure. These advertisements share information about the type of device that is discovered, the name of the devices, and the number and type of the interfaces.

Because most network devices are connected to other devices, CDP can assist in network design decisions, troubleshooting, and making changes to equipment. CDP can also be used as a network discovery tool to determine the information about the neighboring devices. This information gathered from CDP can help build a logical topology of a network when documentation is missing or lacking in detail.

Refer to
Interactive Graphic
in online course

10.1.1.2   Configure and Verify CDP

For Cisco devices, CDP is enabled by default. For security reasons, it may be desirable to disable CDP on a network device globally, or per interface. With CDP, an attacker can gather valuable insight about the network layout, such as IP addresses, IOS versions, and types of devices.

To verify the status of CDP and display information about CDP, enter the **show cdp** command, as displayed in Example 1.

To enable CDP globally for all the supported interfaces on the device, enter **cdp run** in the global configuration mode. CDP can be disabled for all the interfaces on the device with the **no cdp run** command in the global configuration mode.

To disable CDP on a specific interface, such as the interface facing an ISP, enter **no cdp enable** in the interface configuration mode. CDP is still enabled on the device; however, no more CDP advertisements will be sent out that interface. To enable CDP on the specific interface again, enter **cdp enable**, as shown in Figure 2.

Figure 3 shows CDP disabled globally using the command **no cdp run** and re-enabled using the **cdp run** command.

To verify the status of CDP and display a list of neighbors, use the **show cdp neighbors** command in the privileged EXEC mode. The **show cdp neighbors** command displays important information about the CDP neighbors. Currently, this device does not have any neighbors because it is not physically connected to any devices, as indicated by the results of the **show cdp neighbors** command displayed in Figure 4.

Use the **show cdp interface** command to display the interfaces that are CDP enabled on a device. The status of each interface is also displayed. Figure 5 shows that five interfaces are CDP enabled on the router with only one active connection to another device.

Use the Syntax Checker in Figure 6 to practice configuring and verifying CDP.

Refer to
Interactive Graphic
in online course

10.1.1.3   Discover Devices Using CDP

With CDP enabled on the network, the **show cdp neighbors** command can be used to determine the network layout.

For example, consider the lack of documentation in the topology shown in Figure 1. No information is available regarding the rest of the network. The **show cdp neighbors** command provides helpful information about each CDP neighbor device, including the following:

- **Device identifiers** - The host name of the neighbor device (S1)

- **Port identifier** - The name of the local and remote port (Gig 0/1 and Fas 0/5, respectively)

- **Capabilities list** - Whether the device is a router or a switch (S for switch; I for IGMP is beyond scope for this course)

- **Platform** - The hardware platform of the device (WS-C2960 for Cisco 2960 switch)

If more information is needed, the **show cdp neighbors** detail command can also provide information, such as the neighbors' IOS version and IPv4 address, as displayed in Figure 2. By accessing S1 either remotely through SSH or physically through the console port, a network administrator can determine the other devices connected to S1, as displayed in the output of the **show cdp neighbors** in Figure 3.

Another switch, S2, is revealed in the output. The network administrator then accesses S2 and displays the CDP neighbors, as shown in Figure 4. The only device connected to S2 is S1. Therefore, there are no more devices to discover in the topology. The network administrator can now update the documentation to reflect the discovered devices.

Refer to **Packet Tracer Activity** for this chapter

10.1.1.4   Packet Tracer – Map a Network Using CDP

A senior network administrator requires you to map the Remote Branch Office network and discover the name of a recently installed switch that still needs an IPv4 address to be configured. Your task is to create a map of the branch office network. To map the network, you will use SSH for remote access and the Cisco Discovery Protocol (CDP) to discover information about neighboring network devices, like routers and switches.

10.1.2   Device Discovery with LLDP

Refer to **Online Course** for Illustration

10.1.2.1   LLDP Overview

Cisco devices also support Link Layer Discovery Protocol (LLDP), which is a vendor-neutral neighbor discovery protocol similar to CDP. LLDP works with network devices, such as routers, switches, and wireless LAN access points. This protocol advertises its identity and capabilities to other devices and receives the information from a physically connected Layer 2 device.

Refer to **Interactive Graphic** in online course

10.1.2.2   Configure and Verify LLDP

Depending on the device, LLDP may be enabled by default. To enable LLDP globally on a Cisco network device, enter the **lldp run** command in the global configuration mode. To disable LLDP, enter the **no lldp run** command in the global configuration mode.

Similar to CDP, LLDP can be configured on specific interfaces. However, LLDP must be configured separately to transmit and receive LLDP packets, as shown in Figure 1.

To verify LLDP has been enabled on the device, enter the **show lldp** command in the privileged EXEC mode.

Use the Syntax Checker in Figure 2 to practice configuring and verifying LLDP.

Refer to **Interactive Graphic** in online course

10.1.2.3   Discover Devices Using LLDP

With LLDP enabled, device neighbors can be discovered using the **show lldp neighbors** command. For example, consider the lack of documentation in the topology shown in Figure 1. The network administrator only knows that S1 is connected to two devices. Using the **show lldp neighbors** command, the network administrator discovers that S1 has a router and a switch as a neighbors.

Note   The letter B under capability for S2 represents a Bridge. For this output, the word bridge can also mean switch.

From the results of **show lldp neighbors**, a topology from switch S1 can be constructed as depicted in Figure 2. When more details about the neighbors are needed, the **show lldp neighbors detail** command can provide information, such as the neighbors' IOS version, IP address, and device capability.

Refer to
Interactive Graphic
in online course

10.1.2.4   Activity – Compare CDP and LLDP

Refer to
Lab Activity
for this chapter

10.1.2.5   Lab – Configure CDP and LLDP

In this lab, you will complete the following objectives:

■ Build the Network and Configure Basic Device Settings

■ Network Discovery with CDP

■ Network Discovery with LLDP

10.2   Device Management

10.2.1   NTP

Refer to
Online Course
for Illustration

10.2.1.1   Setting the System Clock

The software clock on a router or switch starts when the system boots and is the primary source of time for the system. It is important to synchronize the time across all devices on the network because all aspects of managing, securing, troubleshooting, and planning networks require accurate timestamping. When the time is not synchronized between devices, it will be impossible to determine the order of the events and the cause of an event.

Typically, the date and time settings on a router or switch can be set using one of two methods:

■ Manually configure the date and time, as shown in the figure

■ Configure the Network Time Protocol (NTP)

As a network grows, it becomes difficult to ensure that all infrastructure devices are operating with synchronized time. Even in a smaller network environment, the manual method is not ideal. If a router reboots, how will it get an accurate date and timestamp?

A better solution is to configure the NTP on the network. This protocol allows routers on the network to synchronize their time settings with an NTP server. A group of NTP clients that obtain time and date information from a single source have more consistent time settings. When NTP is implemented in the network, it can be set up to synchronize to a private master clock or it can synchronize to a publicly available NTP server on the Internet.

NTP uses UDP port 123 and is documented in RFC 1305.

Refer to
Online Course
for Illustration

10.2.1.2   NTP Operation

NTP networks use a hierarchical system of time sources. Each level in this hierarchical system is called a stratum. The stratum level is defined as the number of hop counts from the authoritative source. The synchronized time is distributed across the network using NTP. The figure displays a sample NTP network.

NTP servers arranged in three levels showing the three strata. Stratum 1 is connected to Stratum 0 clocks.

Stratum 0

An NTP network gets the time from authoritative time sources. These authoritative time sources, also referred to as stratum 0 devices, are high-precision timekeeping devices assumed to be accurate and with little or no delay associated with them. Stratum 0 devices are represented by the clock in the figure.

Stratum 1

The stratum 1 devices are directly connected to the authoritative time sources. They act as the primary network time standard.

Stratum 2 and Lower

The stratum 2 servers are connected to stratum 1 devices through network connections. Stratum 2 devices, such as NTP clients, synchronize their time using the NTP packets from stratum 1 servers. They could also act as servers for stratum 3 devices.

Smaller stratum numbers indicate that the server is closer to the authorized time source than larger stratum numbers. The larger the stratum number, the lower the stratum level. The max hop count is 15. Stratum 16, the lowest stratum level, indicates that a device is unsynchronized. Time servers on the same stratum level can be configured to act as a peer with other time servers on the same stratum level for backup or verification of time.

Refer to
Interactive Graphic
in online course

10.2.1.3   Configure and Verify NTP

Before NTP is configured on the network, the **show clock** command displays the current time on the software clock. With the **detail** option, the time source is also displayed. As shown in Figure 1, the software clock has been manually configured. Use the **ntp server** *ip-address* command in global configuration mode to configure 209.165.200.225 as the NTP server for R1. To verify the time source is set to NTP, use the **show clock detail** command again.

As shown in Figure 2, use the **show ip ntp associations** and **show ntp status** commands to verify that R1 is synchronized with the NTP server at 209.165.200.225. Notice that R1 is synchronized with a stratum 1 NTP server at 209.165.200.225, which is synchronized with a GPS clock. The **show ntp status** command displays that R1 is now a stratum 2 device synchronized with the NTP server at 209.165.220.225.

The clock on S1 is configured to synchronize to R1, as shown in Figure 3. Output from the **show ntp associations** command verifies that the clock on S1 is now synchronized with R1 at 192.168.1.1 via NTP. R1 is a stratum 2 device and NTP server to S1. Now S1 is a stratum 3 device that can provide NTP service to other devices in the network, such as end devices.

Use the Syntax Checker in Figure 4 to practice configuring and verifying NTP.

Refer to **Packet Tracer Activity** for this chapter

10.2.1.4   Packet Tracer – Configure and Verify NTP

NTP synchronizes the time of day among a set of distributed time servers and clients. While there are a number of applications that require synchronized time, this lab will focus on the need to correlate events when listed in the systems system logs and other time-specific events from multiple network devices.

10.2.2   Syslog Operation

Refer to **Online Course** for Illustration

10.2.2.1   Introduction to Syslog

When certain events occur on a network, networking devices have trusted mechanisms to notify the administrator with detailed system messages. These messages can be either non-critical or significant. Network administrators have a variety of options for storing, interpreting, and displaying these messages, and for being alerted to those messages that could have the greatest impact on the network infrastructure.

The most common method of accessing system messages is to use a protocol called syslog.

Syslog is a term used to describe a standard. It is also used to describe the protocol developed for that standard. The syslog protocol was developed for UNIX systems in the 1980s, but was first documented as RFC 3164 by IETF in 2001. Syslog uses UDP port 514 to send event notification messages across IP networks to event message collectors, as illustrated in the figure.

Many networking devices support syslog, including: routers, switches, application servers, firewalls, and other network appliances. The syslog protocol allows networking devices to send their system messages across the network to syslog servers.

There are several different syslog server software packages for Windows and UNIX. Many of them are freeware.

The syslog logging service provides three primary functions:

- The ability to gather logging information for monitoring and troubleshooting
- The ability to select the type of logging information that is captured
- The ability to specify the destinations of captured syslog messages

Refer to **Online Course** for Illustration

10.2.2.2   Syslog Operation

On Cisco network devices, the syslog protocol starts by sending system messages and **debug** output to a local logging process internal to the device. How the logging process manages these messages and outputs is based on device configurations. For example, syslog messages may be sent across the network to an external syslog server. These messages can be retrieved without the need of accessing the actual device. Log messages and outputs stored on the external server can be pulled into various reports for easier reading.

Alternatively, syslog messages may be sent to an internal buffer. Messages sent to the internal buffer are only viewable through the CLI of the device.

Finally, the network administrator may specify that only certain types of system messages are sent to various destinations. For example, the device may be configured to forward all system messages to an external syslog server. However, debug-level messages are forwarded to the internal buffer and are only accessible by the administrator from the CLI.

As shown in the figure, popular destinations for syslog messages include:

- Logging buffer (RAM inside a router or switch)
- Console line
- Terminal line
- Syslog server

It is possible to remotely monitor system messages by viewing the logs on a syslog server, or by accessing the device through Telnet, SSH, or through the console port.

Refer to **Interactive Graphic** in online course

10.2.2.3 Syslog Message Format

Cisco devices produce syslog messages as a result of network events. Every syslog message contains a severity level and a facility.

The smaller numerical levels are the more critical syslog alarms. The severity level of the messages can be set to control where each type of message is displayed (i.e. on the console or the other destinations). The complete list of syslog levels is shown in Figure 1.

Each syslog level has its own meaning:

- **Warning Level 4 - Emergency Level 0:** These messages are error messages about software or hardware malfunctions; these types of messages mean that the functionality of the device is affected. The severity of the issue determines the actual syslog level applied.

- **Notification Level 5:** The notifications level is for normal, but significant events. For example, interface up or down transitions, and system restart messages are displayed at the notifications level.

- **Informational Level 6:** A normal information message that does not affect device functionality. For example, when a Cisco device is booting, you might see the following informational message: `%LICENSE-6-EULA_ACCEPT_ALL: The Right to Use End User License Agreement is accepted`.

- **Debugging Level 7:** This level indicates that the messages are output generated from issuing various **debug** commands.

In addition to specifying the severity, syslog messages also contain information on the facility. Syslog facilities are service identifiers that identify and categorize system state data for error and event message reporting. The logging facility options that are available are specific to the networking device. For example, Cisco 2960 Series switches running Cisco IOS Release 15.0(2) and Cisco 1941 routers running Cisco IOS Release 15.2(4) support 24 facility options that are categorized into 12 facility types.

Some common syslog message facilities reported on Cisco IOS routers include:

- IP
- OSPF protocol
- SYS operating system

- IP security (IPsec)

- Interface IP (IF)

By default, the format of syslog messages on the Cisco IOS Software is as follows:

```
seq no: timestamp: %facility-severity-MNEMONIC: description
```

The fields contained in the Cisco IOS Software syslog message are explained in Figure 2.

For example, sample output on a Cisco switch for an EtherChannel link changing state to up is:

```
00:00:46: %LINK-3-UPDOWN: Interface Port-channel1, changed state to up
```

Here the facility is LINK and the severity level is 3, with a MNEMONIC of UPDOWN.

The most common messages are link up and down messages, and messages that a device produces when it exits from configuration mode. If ACL logging is configured, the device generates syslog messages when packets match a parameter condition.

Refer to
Online Course
for Illustration

10.2.2.4   Service Timestamp

By default, log messages are not timestamped. For example, in the figure, the R1 GigabitEthernet 0/0 interface is shutdown. The message logged to the console does not identify when the interface state was changed. Log messages should be timestamped so that when they are sent to another destination, such as a Syslog server, there is record of when the message was generated.

Use the command **service timestamps log datetime** to force logged events to display the date and time. As shown in the figure, when the R1 GigabitEthernet 0/0 interface is reactivated, the log messages now contain the date and time.

Note   When using the **datetime** keyword, the clock on the networking device must be set, either manually or through NTP, as previously discussed.

Refer to
Interactive Graphic
in online course

10.2.2.5   Activity – Interpret Syslog Output

10.2.3   Syslog Configuration

Refer to
Interactive Graphic
in online course

10.2.3.1   Syslog Server

To view syslog messages, a syslog server must be installed on a workstation in the network. There are several freeware and shareware versions of syslog, as well as enterprise versions for purchase. In Figure 1, an evaluation version of the Kiwi Syslog Daemon is displayed on a Windows 7 machine.

The syslog server provides a relatively user-friendly interface for viewing syslog output. The server parses the output and places the messages into pre-defined columns for easy interpretation. If timestamps are configured on the networking device sourcing the syslog messages, then the date and time of each message displays in the syslog server output, as shown in Figure 2.

Network administrators can easily navigate the large amount of data compiled on a syslog server. One advantage of viewing syslog messages on a syslog server is the ability to perform granular searches through the data. Also, a network administrator can quickly delete unimportant syslog messages from the database.

Refer to
Interactive Graphic
in online course

10.2.3.2   Default Logging

By default, Cisco routers and switches send log messages for all severity levels to the console. On some IOS versions, the device also buffers log messages by default. To enable these two settings, use the **logging console** and **logging buffered** global configuration commands, respectively.

The **show logging** command displays the default logging service settings on a Cisco router, as shown in the figure. The first lines of output list information about the logging process, with the end of the output listing log messages.

The first highlighted line states that this router logs to the console and includes debug messages. This actually means that all debug level messages, as well as any lower level messages (such as notification level messages), are logged to the console. On most Cisco IOS routers, the default severity level is 7, debugging. The output also notes that 32 such messages have been logged.

The second highlighted line states that this router logs to an internal buffer. Because this router has enabled logging to an internal buffer, the **show logging** command also lists the messages in that buffer. You can view some of the system messages that have been logged at the end of the output.

Refer to
Interactive Graphic
in online course

10.2.3.3   Router and Switch Commands for Syslog Clients

There are three steps to configuring the router to send system messages to a syslog server where they can be stored, filtered, and analyzed:

Step 1.   In global configuration mode, use the **logging** command toconfigure the destination hostname or IPv4 address of the syslog.

Step 2.   Control the messages that will be sent to the syslog server with the **logging trap** *level* global configuration mode command. For example, to limit the messages to levels 4 and lower (0 to 4), use one of the two equivalent commands.

Step 3.   Optionally, configure the source interface with the **logging source-interface** *interface-type interface-number* global configuration mode command. This specifies that syslog packets contain the IPv4 or IPv6 address of a specific interface, regardless of which interface the packet uses to exit the router.

In Figure 1, R1 is configured to send log messages of levels 4 and lower to the syslog server at 192.168.1.3. The source interface is set as the G0/0 interface. A loopback interface is created, then shut down, and then brought back up. The console output reflects these actions.

Shown in Figure 2, the Tftpd32 syslog server has been set up on a Windows 7 machine with IPv4 address 192.168.1.3. As you can see, the only messages that appear on the syslog server are those with severity level of 4 or lower (more severe). The messages with severity level of 5 or higher (less severe) appear on the router console output, but do not appear on the syslog server output, because the logging traplimits the syslog messages sent to the syslog server based on severity.

Refer to
Interactive Graphic
in online course

10.2.3.4   Verifying Syslog

You can use the **show logging** command to view any messages that are logged. When the logging buffer is large, it is helpful to use the pipe option (|) with the **show logging** command. The pipe option allows the administrator to specifically state which messages should be displayed. For example, you can use the pipe to filter only messages that **include changed state to up**, as shown in Figure 1.

Scroll down in the output in Figure 1 to see another filtering example. To view only the messages that were logged to the buffer on or after Jun 12 10:35 PM, you would use the filter **begin June 12 22:35**.

Use the Syntax Checker in Figure 2 to configure and verify the syslog on R1.

Refer to **Packet Tracer Activity**
for this chapter

10.2.3.5   Packet Tracer – Configuring Syslog and NTP

Background/Scenario

In this activity, you will enable and use the Syslog service and the NTP service so that the network administrator is able to monitor the network more effectively.

Refer to
Lab Activity
for this chapter

10.2.3.6   Lab – Configuring Syslog and NTP

In this lab, you will complete the following objectives:

- Part 1: Configure Basic Device Settings
- Part 2: Configure NTP
- Part 3: Configure Syslog

10.3   Device Maintenance

10.3.1   Router and Switch File Maintenance

Refer to
Interactive Graphic
in online course

10.3.1.1   Router File Systems

The Cisco IOS File System (IFS) allows the administrator to navigate to different directories and list the files in a directory, and to create subdirectories in flash memory or on a disk. The directories available depend on the device.

Figure 1 displays the output of the **show file systems** command, which lists all of the available file systems on a Cisco 1941 router. This command provides useful information such as the amount of available and free memory, the type of file system, and its permissions. Permissions include read only (ro), write only (wo), and read and write (rw), shown in the Flags column of the command output.

Although there are several file systems listed, of interest to us will be the tftp, flash, and nvram file systems.

Notice that the flash file system also has an asterisk preceding it. This indicates that flash is the current default file system. The bootable IOS is located in flash; therefore, the pound symbol (#) is appended to the flash listing, indicating that it is a bootable disk.

The Flash File System

Figure 2 displays the output from the **dir** (directory) command. Because flash is the default file system, the **dir** command lists the contents of flash. Several files are located in flash, but of specific interest is the last listing. This is the name of the current Cisco IOS file image that is running in RAM.

The NVRAM File System

To view the contents of NVRAM, you must change the current default file system using the **cd** (change directory) command, as shown in Figure 3. The **pwd** (present working directory) command verifies that we are viewing the NVRAM directory. Finally, the **dir** command lists the contents of NVRAM. Although there are several configuration files listed, of specific interest is the startup-configuration file.

Refer to
Online Course
for Illustration

10.3.1.2   Switch File Systems

With the Cisco 2960 switch flash file system, you can copy configuration files, and archive (upload and download) software images.

The command to view the file systems on a Catalyst switch is the same as on a Cisco router: **show file systems**, as shown in the figure.

Refer to
Online Course
for Illustration

10.3.1.3   Backing Up and Restoring Using Text Files

Backup Configurations with Text Capture (Tera Term)

Configuration files can be saved/archived to a text file using Tera Term.

As shown in the figure, the steps are:

Step 1.   On the File menu, click **Log**.

Step 2.   Choose the location to save the file. Tera Term will begin capturing text.

Step 3.   After capture has been started, execute the **show running-config** or **show startup-config** command at the privileged EXEC prompt. Text displayed in the terminal window will be directed to the chosen file.

Step 4.   When the capture is complete, select **Close** in the Tera Term: Log window.

Step 5.   View the file to verify that it was not corrupted.

Restoring Text Configurations

A configuration can be copied from a file to a device. When copied from a text file and pasted into a terminal window, the IOS executes each line of the configuration text as a command. This means that the file will require editing to ensure that encrypted passwords are in plain text and that non-command text such as "--More--" and IOS messages are removed. This process is discussed in the lab.

Further, at the CLI, the device must be set at the global configuration mode to receive the commands from the text file being pasted into the terminal window.

When using Tera Term, the steps are:

Step 1.   On the File menu, click **Send** file.

Step 2.   Locate the file to be copied into the device and click **Open**.

Step 3.   Tera Term will paste the file into the device.

The text in the file will be applied as commands in the CLI and become the running configuration on the device. This is a convenient method for manually configuring a router.

Refer to
Online Course
for Illustration

10.3.1.4   Backing up and Restoring TFTP

Backup Configurations with TFTP

Copies of configuration files should be stored as backup files in the event of a problem. Configuration files can be stored on a Trivial File Transfer Protocol (TFTP) server or a USB drive. A configuration file should also be included in the network documentation.

To save the running configuration or the startup configuration to a TFTP server, use either the **copy running-config tftp** or **copy startup-config tftp** command as shown in the figure. Follow these steps to backup the running configuration to a TFTP server:

Step 1.   Enter the **copy running-config** tftp command.

Step 2.   Enter the IP address of the host where the configuration file will be stored.

Step 3.   Enter the name to assign to the configuration file.

Step 4.   Press Enter to confirm each choice.

Restoring Configurations with TFTP

To restore the running configuration or the startup configuration from a TFTP server, use either the **copy tftp running-config** or **copy tftp startup-config** command. Use these steps to restore the running configuration from a TFTP server:

Step 1.   Enter the **copy tftp running-config** command.

Step 2.   Enter the IP address of the host where the configuration file is stored.

Step 3.   Enter the name to assign to the configuration file.

Step 4.   Press **Enter** to confirm each choice.

Refer to
Online Course
for Illustration

10.3.1.5   Using USB Ports on a Cisco Router

The Universal Serial Bus (USB) storage feature enables certain models of Cisco routers to support USB flash drives. The USB flash feature provides an optional secondary storage capability and an additional boot device. Images, configurations, and other files can be copied to or from the Cisco USB flash memory with the same reliability as storing and retrieving files using the Compact Flash card. In addition, modular integrated services routers can boot any Cisco IOS Software image saved on USB flash memory. Ideally, USB flash can hold multiple copies of the Cisco IOS and multiple router configurations.

Use the **dir** command to view the contents of the USB flash drive, as shown in the figure.

Refer to
Interactive Graphic
in online course

10.3.1.6   Backing Up and Restoring Using a USB

Backup Configurations with a USB Flash Drive

When backing up to a USB port, it is a good idea to issue the **show file systems** command to verify that the USB drive is there and confirm the name, as shown in Figure 1.

Next, use the **copy run usbflash0:/** command to copy the configuration file to the USB flash drive. Be sure to use the name of the flash drive, as indicated in the file system. The slash is optional but indicates the root directory of the USB flash drive.

The IOS will prompt for the filename. If the file already exists on the USB flash drive, the router will prompt to overwrite, as seen in Figure 2.

Use the **dir** command to see the file on the USB drive and use the **more** command to see the contents, as seen in Figure 3.

Restore Configurations with a USB Flash Drive

In order to copy the file back, it will be necessary to edit the USB R1-Config file with a text editor. Assuming the file name is **R1-Config**, use the command **copy usbflash0:/ R1-Config** *running-config* to restore a running configuration.

Refer to
Interactive Graphic
in online course

10.3.1.7   Password Recovery

Passwords on devices are used to prevent unauthorized access. For encrypted passwords, such as the enable secret passwords, the passwords must be replaced after recovery. Depending on the device, the detailed procedure for password recovery varies; however, all the password recovery procedures follow the same principle:

Step 1.   Enter the ROMMON mode.

Step 2.   Change the configuration register to 0x2142 to ignore the startup config file.

Step 3.   Make necessary changes to the original startup config file.

Step 4.   Save the new configuration.

Console access to the device through a terminal or terminal emulator software on a PC is required for password recovery. The terminal settings to access the device are:

- 9600 baud rate

- No parity

- 8 data bits

- 1 stop bit

- No flow control

With console access, a user can access the ROMMON mode by using a break sequence during the boot up process or removing the external flash memory when the device is powered off.

Note   The break sequence for PuTTY is Ctrl+Break. A list of standard break key sequences for other terminal emulators and operating systems can be found at: http://www.cisco.com/c/en/us/support/docs/routers/10000-series-routers/12818-61.html.

The ROMMON software supports some basic commands, such as **confreg**. The **confreg 0x2142** command allows the user to set the configuration register to 0x2142. With the configuration register at 0x2142, the device will ignore the startup config file during startup. The startup config file is where the forgotten passwords are stored. After setting the configuration register to 0x2142, type **reset** at the prompt to restart the device. Enter the break sequence while the device is rebooting and decompressing the IOS. Figure 1 displays the terminal output of a 1941 router in the ROMMON mode after using a break sequence during the boot up process.

After the device has finished reloading, copy the startup config to the running config, as displayed in Figure 2.

CAUTION: Do *not* enter **copy running-config startup-config**. This command erases your original startup configuration.

Because you are in privileged EXEC mode, you can now configure all the necessary passwords. After the new passwords are configured, change the configuration register back to 0x2102 using the **config-register 0x2102** command in the global configuration mode. Save the running-config to startup-config and reload the device, as shown in Figure 2.

Note   The password **cisco** is not a strong password and is used here only as an example.

The device now uses the newly configured passwords for authentication. Be sure to use **show** commands to verify that all the configurations are still in place. For example, verify that the appropriate interfaces are not shut down after password recovery.

The following link provides detailed instructions for password recovery procedure for a specific device:

http://www.cisco.com/c/en/us/support/docs/ios-nx-os-software/ios-software-releases-121-mainline/6130-index.html

Use the Syntax Checker in Figure 3 to practice password recovery on a router.

Refer to **Packet Tracer Activity** for this chapter

10.3.1.8   Packet Tracer – Backing Up Configuration Files

This activity is designed to show how to restore a configuration from a backup and then perform a new backup. Due to an equipment failure, a new router has been put in place. Fortunately, backup configuration files have been saved to a Trivial File Transfer Protocol

(TFTP) Server. You are required to restore the files from the TFTP Server to get the router back online with as little downtime as possible.

Refer to
Lab Activity
for this chapter

10.3.1.9   Lab – Managing Router Configuration Files with Tera Term

In this lab, you will complete the following objectives:

- Part 1: Configure Basic Device Settings
- Part 2: Use Terminal Emulation Software to Create a Backup Configuration File
- Part 3: Use a Backup Configuration File to Restore a Router

Refer to
Lab Activity
for this chapter

10.3.1.10   Lab – Managing Device Configuration Files Using TFTP, Flash, and USB

In this lab, you will complete the following objectives:

- Part 1: Build the Network and Configure Basic Device Settings
- Part 2: (Optional) Download TFTP Server Software
- Part 3: Use TFTP to Back Up and Restore the Switch Running Configuration
- Part 4: Use TFTP to Back Up and Restore the Router Running Configuration
- Part 5: Back Up and Restore Running Configurations Using Router Flash Memory
- Part 6: (Optional) Use a USB Drive to Back Up and Restore the Running Configuration

Refer to
Lab Activity
for this chapter

10.3.1.11   Lab – Researching Password Recovery Procedures

In this lab, you will complete the following objectives:

- Part 1: Research the Configuration Register
- Part 2: Document the Password Recovery Procedure for a Specific Cisco Router

10.3.2   IOS System Files

Refer to
Online Course
for Illustration

10.3.2.1   IOS 15 System Image Packaging

Cisco Integrated Services Routers Generation Two (ISR G2) 1900, 2900, and 3900 Series support services on demand through the use of software licensing. The Services on Demand process enables customers to realize operational savings through ease of software ordering and management. When an order is placed for a new ISR G2 platform, the router is shipped with a single universal Cisco IOS Software image and a license is used to enable the specific feature set packages, as shown in Figure 1.

There are two types of universal images supported in ISR G2:

- **Universal images with the "universalk9" designation in the image name** - This universal image offers all of the Cisco IOS Software features, including strong payload cryptography features, such as IPsec VPN, SSL VPN, and Secure Unified Communications.

■ **Universal images with the "universalk9_npe" designation in the image name** - The strong enforcement of encryption capabilities provided by Cisco Software Activation satisfies requirements for the export of encryption capabilities. However, some countries have import requirements that require that the platform does not support any strong cryptography functionality, such as payload cryptography. To satisfy the import requirements of those countries, the npe universal image does not support any strong payload encryption.

With the ISR G2 devices, IOS image selection has been made easier because all features are included within the universal image. Features are activated through licensing. Each device ships with Universal image. The technology packages IP Base, Data, UC (Unified Communications), and SEC (Security), are enabled in the universal image using Cisco Software Activation licensing keys. Each licensing key is unique to a particular device and is obtained from Cisco by providing the product ID and serial number of the router and a Product Activation Key (PAK). The PAK is provided by Cisco at the time of software purchase. The IP Base is installed by default.

Refer to
Interactive Graphic
in online course

10.3.2.2   IOS Image Filenames

When selecting or upgrading a Cisco IOS router, it is important to choose the proper IOS image with the correct feature set and version. The Cisco IOS image file is based on a special naming convention. The name for the Cisco IOS image file contains multiple parts, each with a specific meaning. It is important to understand this naming convention when upgrading and selecting a Cisco IOS Software.

As shown in Figure 1, the **show flash** command displays the files stored in flash memory, including the system image files.

Figure 2 illustrates the different parts of an IOS 15 system image file on an ISR G2 device:

■ **Image Name (c1900)** - Identifies the platform on which the image runs. In this example, the platform is a Cisco 1900 router.

■ **universalk9** - Specifies the image designation. The two designations for an ISR G2 are universalk9 and universalk9_npe. Universalk9_npe does not contain strong encryption and is meant for countries with encryption restrictions. Features are controlled by licensing and can be divided into four technology packages. These are IP Base, Security, Unified Communications, and Data.

■ **mz** - Indicates where the image runs and if the file is compressed. In this example, mz indicates that the file runs from RAM and is compressed.

■ **SPA** - Designates that file is digitally signed by Cisco.

■ **152-4.M3** - Specifies the filename format for the image 15.2(4)M3. This is the version of IOS, which includes the major release, minor release, maintenance release, and maintenance rebuild numbers. The M indicates this is an extended maintenance release.

■ **bin** - The file extension. This extension indicates that this file is a binary executable file.

The most common designation for memory location and compression format is mz. The first letter indicates the location where the image is executed on the router. The locations can include:

- **f** - flash
- **m** - RAM
- **r** - ROM
- **l** - relocatable

The compression format can be either z for zip or x for mzip. Zipping is a method Cisco uses to compress some run-from-RAM images that is effective in reducing the size of the image. It is self-unzipping, so when the image is loaded into RAM for execution, the first action is to unzip.

Note   The Cisco IOS Software naming conventions, field meaning, image content, and other details are subject to change.

Memory Requirements

On most Cisco routers including the integrated services routers, the IOS is stored in compact flash as a compressed image and loaded into DRAM during boot-up. The Cisco IOS Software Release 15.0 images available for the Cisco 1900 and 2900 ISR require 256MB of flash and 512MB of RAM. The 3900 ISR requires 256MB of flash and 1GB of RAM. This does not include additional management tools such as Cisco Configuration Professional (Cisco CP). For complete details, refer to the product data sheet for the specific router.

10.3.3   IOS Image Management

10.3.3.1   TFTP Servers as a Backup Location

Refer to
Online Course
for Illustration

As a network grows, Cisco IOS Software images and configuration files can be stored on a central TFTP server. This helps to control the number of IOS images and the revisions to those IOS images, as well as the configuration files that must be maintained.

Production internetworks usually span wide areas and contain multiple routers. For any network, it is good practice to keep a backup copy of the Cisco IOS Software image in case the system image in the router becomes corrupted or accidentally erased.

Widely distributed routers need a source or backup location for Cisco IOS Software images. Using a network TFTP server allows image and configuration uploads and downloads over the network. The network TFTP server can be another router, a workstation, or a host system.

Refer to
Interactive Graphic
in online course

10.3.3.2   Steps to Backup IOS Image to TFTP Server

To maintain network operations with minimum down time, it is necessary to have procedures in place for backing up Cisco IOS images. This allows the network administrator to quickly copy an image back to a router in case of a corrupted or erased image.

In Figure 1, the network administrator wants to create a backup of the current image file on the router (c1900-universalk9-mz.SPA.152-4.M3.bin) to the TFTP server at 172.16.1.100.

To create a backup of the Cisco IOS image to a TFTP server, perform the following three steps:

Step 1.   Ensure that there is access to the network TFTP server. Ping the TFTP server to test connectivity, as shown in Figure 2.

Step 2.   Verify that the TFTP server has sufficient disk space to accommodate the Cisco IOS Software image. Use the **show flash0:** command on the router to determine the size of the Cisco IOS image file. The file in the example is 68831808 bytes long.

Step 3.   Copy the image to the TFTP server using the **copy** *source-url destination-url* command, as shown in Figure 3.

After issuing the command using the specified source and destination URLs, the user is prompted for the source file name, IP address of the remote host, and destination file name. The transfer will then begin.

Use the Syntax Checker in Figure 4 on R2 to copy the IOS to a TFTP server.

Refer to
Interactive Graphic
in online course

10.3.3.3   Steps to Copy an IOS Image to a Device

Cisco consistently releases new Cisco IOS software versions to resolve caveats and provide new features. This example uses IPv6 for the transfer to show that TFTP can also be used across IPv6 networks.

Figure 1 illustrates copying a Cisco IOS software image from a TFTP server. A new image file (c1900-universalk9-mz.SPA.152-4.M3.bin) will be copied from the TFTP server at 2001:DB8:CAFE:100::99 to the router.

Follow these steps to upgrade the software on the Cisco router:

Step 1.   Select a Cisco IOS image file that meets the requirements in terms of platform, features, and software. Download the file from cisco.com and transfer it to the TFTP server.

Step 2.   Verify connectivity to the TFTP server. Ping the TFTP server from the router. The output in Figure 2 shows the TFTP server is accessible from the router.

Step 3.   Ensure that there is sufficient flash space on the router that is being upgraded. The amount of free flash can be verified using the **show flash0:** command. Compare the free flash space with the new image file size. The **show flash0:** command in Figure 3 is used to verify free flash size. Free flash space in the example is 182,394,880 bytes.

Step 4.   Copy the IOS image file from the TFTP server to the router using the **copy** command shown in Figure 4. After issuing this command with specified source and destination URLs, the user will be prompted for IP address of the remote host, source file name, and destination file name. The transfer of the file will begin.

Refer to
Interactive Graphic
in online course

10.3.3.4   The boot system Command

To upgrade to the copied IOS image after that image is saved on the router's flash memory, configure the router to load the new image during bootup using the **boot system** command, as shown in Figure 1. Save the configuration. Reload the router to boot the router with new image. After the router has booted, to verify the new image has loaded, use the **show version** command, as shown in Figure 2.

During startup, the bootstrap code parses the startup configuration file in NVRAM for the **boot system** commands that specify the name and location of the Cisco IOS Software image to load. Several **boot system** commands can be entered in sequence to provide a fault-tolerant boot plan.

If there are no **boot system** commands in the configuration, the router defaults to loading the first valid Cisco IOS image in flash memory and running it.

Refer to **Packet
Tracer Activity**
for this chapter

10.3.3.5   Packet Tracer – Using a TFTP Server to Upgrade a Cisco IOS Image

Background/Scenario

A TFTP server can help manage the storage of IOS images and revisions to IOS images. For any network, it is good practice to keep a backup copy of the Cisco IOS Software image in case the system image in the router becomes corrupted or accidentally erased. A TFTP server can also be used to store new upgrades to the IOS and then deployed throughout the network where it is needed. In this activity, you will upgrade the IOS images on Cisco devices by using a TFTP server. You will also backup an IOS image with the use of a TFTP server.

Refer to **Video**
in online course

10.3.3.6   Video Demonstration – Managing Cisco IOS Images

10.3.4   Software Licensing

Refer to
Interactive Graphic
in online course

10.3.4.1   Licensing Overview

Beginning with Cisco IOS Software release 15.0, Cisco modified the process to enable new technologies within the IOS feature sets. Cisco IOS Software release 15.0 incorporates cross-platform feature sets to simplify the image selection process. It does this by providing similar functions across platform boundaries. Each device ships with the same universal image. Technology packages are enabled in the universal image via Cisco Software Activation licensing keys. The Cisco IOS Software Activation feature allows the user to enable licensed features and register licenses. The Cisco IOS Software Activation feature is a collection of processes and components used to activate Cisco IOS software feature sets by obtaining and validating Cisco software licenses.

Figure 1 shows the technology packages that are available:

- IP Base
- Data
- Unified Communications (UC)
- Security (SEC)

Click the buttons in Figure 2 to learn more about technology packages.

Note The IP Base license is a prerequisite for installing the Data, Security, and Unified Communications licenses. For earlier router platforms that can support Cisco IOS Software release 15.0, a universal image is not available. It is necessary to download a separate image that contains the desired features.

Technology Package Licenses

Technology package licenses are supported on Cisco ISR G2 platforms (Cisco 1900, 2900, and 3900 Series routers). The Cisco IOS universal image contains all packages and features in one image. Each package is a grouping of technology-specific features. Multiple technology package licenses can be activated on the Cisco 1900, 2900, and 3900 series ISR platforms.

Note Use the **show license feature** command to view the technology package licenses and feature licenses supported on the router.

Refer to
Online Course
for Illustration

10.3.4.2 Licensing Process

When a new router is shipped, it comes preinstalled with the software image and the corresponding permanent licenses for the customer-specified packages and features.

The router also comes with the evaluation license, known as a temporary license, for most packages and features supported on the specified router. This allows customers to try a new software package or feature by activating a specific evaluation license. If customers want to permanently activate a software package or feature on the router, they must get a new software license.

The figure shows the three steps to permanently activate a new software package or feature on the router.

Refer to
Online Course
for Illustration

10.3.4.3 Step 1. Purchase the Software Package or Feature to Install

The first step is to purchase the software package or feature needed. This may be adding a package to IP Base, such as Security.

Software Claim Certificates are used for licenses that require software activation. The claim certificate provides the Product Activation Key (PAK) for the license and important information regarding the Cisco End User License Agreement (EULA). In most instances, Cisco or the Cisco channel partner will have already activated the licenses ordered at the time of purchase and no Software Claim Certificate is provided.

In either instance, customers receive a PAK with their purchase. The PAK serves as a receipt and is used to obtain a license. A PAK is an 11 digit alpha numeric key created by Cisco manufacturing. It defines the Feature Set associated with the PAK. A PAK is not tied to a specific device until the license is created. A PAK can be purchased that generates any specified number of licenses. As shown in the figure, a separate license is required for each package, IP Base, Data, UC, and SEC.

Refer to
Interactive Graphic
in online course

10.3.4.4   Step 2. Obtain a License

The second step is to obtain the license, which is actually a license file. A license file, also known as a Software Activation License, is obtained using one of the following options:

- **Cisco License Manager (CLM)** - This is a free software application available at http://www.cisco.com/go/clm. Cisco License Manager is a standalone application from Cisco that helps network administrators rapidly deploy multiple Cisco software licenses across their networks. Cisco License Manager can discover network devices, view their license information, and acquire and deploy licenses from Cisco. The application provides a GUI that simplifies installation and helps automate license acquisition, as well as perform multiple licensing tasks from a central location. CLM is free of charge and can be downloaded from CCO.

- **Cisco License Registration Portal** - This is the web-based portal for getting and registering individual software licenses, available at http://www.cisco.com/go/license.

Both of these processes require a PAK number and a Unique Device Identifier (UDI).

The PAK is received during purchase.

The UDI is a combination of the Product ID (PID), the Serial Number (SN), and the hardware version. The SN is an 11 digit number which uniquely identifies a device. The PID identifies the type of device. Only the PID and SN are used for license creation. This UDI can be displayed using the **show license udi** command shown in Figure 1. This information is also available on a pull-out label tray found on the device. Figure 2 shows an example of the pull-out label on a Cisco 1941 router.

After entering the appropriate information, the customer receives an email containing the license information to install the license file. The license file is an XML text file with a .lic extension.

Use the Syntax Checker in Figure 3 to determine the UDI on router R2.

Refer to
Interactive Graphic
in online course

10.3.4.5   Step 3. Install the License

After the license has been purchased, the customer receives a license file. Installing a permanent license requires two steps:

Step 1.   Use the **license install** *stored-location-url* privileged exec mode command to install a license file.

Step 2.   Reload the router using the privileged exec command **reload**. A reload is not required if an evaluation license is active.

Figure 1 shows the configuration for installing the permanent license for the Security package on the router.

Note   Unified Communications is not supported on 1941 routers.

A permanent license is a license that never expires. After a permanent license is installed on a router, it is good for that particular feature set for the life of the router, even across IOS versions. For example, when a UC, SEC, or Data license is installed on a router, the subsequent features for that license are activated even if the router is upgraded to a new IOS release. A permanent license is the most common license type used when a feature set is purchased for a device.

Note   Cisco manufacturing preinstalls the appropriate permanent license on the ordered device for the purchased feature set. No customer interaction with the Cisco IOS Software Activation processes is required to enable that license on new hardware.

Use the Syntax Checker in Figure 2 to install a permanent license file on router R2.

10.3.5   License Verification and Management

Refer to
Interactive Graphic
in online course

10.3.5.1   License Verification

After a new license has been installed the router must be rebooted using the **reload** command. As shown in Figure 1, the **show version** command is used after the router is reloaded to verify that license has been installed.

The **show license** command in Figure 2 is used to display additional information about Cisco IOS software licenses. This command displays license information used to help with troubleshooting issues related to Cisco IOS software licenses. This command displays all the licenses installed in the system. In this example, both the IP Base and Security licenses have been installed. This command also displays the features that are available, but not licensed to execute, such as the Data feature set. Output is grouped according to how the features are stored in license storage.

The following is a brief description of the output:

- **Feature** - Name of the feature

- **License Type** - Type of license; such as Permanent or Evaluation

- **License State** - Status of the license; such as Active or In Use

- **License Count** - Number of licenses available and in use, if counted. If non-counted is indicated, the license is unrestricted.

- **License Priority** - Priority of the license; such as high or low

Note   Refer to the Cisco IOS 15 command reference guide for complete details on the information displayed in the **show license** command.

Refer to
Interactive Graphic
in online course

10.3.5.2   Activate an Evaluation Right-To-Use License

Evaluation licenses are replaced with Evaluation Right-To-Use licenses (RTU) after 60 days. An Evaluation license is good for a 60 day evaluation period. After the 60 days, this license automatically transitions into an RTU license. These licenses are available on the honor system and require the customer's acceptance of the EULA. The EULA is automatically applied to all Cisco IOS software licenses.

The **license accept end user agreement** global configuration mode command is used to configure a one-time acceptance of the EULA for all Cisco IOS software packages and features. After the command is issued and the EULA accepted, the EULA is automatically applied to all Cisco IOS software licenses and the user is not prompted to accept the EULA during license installation.

Figure 1 shows how to configure a one-time acceptance of the EULA:

```
Router(config)# license accept end user agreement
```

In addition, Figure 1 shows the command to activate an Evaluation RTU license:

```
Router# license boot module module-name technology-package package-name
```

Use the **?** in place of the arguments to determine which module names and supported software packages are available on the router. Technology package names for Cisco ISR G2 platforms are:

- **ipbasek9** - IP Base technology package

- **securityk9** - Security technology package

- **datak9** - Data technology package

- **uck9** - Unified Communications package (not available on 1900 series)

Note   A reload using the **reload** command is required to activate the software package.

Evaluation licenses are temporary, and are used to evaluate a feature set on new hardware. Temporary licenses are limited to a specific usage period (for example, 60 days).

Reload the router after a license is successfully installed using the **reload** command. The **show license** command in Figure 2 verifies that the license has been installed.

Use the Syntax Checker in Figure 3 to accept the EULA and activate an Evaluation RTU data package license on the 1900 router.

Refer to
Interactive Graphic
in online course

10.3.5.3   Back up the License

The **license save** command is used to copy all licenses in a device and store them in a format required by the specified storage location. Saved licenses are restored by using the **license install** command.

The command to back up a copy of the licenses on a device is:

```
Router#  license save file-sys://lic-location
```

Use the **show flash0:** command to verify that the licenses have been saved (Figure 1).

The license storage location can be a directory or a URL that points to a file system. Use the **?** command to see the storage locations supported by a device.

Use the Syntax Checker in Figure 2 to save all license files on router R2.

Refer to **Interactive Graphic** in online course

10.3.5.4 Uninstall the License

To clear an active permanent license from the Cisco 1900 series, 2900 series, and 3900 series routers, perform the following steps:

Step 1. **Disable the technology package.**

- Disable the active license with the command:

  ```
  Router(config)# license boot module module-name technology-
  package package-name disable
  ```

- Reload the router using the **reload** command. A reload is required to make the software package inactive.

Step 2. **Clear the license.**

- Clear the technology package license from license storage.

  ```
  Router# license clear feature-name
  ```

- Clear the **license boot module** command used for disabling the active license:

  ```
  Router(config)# no license boot module module-name
  technology-package package-name  disable
  ```

Note Some licenses, such as built-in licenses, cannot be cleared. Only licenses that have been added by using the **license install** command are removed. Evaluation licenses are not removed.

Figure 1 shows an example of clearing an active license.

Use the Syntax Checker in Figure 2 to uninstall the security license on router R2.

Refer to **Video** in online course

10.3.5.5 Video Demonstration – Working with IOS 15 Image Licenses

10.4 Summary

Refer to **Packet Tracer Activity** for this chapter

10.4.1.1 Packet Tracer – Skills Integration Challenge

In this challenge activity, you will finish the addressing scheme, configure routing, and implement named access control lists.

Refer to **Online Course** for Illustration

10.4.1.2 Device Discovery, Management, and Maintenance

In this chapter, you learned and practice skills that network administrators use for device discovery, management, and maintenance.

CDP is a Cisco proprietary protocol for network discovery on the data link layer. It can share information such as device names and IOS versions, with other physically connected Cisco devices. LLDP is vendor-neutral protocol on the data link layer for network discovery. The network devices advertise information, such as their identities and capabilities to their neighbors.

NTP synchronizes the time of day among a set of distributed time servers and clients. This allows networking devices to agree on the time a specific event occurred, such as the lose of connectivity between a router and a switch. Syslog messages can be trapped and sent to a syslog server where the network administrator can investigate when the link failed.

Device maintenance includes the tasks of backing up, restoring, and upgrading IOS images and configuration files. Upgrading an IOS image also includes tasks related to software licensing.

Go to the online course to take the quiz and exam.

Chapter 10   Quiz

This quiz is designed to provide an additional opportunity to practice the skills and knowledge presented in the chapter and to prepare for the chapter exam. You will be allowed multiple attempts and the grade does not appear in the gradebook.

Chapter 10   Exam

The chapter exam assesses your knowledge of the chapter content.

Your Chapter Notes

Index

Numbers

A

Notes

Notes

Notes

Notes

Notes

Notes

CISCO

Connect, Engage, Collaborate

The Award Winning Cisco Support Community

Attend and Participate in Events

Ask the Experts
Live Webcasts

Knowledge Sharing

Documents
Blogs
Videos

Top Contributor Programs

Cisco Designated VIP
Hall of Fame
Spotlight Awards

Multi-Language Support

https://supportforums.cisco.com

REGISTER YOUR PRODUCT at CiscoPress.com/register

Access Additional Benefits and SAVE 35% on Your Next Purchase

- Download available product updates.
- Access bonus material when applicable.
- Receive exclusive offers on new editions and related products.
  (Just check the box to hear from us when setting up your account.)
- Get a coupon for 35% for your next purchase, valid for 30 days.
  Your code will be available in your Cisco Press cart. (You will also find
  it in the Manage Codes section of your account page.)

Registration benefits vary by product. Benefits will be listed on your account page under Registered Products.

CiscoPress.com – **Learning Solutions for Self-Paced Study, Enterprise, and the Classroom**
Cisco Press is the Cisco Systems authorized book publisher of Cisco networking technology, Cisco certification self-study, and Cisco Networking Academy Program materials.

At CiscoPress.com you can
- Shop our books, eBooks, software, and video training.
- Take advantage of our special offers and promotions (ciscopress.com/promotions).
- Sign up for special offers and content newsletters (ciscopress.com/newsletters).
- Read free articles, exam profiles, and blogs by information technology experts.
- Access thousands of free chapters and video lessons.

Connect with Cisco Press – Visit CiscoPress.com/community
Learn about Cisco Press community events and programs.

Cisco Press

ALWAYS LEARNING

PEARSON